"Kathryn's approach is practical, intuitive and full of empathy and support. She has transformed my son's eating and our approach to mealtimes. I only wish I had found her sooner!"

Emily, Fulham

"Kathryn is fantastic! Not only did she solve our one-year-old's sleep problems in a very gentle and kind manner, she also gave lots of tips on other topics and was simply lovely to have around!"

Anna, Parsons Green

"We all loved having Kathryn in our home. She sat with Lucien and they created a weekend menu together and cooked all of the weekend food. She believes in children making their own choices rather than feeling food is forced upon them."

Rosie Millard, Daily Telegraph journalist and author

"Before Kathryn's arrival I was dreading the moment ... but it all ended up like a three-day holiday! She trained us as parents to WAIT, understand, listen and recognise her voice. The result: my child now sleeps on average from 7.30pm to 7.15am!"

Veronica, Wimbledon

"Welcoming Kathryn into our home was the most pain-free method of smoothing out our family wrinkles!"

Emma, Battersea

I dedicate this book to my mother:
my mentor, my guide and my sounding board,
the major influence who made me what I am today.
With love and thanks,
Kathryn x

The 3 Day NANNY

Simple Three-Day Solutions for Sleeping, Eating, Potty Training & Behaviour Challenges

Kathryn Mewes

Vermilion
LONDON

5 7 9 10 8 6 4

Published in 2012 by Vermilion, an imprint of Ebury Publishing
A Random House Group company

The Random House Group Limited Reg. No. 954009

Addresses for companies within the Random House Group can be found at
www.randomhouse.co.uk

The Random House Group Limited supports the Forest Stewardship
Council® (FSC®), the leading international forest-certification organisation.
Our books carrying the FSC label are printed on FSC®-certified paper. FSC is
the only forest-certification scheme supported by the leading environmental
organisations, including Greenpeace. Our paper procurement policy can be
found at www.randomhouse.co.uk/environment

Designed and set by seagulls.net

Printed and bound by CPI Group (UK) Ltd, Croydon, CR0 4YY

ISBN 9780091939939

To buy books by your favourite authors and register for offers visit
www.randomhouse.co.uk

Note: 'He' and 'she' are used interchangeably to refer to the child throughout this
book, but all advice applies equally to both sexes. When talking about the parent
who will take the lead in the three-day plans, the term 'Mummy' is most often used,
but fathers or any other primary carer may just as easily take the lead role.

Contents

Acknowledgments

Grateful thanks to Susanna Abbott for the opportunity to write this book.

To Gill Paul for editing and helping with the creation of the book.

To all of the families I have helped with The 3-Day Plan.

Your input and suggestions for the book have been fundamental to the final product.

Introduction

For the last twenty years, I have been helping and guiding parents to raise their children, and during that time I've come to the conclusion that there is no job more challenging than that of a mother or father.

Children don't come with instruction manuals attached to the umbilical cord. It's assumed that if you've made the decision to have babies, you should know what to do with them when they arrive, but of course they come in all shapes and sizes, with their own unique personalities. They don't understand anything at all and it's up to you to teach them. How best can you do that? How are you, the parent, supposed to know the most successful methods? And what can you do if it doesn't all go according to plan? There's plenty of guidance out there when you are pregnant and then for the first months of baby's life, but it can be difficult to know where to go and who to ask if obstacles arise thereafter – and they almost certainly will.

I believe that asking for help and guidance is a positive step parents should feel good about taking. Conscientious parents strive to be the best they can be, and sometimes that will involve seek-

> The easy choice is often the wrong one in life, while the difficult choice holds the reward.

ing outside advice. In my role as a 'Bespoke Nanny', I go to people's homes for three days only and help them to address any challenges their family faces. Before we start work I always congratulate the parents on taking that first step, putting their own emotions to one side and deciding to make a change that will enhance their family life. By picking up this book and starting to read, you have already proved that you are a conscientious parent, so congratulations to you too!

This book covers children from the age of six months to six years, a period when they are taking on board the basic information that they will need to thrive at school and in social situations outside the home, as well as laying down the foundations for their future health. All parents want the same basic things for their little ones: for them to sleep, eat and behave well. This makes the parent feel happy and confident, which in turn makes for a happy and confident child. However, when they don't do these three things, a happy family can quickly become a very stressed one. Sleep problems, worry about whether a child is taking in enough nutrition, or disruptive behaviour can make parents very anxious, and their anxiety is picked up by the child until it all becomes a vicious circle.

That's where this book comes in. My step-by-step guides will show you how to get your child to sleep through the night in his own bed, eat a range of nutritious foods, and learn some self-control when it comes to behaviour. The plans will turn a 'family challenge' into an exciting project and if you follow them exactly, you will see some astounding results in just three days. That's all it need take to make changes that will last. I put the three-day programme into practice every single week so I *know* it works. Now it's your turn to find out.

WHY THREE DAYS?

I'm often asked why my programme takes three days, and I explain by using two different scenarios.

Imagine you are starting a new job. You may have a restless night before the big day as you worry about all the new challenges you will face. The first day itself involves a huge amount of information being thrown at you, new faces and names to remember, navigating your way around unfamiliar surroundings – and remembering to be enthusiastic about this great change! By the end of the first day you are simply exhausted and mentally drained. You may even question whether you'll be able to return the following day … but you do.

On Day Two you are equipped with some knowledge, you start to find your way from A to B and a few faces are familiar. You begin to relax and accept your new environment and role, although you are still learning.

By Day Three you feel you have a presence in the workplace. You are able to do your job without asking so many questions as on Day One, and you have broken the ice with at least one other member of staff. Things are falling into place and a new routine in your life has been formed. You still have a lot to learn but the main hurdles have been jumped and you are striding on.

Another scenario might be starting a new exercise class. We all feel apprehensive as we push open the door and walk in. That's why we immediately head to the back of the room, as far away from the mirrors as possible. You notice there are people standing at the front of the room 'stretching out' who have clearly been coming their entire life, and that makes you even more self-conscious.

Before you know it the music has started and the routines have begun. You are desperately trying to copy the instructor but often find yourself heading in the opposite direction to the rest of the class. You are screaming "Arggghh!"

> In just 72 hours you have made a dramatic life change. You have walked the path of a three-day miracle!

inside your head but you're there and somehow have to get through to the end of the class. You lose count of the number of times you look at the clock and by the time it is all over, you are seriously contemplating remaining on the sofa this time next week.

But Week Two arrives and you find yourself entering the class again, a little more 'in the know' this time. You make eye contact with someone and manage a half smile. There may even be someone starting out as a 'newbie' who knows even less than you! The music starts, you remember a few moves, and you even manage to glance at yourself in the mirror. You still have a lot to learn but you feel confident enough to continue.

By Week Three you know the drill and are ready for a workout. You may strike up a conversation with someone before the class begins, and you remember a lot of the moves. You might even enjoy yourself this time!

You have started something new and in just three consecutive weeks a different routine has formed … your own three-week miracle!

Young children learning new lessons will go through exactly the same trajectory of emotions, with fear and a desire to run away from it all on Day One, greater understanding and a gradual acceptance of change on Day Two, and by Day Three they are showing clear signs of accepting the change and have all but forgotten the old ways.

Think back to situations in your own life in which you have had to make changes and you will understand the emotions you and your family are likely to experience when you undertake one of my three-day plans. The journey will not be easy to start with but if you remain consistent and keep to the plan, I'm sure you will see huge improvements after just 72 hours.

WHICH THREE-DAY PLAN DO YOU NEED?

This book gives advice on guiding children aged between six months and six years, but obviously there is a fundamental difference in the abilities within that age range, from babies who can't walk or talk through to schoolchildren. That's why I have broken them down into three age groups:

- In Chapter 3, you will find the three-day plans for children aged between six and eighteen months. Within the chapter there are separate plans for children who have sleeping problems, eating problems and behaviour problems.

- In Chapter 4, you will find three-day plans for children aged between eighteen months and three years, and once again there are separate plans for sleeping, eating, and behaviour.

- In Chapter 5, you will find three-day plans for children aged between three and six years, addressing their sleeping, eating and behaviour.

If your child is on the cusp between two age bands, think about her level of maturity and decide whether it will be easier to use the plan for a younger or older child.

If your child has problems in two separate areas, say she is sleeping poorly and behaving badly, you need to address these separately. Generally, you should aim to have your child sleeping through the night before you tackle other problems, because not sleeping well will adversely affect her eating and behaviour. Ensure she's had five consecutive nights of good sleep before starting any other plan, then choose the issue that is most challenging to your child and to the family as a whole.

🦋 In Chapter 6, I have addressed the issue of potty training, which can be another problem area for some parents. The age at which a child is able to use the toilet on his own varies a lot from one individual to another and should never be forced – that's why I didn't address it in one of the age-related chapters. You only need read this chapter if you are worried about training your child to use the toilet.

Before you start any plans, though, you should read Chapters 1 and 2, which explain my approach to successful parenting and give you some of the tools you will need to follow the plans successfully. After that, you

You should only follow one plan at a time.

can go straight to the three-day plan you need. You'll find the page numbers for each on the Contents page.

WANTING AND BELIEVING IN CHANGE

If you've been struggling for a while with a child who won't stay in his own bed, a fussy eater or a chronic tantrum-thrower, you may find it hard to believe that change can be achieved in just three days – but it will be if you give the plan your undivided attention and full dedication. Wanting to change and committing whole-heartedly to it come first. Half measures won't do. If you work full-time, you can begin the plan over a weekend but you will have to take Monday off to see it through. Alternatively, you can do a three-day plan in the holidays. You may have to cancel social events, or change the whole family's routine. You must truly need to, want to and have to make a change. Until you feel this way, do not follow one of my programmes – but if you are ready to 'give it your all', read on!

The next thing I require from you is a genuine belief that it will work. Don't just read the words. Believe in the changes you can make for your family. Believe in yourself. Look at your reflection in the mirror and say "I can do this, I want to do this and I will make the change." These programmes are not about hoping and wishing; they are about trusting and believing.

The second step involves you believing in yourself and your partner or any other person who helps with the care of your child on a regular basis (such as a grandparent, nanny or childminder).

Step three: most importantly, you need to believe in your child. You have been living in a cloud of doubt and disbelief and you may even have reached a stage of feeling as if this is just the way life is going to be. You need to shift this thought and turn it around. Now it is time to believe in your child. He will begin to sense your confidence in him and this will make him start to believe in his own ability to change. Your emotions and feelings will often spill into your child's mind without you even realising it.

I am asking you for three consecutive days. Not one and then a pause, or two and then an adjustment to the plan. For three days you need to remain completely consistent in your approach. After that, you will need to make a shift in your parenting – a shift for life. Results will be seen in three days but this does not mean returning to your old ways on Day Four. Continuity and consistency are compulsory. Think of it in the same way as starting a diet. If you drop the weight in three days and then

> Once you believe that a change truly needs to be made and you are confident about the programme, you have taken the first step.

return to your old eating habits on Day Four, we all know what is going to happen!

But the rewards for you, your child and your family are so great that I know you will think it worthwhile. I practise these plans every week with different parents. I know they work for them and, with the right state of mind, I know they will work for you too.

With your positive energy and enthusiasm you can turn your family life around.

Go on... Do it! You've got this far. I believe you will succeed – and the chances are you are even going to enjoy it!

Now is the time for you to exude positive energy ... and pass it on to your child.

CHAPTER I

The basics of successful parenting

There are certain key life skills you need to instil in your children between the ages of six months and six years to enable them to move with confidence into the world of school, friendships, hobbies and interests outside the home. The basics of eating and sleeping well are obviously crucial for their physical health, but it is also important that they grow up to feel they are capable of meeting the challenges life throws at them, and that they are likeable, interesting little people.

That's why parenting shouldn't be about laying down the law, shouting orders and expecting instant obedience. As you'll see, my Bespoke Nanny methods are about helping children to make choices, then praising and rewarding them when they make the correct choice. If they don't, I help them to pause, reflect and understand that there will be consequences. The methods vary slightly according to the age of your child, but the principles remain the same.

Children thrive when they have a regular routine. This makes life easier for them because they know what to expect and new experiences can be introduced one at a time. When you have an established routine, your child will know what is going to happen at each stage of the day and what is expected of them. If there are variations to the routine, you can explain them in advance, giving the child time to get used to the idea.

Without routine, it is very likely that you are going to see signs of uncertainty and even panic in children. For example, if a child is hungry and unsure when their next meal is due, it can cause tears and tantrums. If a child's bedtime varies, you are likely to miss the period when they are ready to settle naturally and move into a period when they become over-tired and fractious. This will cause frustration in your child, which will then affect your mood, and all kinds of confrontational situations can arise.

A sequence of events, a routine, will prevent uncertainty and encourage confidence and independence. Your child should know at any given time who will be looking after him, whether it's you or a babysitter; when he will be eating meals; and what time he will go to bed. Long before he is able to tell the time himself, he will pick up signs (such as knowing that he has an afternoon rest straight after lunch, or that bedtime comes after bath-time and a story).

Routine is good for your child, and it's good for you too, as you can schedule in your own personal time to reply to emails, make phone calls, prepare meals or even put your feet up for five minutes! A routine in which each family member has their own space will make living together much easier.

In this chapter, we'll look at the type of routine your child needs in order to thrive, and we'll start by looking at that most precious commodity of all for parents – sleep!

GETTING A GOOD NIGHT'S SLEEP

Sleep is vital for your children's healthy growth and development. From when they are babies, they need to learn to settle themselves in their own beds when they are first put down, and to get themselves back to sleep again if they wake up in the middle of the night when it's still pitch dark. Apart from anything else, teaching this skill is vital if you want to get a good night's sleep yourself.

Some parents fall into the trap of taking babies and young children into bed with them to help settle them in the night. By doing this, you should be aware that you are introducing a precedent. If your child learns that when they waken in the night they get to come into Mummy's bed, they will start naturally wakening in the night more and more often. At some stage they need to learn to sleep in their own beds, and it will be much easier to teach this at six months than at six years!

There are some exceptions to the rule. When your child is ill, you may want them beside you during the night. You may have to share a bed when you're on holiday, or visiting someone else's home. But if this happens, you should explain to your child that it is an exception and that the routine will return to normal when they are well again or when you are back home (assuming they are old enough to understand).

The table below is a basic guide to the number of hours a child should sleep, but every child is different, so do let your child guide you as to how much sleep they require. Adults differ in their sleep requirements and so do children. You will soon realise if your child is not getting enough sleep because he will become whiney, short-tempered and unreasonable due to tiredness. However, if he seems to function perfectly well on less sleep than I've indicated here, that is fine.

AGE OF CHILD	DAYTIME SLEEP	NIGHT SLEEP	TOTAL
6–12 MONTHS	AROUND 2 HOURS	11–12 HOURS	13–14 HOURS
1–3 YEARS	1–2 HOURS	10–12 HOURS	11–14 HOURS
3–6 YEARS		10–12 HOURS	10–12 HOURS

THE SLEEP/WAKE CYCLE

We all wake on average six times a night – both adults and children. This is why it is fundamentally important that we teach children to settle themselves again as soon as possible. Otherwise, we can find ourselves jumping out of bed to settle them each time.

In general, the sleep/wake cycle is as follows:

🦋 It should take ten to fifteen minutes to fall to sleep.

🦋 The first ten minutes are spent in a light sleep.

🦋 During the next twenty minutes, your body temperature reduces and your heartbeat begins to slow down. This is mid sleep.

You then go into sleep cycles lasting between 70 and 90 minutes, with a period of deep sleep and a period of REM (rapid eye movement) in each.

REM is a lighter state of sleep, during which we are most likely to dream, and some people sleep-talk or sleep-walk. Each episode of REM gets longer as the night progresses, and children aged between six months and six years will spend 30 per cent of their sleep in REM.

When babies are younger, we give them feeds at regular intervals through the night, at say 10.30pm, 1am and 3am, because these are the times when their sleep is lighter and hunger is more likely to wake them up.

At the beginning of the night, the periods of deep sleep are longer and the REM periods are shorter, but as morning approaches, there is more time spent in light sleep. Around 5am can be a challenging time in many households as children wake during a period of REM, but they are still tired and need more sleep (as do you). They need to be guided to get back to sleep and stay asleep for a further one or two hours after this.

Here's a little trick of the trade. If your child wakes at 5am and can see daylight round the edges of the curtains, she will think that it is time to rise rather than settle herself back to sleep. A dark room with black-out curtains can make all the difference. I have guided countless parents to help their children sleep through the night, and one item I always carry in my case is a roll of tin foil. Yes, tin foil. If you sprinkle your window with water and press the foil onto the glass it will stick, making the room nice and dark. If you go away for the weekend or on holiday, I recommend taking a roll with you so you can create instant black-out conditions wherever you are.

I am also a great believer in putting younger children (under the age of two) into a sleep sack (or 'Gro-bag'). This is a sleeping bag,

> Sleep is fundamentally important for the development of your child's body and mind.

which means they don't need sheets or blankets in their cot. They come in different thicknesses for different seasons. The legs and body are enclosed while the arms come out through armholes, so in winter you'll need to put your child in a long-sleeved baby-gro as well so their arms don't get cold. The advantage of sleep sacks is that children can't kick off the covers in the night and then get too cold. They also give a lovely feeling of being securely tucked in.

It's crucial that we give children the guidance and skill to settle themselves back to sleep again, both for their health and for your sanity! Poor sleep as a child can make you more likely to suffer from insomnia as an adult, which is yet another reason to deal with it early.

THE BEDTIME ROUTINE

I think of the end of the day as 'run the gauntlet time'. We need to get tea on the table around 5pm and watch at least half of it be consumed, then there's down time, bath, books and bed around 7pm. If you can settle your child for the night, you will have the next ten to twelve hours for yourself, so it's worth establishing a routine that works. If you are not home from work by 5pm, ask whoever is caring for your child to follow the routine until you get in and can take over.

It is important that this time of day is not rushed or hurried and the key is to get the dinner on the table by 5pm. If it's nearer to 6pm there is no way bedtime can take place at 7pm without hurrying. People feel stressed and panicked when they are told to hurry and rush, and this is not the state we want to send a child to bed in. The hour before bedtime should not be a 'rush hour'.

The key is to think ahead of time. Plan in the morning what the evening meal for the children is going to be. As we'll discuss later in this chapter, you want to work towards your child eating the same meal as the rest of the family, so it can be a good idea to save a portion of whatever you had the night before and give it to them for dinner. It is a great time-saver for you, and once they get used to trying a variety of flavours, your child will like the idea that you eat the same as them.

Here's an ideal routine for the run-up to bedtime:

4.30pm	Start preparing the dinner
5pm	Dinner is served
5.30pm	Tidy-up time for parent/carer and free play for the child(ren)
6pm	Bath-time (whether they are dirty or not, this is a good way to make young children relax and calm down)
6.30pm	Milk and stories (maybe your older child has a drink of milk in front of the TV while you feed your younger child)
6.45pm	Visit the loo, brush teeth
7–7.15pm	Stories for older children and lights out

After saying goodnight and having a last cuddle, you should be able to leave your child to settle themselves to sleep over the next ten to fifteen minutes.

Stick to this routine as closely as possible, even on holidays, and you will find your child accepts it as natural and seldom resists. (Although make sure distractions are kept to a minimum and they can't hear the sounds of older children still playing fun games downstairs.)

If your child is having trouble with any aspect of sleeping: settling himself when he first goes to bed, wakening frequently at night or too

Don't underestimate your child's ability. He will be able to settle himself to sleep given the right guidance.

early in the morning, it may be time to try my three-day plan for sleeping (see pages 44–48 for a general introduction to this). It could make all the difference to your child's health and happiness – and to your own as well.

Now for the next important plank in your child's development: eating well.

INTRODUCING YOUR CHILD TO A HEALTHY DIET

I have never met anyone who is happy to eat anything and everything. We all have our own likes and dislikes when it comes to flavours and textures, as well as our preferred times to eat. For example, some people want to eat their main meal at lunchtime, others want to skip breakfast, while some are 'grazers' who eat little and often throughout the day.

As adults we only tend to think about what we eat if we need to for health reasons, or because the summer holiday is approaching and we want to drop a few pounds before getting into swimwear. But when your baby reaches the 'weaning' stage at six months old, your head will be full of the importance of vegetables and fruit, protein and carbohydrate, and you'll start to see 'a balanced diet' in a whole new light.

You might find it alarming when your child decides they don't like a particular flavour or type of food, but remember that adults have preferences too. Still, it's important for children to learn from an early stage that not every meal produced will be their 'favourite'. They need to realise that their bodies need a varied balanced diet so they won't be getting sausages for breakfast, lunch and dinner.

In years gone by parents could be heard saying "Eat your greens – they make you big and strong.""Carrots will help you see in the dark.""Drink your milk; it's good for your bones." I remember watching *Popeye* and understanding the importance of that tin of spinach because his muscles grew once he had consumed the green leaves!

Now we are faced with more convenience and fast food than ever before, in packaging that is deliberately attractive to children. Television advertisements attract children to products full of artificial colours and preservatives, high salt and sugar levels. No longer is 'spinach' promoted to children as it used to be!

With such a wide variety of foods available, your children might try to dictate what they want to eat and begin to challenge the meals you prepare for them. With a six-month-old, this could involve spitting it out or refusing to let the spoon in their mouth. With a six-year-old it could involve sulks and noisy protests. On the one hand, to look at this in a positive light, it is wonderful to have a child who challenges life. Questioning is how we learn. Children will often use mealtimes to show you that they do have some control over their lives. They can choose what they want to eat and not eat. The important message is to:

Stay calm and accept their decision … for today!

Over time, if you follow my eating programme, you will be able to persuade your child to try foods they are convinced they don't like, but in the first instance it's important to let them make their own decisions and trust that, with the right guidance, they will eventually make the decisions that are best for their growth and development.

I have seven key principles when it comes to feeding young children, and I include them here because I suggest you follow them whether your child has 'issues' with food or not. You'll be laying the foundations for them growing up with a healthy relationship to food that will stay with them into adulthood.

- Set a good example
- Serve realistic portions
- Explain what they are eating and why
- Involve your child in food preparation
- Have conversations at mealtimes
- Introduce new foods each week
- Offer healthy snacks

Let me explain what I mean by each of these.

SET A GOOD EXAMPLE

The most important person in a young child's life are their parents. You are their role model and they learn by imitating you. This means that you need to guide your child by example when it comes to mealtimes. Why should a child enthusiastically eat a meal if you are not eating it alongside him? From when your child is about a year old,

I suggest you serve yourself a small portion of the food your child is eating and let her see you consume it. Young children want to be like their mummy or daddy, and they are more likely to try a food if they see that you are eating the same thing. Of course, when they are weaning I don't expect you to sit with a bowl of mashed sweet potato, but you can munch on breadsticks and carrot sticks and share these with your child.

Over time, you should work towards feeding your child the meals you and your partner, or whoever else lives with you, like to eat. Discuss meal options with them and try to come up with fourteen days' worth of meals that both you, the other people in the house and your child will enjoy.

The dinner table is the heart of the family, the place where you all congregate. This is where family topics are discussed and you share your opinions and discuss life questions.

Eating together as a family is hugely beneficial to your child's attitude to food. If you make positive comments about the food, such as "I love carrots; they are so sweet and crunchy" or "This beef is full of protein; that's what makes my muscles strong", you will be helping your child to learn what is good for them. Even if she is too young to understand your words, she will be observing your positive energy towards food and this will build her own confidence about trying different flavours.

The main aim is that as your child gets older she begins to eat with you more and more often.

When the family is eating together I always encourage everyone to say 'thank you' to the person who cooked the meal, and then to place their knife and fork together and ask to leave the table. You can start working towards this when a child is as young as one year old. Before you lift your child from his high-chair, wipe his hands and face then look into his eyes and say "Thank you, Mummy, for my lunch. Please may I get down?" If your child hears this three times a day, after every meal, it will become routine and once he starts talking he will copy what you have taught him. It is a wonderful moment when your child spontaneously says 'thank you' for his meal for the first time.

As your child gets older, eating becomes more of a social activity. Children as young as three might be invited on play dates at friends' houses, meals may be eaten at nursery school and you may also be invited as a family to eat in restaurants or at relatives' houses. Every parent wants to feel

> Introducing a child to a wide variety of foods from an early age will enhance their confidence about eating socially.

confident that their child will consume at least some of the meal that has been provided in a strange location. If you offer a wide variety of foods at home your child will always recognise something he likes to eat when he is elsewhere.

SERVE REALISTIC PORTIONS

Think about how overwhelming it feels if you are presented with a meal that looks as though it could easily feed two people. It puts you off and makes you lose your appetite. This is exactly how a child feels when they are presented with an oversized meal. That's why I always advise giving children a small portion of just a few spoonfuls and letting them tell you if they want more.

Think of the size of the palm of your child's hand, and imagine covering this area with a portion of protein, carbohydrate and vegetable. For example, a twelve-month-old's palm might contain roughly a quarter of a small chicken breast, one or two tiny new potatoes, a small floret of broccoli and two carrot sticks.

The table below gives a rough guide to portion size for one-pot foods such as stir-fries, curry or pasta.

CHILD AGED 6–12 MONTHS	1–2 TABLESPOONS
CHILD AGED 12–18 MONTHS	2 TABLESPOONS
CHILD AGED 18 MONTHS–3 YEARS	3 TABLESPOONS
CHILD AGED 3–6 YEARS	4 TABLESPOONS

Don't feel you have to stick rigidly to these guidelines, though. Your child will let you know how much she needs.

Children feel a huge sense of achievement when they finish everything on the plate, and this should not go unremarked. Praise them for completing their meal and ask them if they need more to "help make their body nice and strong". That way you are setting up positive associations with food that they will keep for life.

I work on the principle that the size of your dessert should reflect how much of your main meal you have eaten. In other words, a small amount of main course means you get a small dessert. If nothing has been eaten for the main course, I would just offer fruit for dessert.

Your child will not starve if they eat nothing at one meal. In fact, it is likely to make them more enthusiastic about the next meal. You can give a between-meals snack, but ensure that it is not too large. It is not a meal substitute, simply an energy boost. That way, they will be more likely to eat what is put in front of them at the next meal.

EXPLAIN WHAT THEY ARE EATING AND WHY

Children all reach an age when 'what' and 'why' appear to be their favourite words. It is important to educate your children about why they eat certain foods from as early as two years of age, so questions are to be encouraged. Keep the answers in terms they can easily understand.

> "We eat our vegetables because they keep us healthy and fight away the germs that give us coughs and colds."

> "We eat fish and meat for protein which makes our muscles strong."

> "We eat pasta, bread and rice because they give us energy to hop, skip and run fast."

However, be careful not to classify foods as 'good' and 'bad', or 'reward' and 'punishment'. If they are told "You can have an ice cream if you eat your broccoli", children get the message that some foods are more 'desirable' than others and you can bet those are the foods she will steer towards in future. Avoid classifying foods as 'treats' unless you want your child to pester you for them!

INVOLVE YOUR CHILD IN FOOD PREPARATION

I encourage parents to involve their children in the preparation of the meal as soon as they are old enough. Children love to take responsibility and feel needed.

When I first start one of my three-day programmes with a child who has a limited diet, the first thing I introduce is shopping for foods and cooking together.

In the fast-paced modern world, it's great that we can get groceries delivered direct to the door. I'm all for it. However, if you do get the opportunity to visit food shops, or ideally a market, it's a fantastic opportunity for your child to learn about food and also make some choices of their own.

> "Shall we buy some chicken to make curry or some minced beef to make a lasagne?"

> "What do you think Daddy would like for his dinner? Shall we go and choose some fish?"

By involving your child in choosing the food you eat in your home, you give them a modicum of control over what they eat.

To help them discover different foods, I advise that you unload the shopping together. If the fruit and vegetables are pre-wrapped, unwrap them and smell them, talk about them, even wash and taste them. Bite into an apple, nibble on a carrot or munch on some seeds.

When it comes to cooking, there are lots of jobs your children can help with: mixing and stirring, tearing up lettuce for a salad, maybe rolling fish in breadcrumbs. Once they are old enough they could use a knife to chop softer fruits and vegetables, such as bananas or mushrooms. All of these tasks will help to give children a greater understanding of food. It is important they know what they are eating, and the best way to learn is from scratch.

Children need to understand and learn about food … not just be told to eat it.

Children take ownership of food they have created and feel proud when you sit down as a family and consume what they have cooked.

Praise your child for her efforts in the kitchen and thank her for helping you. Who knows? She may end up becoming the family chef!

I also recommend letting children help themselves to their own portions of food when they are old enough. This helps you to understand how hungry they are and you may be pleasantly surprised. I remember arranging self-service in one household where a five-year-old boy astonished his mother – and me! – by piling his plate high with broccoli.

> Building your children's understanding of food is something they will take with them through their lives.

When letting children help themselves, ensure they place a little of everything on their plate, even if it is just one carrot stick or half a dozen peas. They need to get used to seeing that food on their plates so that it becomes familiar, and eventually they will try a little of it.

I've found that offering little pots of ketchup or sweet chilli sauce, soy sauce, mustard or hummus can encourage children to eat something unfamiliar, because they can dip it into their familiar condiment. Never let them add their own salt to food though. They shouldn't be taking salt because their kidneys are not able to cope with it. And don't let it get to a stage when you are serving tomato ketchup with every meal, because it's full of sugar. Save it for occasions when they are trying something new.

HAVE CONVERSATIONS AT MEALTIMES

When I am sitting in a café or restaurant at lunchtime I look around at the people who are dining alone. They are usually entertaining themselves in some way, perhaps balancing a phone between their ear and their shoulder as they eat, reading a book or the newspaper, texting or checking their emails. The point I am trying to make is that it is a tall order to expect your child to sit alone at the table and simply eat their meal. If we can't do it, why should they?

However, I'm not recommending that you introduce technology to mealtimes, especially the television. It is one thing for us to eat as we watch the screen, but it is too much for a child. She will do one or the other. In my experience when the TV is on, a child's mouth tends to be firmly closed. The meal then goes cold and is left untouched. Mealtimes are a social event and *you* should be your child's entertainment. Sit together and communicate as you eat and there will be no need for a television. By the time they are teenagers, they too will be texting, checking emails and living a busy life, but for now let them simply eat and communicate with the most important people in their lives – their family.

Nobody wants to feel that they are being watched when they eat so don't keep up a running commentary on what your child is putting in her mouth. Simply place the food on the table and begin eating yourself. Spark up a conversation that does not involve food and give your child time. She may need a moment before she takes her first mouthful. When she begins to eat, don't draw attention to it as you might slow her down. Continue conversing, without drawing attention to the job in hand – eating.

When the meal is finished, even if your child has only taken a few mouthfuls, praise her. She sat at the table and conversed with you and managed to eat some food. This is a small step towards eventually eating an entire meal.

INTRODUCE NEW FOODS EACH WEEK

It's good to get your child used to trying new flavours – but choose your moment. This may sound obvious but there is no point in introducing food to a child if she is not hungry. Watch for signs of hunger, such as becoming tired and irritable, behaving unreasonably, continually asking for snacks or even having physical accidents, such as tripping up or walking into things. However, don't wait until your child is so tired and irritable at the table that she rejects the new food that is placed in front of her as a matter of course. You need to choose your moment carefully.

It's possible that a new food won't be tried when it is first offered, but it is now recognised and in time it will be tried. Make a note of when this food was introduced and reintroduce it in a week's time.

If possible, try to involve your child in preparing the new food and make sure that you sit down together to eat it. It will help if there are other foods on her plate that she does recognise and like. For example, if you know your child likes rice and you are trying to introduce a curry, keep the two parts of the meal separate on the plate and accept that only the rice may be eaten. This means that there is always part of the meal they will eat.

If your child refuses the meal outright, don't worry. Leave it on the table and offer a small yoghurt or some fruit, but not a huge amount. This is not a substitute for the main meal. Once she has eaten her small dessert, she might return to her main meal. This is something I have observed many two- to four-year-olds do.

> Please don't make her another meal if she refuses the first one.

Most parents worry that hunger might make their child wake in the middle of the night but I have never known this to happen. You will probably find that she wakes promptly the following morning and will want breakfast. This is simply the start of a new day and you will be serving another meal that is familiar to your child.

Finally, I advise that only one new food type or meal is tried each week. Don't bombard your child with new foods. She needs to see what she is familiar with as well. So if you try a new meal on Monday, make sure you offer familiar meals for the rest of the week.

Guide your child to try the food but don't force it:

"Just see if you can put a small amount in your mouth."

"I am sure you are bursting to know what it tastes like."

"I will leave it up to you and see if you can surprise me!"

Accept that the food may not be eaten or even tried but praise her for placing it on her plate and make her aware that you will be having it again next week. Maybe she'll feel like eating a little of it then.

OFFER HEALTHY SNACKS

Some people don't agree with eating between meals, but I'm not one of them! I simply couldn't survive without my 3.30pm cup of Earl Grey and a biscuit. Every family I have helped knows this. And if I am having a mid-afternoon snack, it would be wrong of me to deny one to a child I'm looking after.

Children usually need refuelling when they get home from school, and when young children wake from their afternoon nap they usually need a drink and a piece of fruit to bring them back into the world of the living! I suggest dedicating a shelf in your food store to healthy snacks, such as savoury crackers, nuts and seeds, dried fruit and home-made flapjacks. Crudités and dips or fruit could also be offered. Do read the ingredients labels on shop-bought 'healthy snacks' because some of them contain a lot of sugar (fruit and cereal bars can be guilty of this) while others might have mysterious E numbers.

I am not saying that snacks should only ever be of the healthy kind. Most children love a cake or biscuit, and these can be given if the rest of the diet is balanced and healthy.

If you don't know what an ingredient is … put the item back on the shop shelf!

I think it's a good idea to have clear-cut snack times so that your child knows when she will be getting something to eat. If you don't make this clear, you could have her asking continually "Can I have a snack? Can I have a snack?"

The ideal snack times are mid-morning (10.30–11am) and mid-afternoon (3–3.30pm). If your child can't yet tell the time, give her an event to associate the snack with. If she is told what her snack will be, she is less likely to argue when it is presented to her.

"After our morning walk in the park we will stop on a bench for a fruit snack."

"Let's play in the garden, then read two stories, then have a cracker snack."

"I will bring you a flapjack snack when I collect you from school."

I advise that you leave one and a half hours after every snack before the next meal. Make sure a snack is not too big. Explain to your child that it is just a little 'energy boost' and not a main meal.

By following these basic principles from the time your child is six months old, you will be setting up good habits around food, which will make life much easier for you all. However, if your child is unduly picky, or mealtimes frequently seem to become a battleground, follow the three-day plan that is appropriate for the child's age (pages 80–97 for six to eighteen months, pages 128–143 for eighteen months to three years, pages 190–205 for three to six years). I've tried them on children with all kinds of eating problems and they haven't failed me yet!

ENCOURAGING GOOD BEHAVIOUR

It's very stressful having to ask your child not to do something, and figuring out how to react when they don't listen – or they do listen and choose to disobey. I have worked with many mothers who have successful careers in which they manage lots of staff, and they often say to me, "I can discipline and be firm at work, but it is completely different with my little boy."

I've also met lots of fathers who simply want to be the 'Fun Weekend Daddy'. They tell me they feel guilty because they've been at work all week long and the last thing they want to do is be the bad guy at the weekend.

The big picture is that you are working towards teaching your child self-discipline.

Discipline sounds like such a severe word. It conjures up loud voices of authority that scare us into 'doing as we are told'. I would like to think that those days are gone. Rather than using the word 'discipline' I advise that in your mind you think about guiding your child to make the right choices.

In life, once you know right from wrong you can live a happy and enriching life. This is what you are guiding your child to do and I feel strongly that these lessons should start early, even before your child can speak. In general they should be ready from around the age of fourteen months. By this stage they will be mobile, either crawling or walking around, and they will start exploring things that you may not want them to touch, such as buttons on the washing machine, the television remote – oh, and a popular one for little fingers, the loo brush! This is when you need to start setting boundaries and helping your child to recognise them.

ESTABLISHING BOUNDARIES

In adult life, we are surrounded by rules and regulations. We know our own boundaries and your child must learn to know his. From an early stage, and certainly by the time your child is able to crawl, I suggest you sit down with your partner or any other people who care for him on a regular basis and agree a set of rules and boundaries together. Write them down if you like.

It's absolutely vital that you are singing from the same hymn sheet so that your child isn't confused by getting one set of boundaries from one parent and a different set from the other. This is a discussion that will often lead to you talking together about your own childhoods and the way you were raised. There will be elements of your upbringing that you want to imitate and perhaps others that you want to avoid, and your partner will feel the same about his upbringing. You may need to compromise to arrive at the set of rules you want for your child.

The type of questions you might want to discuss could include:

- How often will you eat together as a family?
- Should your child stay seated at table until everyone has finished eating?
- Will you let your child walk around the house eating and drinking?
- Will you let your child open cupboards and drawers around the house?

🌿 Can snacks be eaten in the car? If so, what?

🌿 Is it important to you that your child always says 'please' and 'thank you'?

🌿 How often do the toys get tidied away? Will you encourage your child to help?

🌿 Will you teach your child to say 'sorry' after an incident that was their fault?

🌿 Is your child allowed to jump on the bed?

🌿 Do you promote sharing of toys?

🌿 Snacks and sweets – how often?

🌿 How many stories will you read to your child before bed?

🌿 Does he sleep with the light on or off?

The rules need to be simple and you must be in agreement, which is why this discussion is so important. However, children are constantly developing and discovering so new boundaries will have to be set from time to time and you and your partner will have to communicate about this.

I worked with a family in which the two-year-old girl was fascinated by the kitchen cupboards and continually wanted to 'help cook' when her mother was in the kitchen. The mother simply wanted to get the task done and didn't have time for her daughter to help every time a meal was being prepared. We solved the problem by emptying out a cupboard and filling it with the little girl's plastic foods and tea set, which she could play with while her mother cooked. This was a great success and led to a contented mother and daughter. However, when the weekend came, the mother had a lie-in and the little girl came downstairs with her father. He didn't know the new arrangement so every time the girl went to open the cupboard, her father removed her. This led to tears and frustration, until the mother got up and came downstairs to explain.

I suggest to families that they write down new strategies in case the parent at home forgets to relay them. Keeping a notebook in a prearranged place will reinforce the rule you are implementing and ensure that both parents are aware of the change. Here are some examples:

DATE	INCIDENT	SYSTEM IN PLACE
05/05	JOSH KEEPS TRYING TO CLIMB ON THE KITCHEN CHAIRS.	HE IS GUIDED TO CLIMB ONLY ON HIS LITTLE RED CHAIR. REMOVE HIM FROM THE LARGE CHAIR AND TAKE HIM TO HIS LITTLE ONE, OFFERING PRAISE.
06/05	WHY DOES HE LOVE THE LOO BRUSH SO MUCH?	OUR LOO BRUSH NOW SITS ON THE BACK OF THE CISTERN. IT LOOKS UGLY BUT IT STOPS OUR SON DRINKING THE BLEACH IN ITS BASE!
07/05	JOSH ONLY EVER WANTS TO WEAR HIS BROWN SHOES.	WHEN YOU WANT HIM TO WEAR ANY OTHERS, PLEASE INFORM HIM THAT THE BROWN ONES ARE IN THE WASH AND WILL BE BACK AFTER 'ONE SLEEP' (I.E. TOMORROW).

Children grasp very quickly that if they ask their mother for a biscuit and she says 'no' that it might be a good idea to go and ask their father because he tends to say 'yes'. If your child gets the impression that you are not a united front, he can play one of you against the other. That's why it's vital that you let the child know that you make decisions together: "Have you asked your mother? If she says it's alright, then you can have a biscuit but not otherwise." Let him know you are a team.

Always support your partner in any decision they have made. You may not agree at the time but this can be discussed later and an alternative system created. If you undermine your partner, it teaches your child to lack respect for them too.

Little things to us mean a lot to a child. Continuity of care is fundamentally important to stop your child becoming confused by mixed messages.

FIND YOUR FIRM TONE OF VOICE

Until your baby is crawling, you have probably talked to her in a very gentle way. Your voice has mirrored her. You have seen her as tiny and vulnerable so you have trodden carefully. But when this little being becomes more robust, it is time for you to find your firm voice. By this I don't mean a shout. Shouting is exhausting and draining for all parties. Raising your voice indicates to your child that you have lost control and is totally counter-productive.

A firm voice will often be slightly deeper than your typical voice and when you use it you are giving an instruction.

Deep voice + clear statement = firm instruction

I advise that you practise this in front of the mirror. It's an interesting exercise and I would continue until you genuinely think "Yes, I would listen to that person in the mirror. She means it!" Try the following:

"Right, stop that now. Let's find something else to do."

"Leave that, thank you. Now, where are your books?"

"Come away. Let's sing a song instead."

Can you see how the first part of the sentence is the instruction and the second part is the guiding away? You need to keep your firm voice for the entire sentence, with a slight pause in the middle for your child to acknowledge what you have said to them.

You will know when you have found your firm voice because when you use it your child will respond. She may get tearful at first but this is a sign that she knows you mean what you are saying.

Everyone wants their child to be happy, of course. Some parents tell me they're worried that disciplining their child will upset him: "Won't this make him sad? Will it cause him to dislike me?"

I answer that the love between parent and child should be unconditional but you need to earn and build the respect your child has for you, and that means both giving and receiving respect.

MAKE EYE CONTACT

We have all been in situations in which we have found ourselves speaking to someone who is not making eye contact. It leaves us feeling uncomfortable, and not always sure that the person was interested in what we were saying. I believe that it is very important to guide your child with eye contact from a very young age. We can tell a lot about a person by their eyes, and it adds emphasis to whatever message you are trying to impart.

You will find there are times when you need to discipline your child and eye contact is crucial to underline the message. Bend down to his level and make eye contact, ensuring that he meets your eyes as well. Please remember my simple rule:

> If your child is not looking at you, he is not fully listening. Your voice is simply background noise.

Hold his arms so that he is facing you then use your firm clear voice. Speak to him in a way that shows you are genuinely disappointed in the choice he has made. It is not enough to glance over your shoulder and say "Don't do that!" because he won't respect a half-hearted effort.

After the incident you can explain and then hug and carry on with your day. I guarantee that your child will have forgotten about it before long. I have never seen a young child bearing a grudge when discipline was deserved.

WHO CARES WHAT OTHERS THINK?

I speak to many parents who tell me that while they can be firm and direct in the comfort of their own home, they are less confident when they are in social environments outside the house. The fact of the matter is that you must be consistent in the way you discipline and guide your child. He can't be led to believe that when he is out of the house the boundaries widen. If you give this impression, your child will push the boundaries further and start to challenge you more and more, until you reach the stage where you dread leaving the house for fear of being 'watched by others'.

The fact is that most people are busy with their own lives. They are travelling from one place to another or concentrating on their meal in the restaurant, not yours! Simply live your life and guide your child in the way he needs to be guided. Ignore the rest, because the chances are that they are ignoring you.

It's true that sometimes people will watch and wonder how you are going to manage a particular situation with your child, but realise that they are not judging your child's behaviour – they are looking to see how you manage it. If you face the situation 'head on' you are likely to impress an onlooker. It is the parents who take the easy option and ignore bad behaviour who are frowned upon.

I was walking home through a park one day after meeting a friend for lunch and a mother was walking along with her son (aged about two years). He decided that he didn't want to walk any further and he sat down on the grass leaving his mother standing with his scooter.

"Now, you can jump back on the scooter and I will run next to you back to our house," she told him, *"or you can stay there for the night and wait for a policeman to come and talk to you and he will bring you home!"*

She started to walk away and didn't look back. It was clear that she believed 100 per cent in her child and trusted him to make the right decision.

He sat for a few moments' protest as his mother strode away, and then realised he needed to catch up with her fast. He jumped up and scooted off into the distance until he was alongside her again, and they made their way home with her jogging by his side.

This parent had clearly used similar methods before and she had a clear understanding of her child. She believed he would make the right decision and wouldn't want to be walked home by a policeman. Maybe one or two observers might have thought she was taking a risk in leaving her child, but most people watching would have thought 'Good parenting!'

BELIEVE IN YOURSELF, BELIEVE IN YOUR CHILD

In my opinion, the single most important lesson when it comes to guiding your child towards good behaviour is to *believe* that you are able to teach this lesson and that your child is capable of learning and acting on it. If you tell him 'no' and try to engage him in something else, truly *believe* that he will follow your direct guidance.

I often say to parents that your child can sense your feelings. They know you better than you think. So with this in mind you need to realise that if you ask your child not to do something, you need to truly believe that your child will make the correct decision. Make your directions and your belief clear, and good behaviour will follow.

If you do not believe he will respond correctly, he will sense your doubt. This will cause him to lose belief in himself and the instruction will go unheard. When you ask him to do something, say "I know you can do this because you are my super-good boy." Say it and believe it.

Parents' doubt = child's self-doubt

Parents' belief = child's self-belief

When he is old enough to understand the reasons for an instruction then it is a good idea to give them, but don't feel you need to state the obvious. For example, there's no need to tell him why he shouldn't hit his little sister, but you should probably explain why stepping onto the ice on a pond is a bad idea. You want him to learn, but there are also times when he simply needs to obey.

If your child consistently behaves badly in a particular circumstance, you can address the behaviour by following an age-appropriate three-day plan. If his behaviour is bad in several different respects, deal first with the aspect that causes most disruption to the family and establish new routines regarding that behaviour before continuing to address something else. You'll find the plan for children aged six to eighteen months on page 97, for children aged eighteen months to three years on page 143 and for three- to six-year-olds on page 205.

SPACE AND INDEPENDENCE

Everybody, young and old, needs their own space. Time on your own allows you to stop, think and reflect. For many parents the only time they have to themselves is a few brief minutes in the bathroom and then the couple of moments when their head hits the pillow at night before they fall asleep – but it doesn't have to be this way. You are not the only family member who needs space. You all do – including your child.

It's obvious that your child needs one-to-one time with you when you play and chat together because this is an important part of the learning process, as well as building on the bond between you. Choose activities in which you can teach him new skills, such as baking, doing jigsaw puzzles, creative artwork, making playdough figures, or even learning letters and numbers. This time helps you to understand your child's capabilities and personality, and creates closeness between you.

Don't feel you need to do this throughout your child's waking hours, though.

As time passes, your child will be less willing to play by himself and will continually ask for tasks, activities and entertainment to be laid on. He will grow to feel that he always needs company, and will struggle to cope with time alone.

Some parents feel they need to keep young children occupied from dawn to dusk, but over-stimulating your child can have adverse effects in the long term.

I've found that giving twenty minutes of your time is enough before you can explain that you need to do something else:

> "We have had a lovely time with the playdough together. Thank you for letting me play. Now maybe you could make me a playdough cake while I make a phone call and then we can plan what we are going to do next in our day."

Balancing periods of independent play with periods of structured play makes for a contented and balanced child.

There will always be times in our lives when we have to manage independently, so children need to learn from an early age to appreciate the pleasure of personal space, independence and their own achievements. I feel a sense of joy when I walk into a family kitchen and see a child happily colouring at the kitchen table and a parent busy preparing a meal or checking their emails. In this situation both parent and child have their own space. One is not relying on the other. They are both in their own worlds for as long as the moment lasts.

Whatever age your child is, you don't always have to be in the same room as them. The environment they are in must be safe, of course, but they don't need constant supervision. If you are going to leave your child for a moment to go into another room, tell them where you are going and that you will be back in a minute. You have reassured your child of the situation and they should feel comfortable with this arrangement.

As your child gets older he will start to choose to play independently, either going into the garden or retreating to his bedroom to achieve something alone. Instil in your child that he must tell you where he is going and what he is planning to do (if he knows), in the same way you do when you leave him for your own independent space.

Here are some tips on helping your child to learn to appreciate their own independence – and give you space at the same time.

AGE 6 MONTHS TO 2 YEARS

When your child wakes in the morning, give him some toys to play with in his cot and if he is able to feed himself from a bottle, you could give him his morning milk. Let him know where you are going and that you will be back in a little while. Leave the bedroom door open so that he can hear you. He needs to know that it is not night-time but that he is starting his day with 'independent play'. When you return to his room, praise him for the time alone.

The average length of time a child can manage independent play at this age is fifteen minutes. As well as first thing in the morning, this can also be done after your child's morning or afternoon sleeps.

Another time when you can leave your child to enjoy some independent play is when he is sitting safely in a high-chair. Offer some activities before you leave the room, such as the following:

6 MONTHS – I YEAR	I YEAR – 18 MONTHS	18 MONTHS – 2 YEARS
WATER BEAKER AND RICE CAKE	WATER BEAKER AND FRUIT	WATER BEAKER AND RAISINS
RATTLES AND MUSICAL TOY	MUSICAL INSTRUMENTS	PLAYDOUGH
PICTURE BOOKS	NOISY STORYBOOKS	STICKER/ACTIVITY BOOKS
FAVOURITE CUDDLY TOYS	CARS AND TRAINS	MATCHBOX CARS
STRINGS OF LARGE WOODEN BEADS	CHUNKY CRAYONS AND PAPER*	PAINTS/PENS AND PAPER*

* SELLOTAPE THE PAPER ONTO THE HIGH-CHAIR TABLE SO THAT IT DOESN'T FALL TO THE FLOOR.

I don't recommend leaving your child alone in a high-chair for longer than three to five minutes. You'll probably find that he starts to object after this length of time anyway.

Do you have an outdoor space that your child could take ownership of? If you have a garden, devote part of it to a flowerpot full of their garden toys, a sandpit, a ball pit, or a playhouse. When your child learns to enjoy his own outdoor space, you can take the opportunity to sit on a bench with a magazine, make a phone call or hang out the washing. Remember to make your child aware of what you are doing by telling him first.

> "Well done for sitting on your play mat with your lovely toys. Mummy is just going to hang out the washing."

> "You are doing some brilliant digging there. I am just going inside to make a cup of tea and then I will be straight back."

If you are leaving your child in the garden alone for a moment you must feel confident that he is in a safe and secure environment. Make sure no passers-by or stray dogs could get in, and that there is nothing lying around that he could hurt himself with, such as a lawnmower, garden tools or plants that could be poisonous if eaten. Create a safe area, using barriers if necessary.

AGE TWO TO THREE YEARS

At this age, you can encourage your child to get out of bed and play in his room with his toys when he wakes in the morning. You could have made a train track the night before, started a tower of Duplo bricks or tidied the dolls' house. Alternatively you could lay out some books with a beaker of water. Children of this age can manage independent play for fifteen or twenty minutes.

During the day you should be able to leave him at the table with some absorbing activity such as painting, colouring, playdough, sticker books, large Lego blocks, bead threading, baking and mixing, or posting pennies into a money box while you are within close range yet carrying out your own tasks for the day. Keep an eye on him if there are small pieces he could swallow. I find children aged nine to eighteen months are most likely to try to swallow small objects, and that children over two are more responsible, but stay close at hand just in case. Children should be able to sit alone at the table during snack time as well but stay nearby in case of choking.

This is the age when you can encourage your child to do his own planting and growing. It's lovely to explain to your child about the wonders of nature and ways in which we can get back to the land. Start by growing a pot of cress, which offers fast results. Tomato plants can also be good. They need frequent watering in the summer months but then your child can help to pick (and taste) the juicy red tomatoes.

Children of this age love to have their own little 'den' and it doesn't have to cost anything. Blankets can be arranged over a tree, bush or clothes horse with the help of some clothes pegs. Hung with a splash of creativity and imagination, this can make for a great space in which to develop your child's independence. If you build the den together you may find that he spends a large proportion of the day in it, giving you your own space.

Soon you will find that your child is happy to play in one room while you are in another. Perhaps he will be in the living room with his toys while you are in the kitchen. This is part of learning independence, and all you need do is call through from time to time to check he is OK.

AGE THREE TO SIX YEARS

By the age of three, your child should be able to dress himself (of sorts!), put on his shoes and take them off. He can feed himself and find activities to entertain himself.

By three years old, you can encourage your child to play alone in his bedroom. Keep certain toys there to entice him upstairs, so long as he is confident and competent at climbing and descending the stairs alone.

Craft activities such as sticking and glueing, painting and colouring can be done sitting up at the table by himself. You can even encourage your child to make his own lunchtime sandwich, spreading butter on bread and choosing his own fillings. This is an activity, mealtime and lesson in independence all rolled into one!

You should find that your child will now engage fully with other children so 'play dates' can be arranged. So long as the children play harmoniously together, this will give you a little more space of your own.

TRICKS OF THE TRADE: THE EGG TIMER

The concept of time is seldom clear to a child under the age of six. It means nothing to them when you say "In a minute" or "We'll do that later". They are not satisfied with this and will continue to ask the same question until they get an answer they understand.

The move from one activity to another can be stressful for them. When are you going to drag them away from the park? When is it time for tea? I find it useful to use an egg timer to help explain to a small child when something will happen. Here's an example.

Small child: "Can we go to the park now?"

Mother: "I need to finish preparing the dinner. Let's get the timer."

The mother sets the egg timer for the amount of time she needs (it's best to make 30 minutes the maximum if you can).

Mother: "You've got time to build something with your Lego and look at your books and then the alarm will ring to tell us that it is park time!"

Place the alarm out of your child's reach so that they cannot tamper with it. This is a tool that only adults have control of.

Another time when the egg timer can be useful is if the children are engaged in an enjoyable activity that you want to limit, such as watching TV, playing with a games console or playing on the computer. As before, make your child aware that you are setting the timer and that when the alarm sounds their screen will be turned off.

I think that every parent is aware of time slipping away from them. Using an egg timer makes you aware of how long it takes to do things and you'll stop yourself saying 'In a minute' when you realise that 60 seconds is actually no time at all!

PRAISE PHRASES

Parents often say to me that they keep re-using the same phrases when praising their child and it stops sounding genuine after a while. I believe that praise should be given only when praise is due and for a particular act. This means that you need to identify the act in the praising statement.

> "I think you are great to share your cars with your brother. Sharing is caring!"

> "Thank you for listening to me and playing on your own for ten minutes just as I asked you to."

> "You make me so happy when I see you making the right choices, such as [state act]."

> "You are a fantastic big brother. You show [sibling's name] how to behave brilliantly."

> "I love you for being you. It was very kind of you to help me tidy up the kitchen."

> "You have done that entire puzzle on your own. You are a true whizz!"

TEACHING INDEPENDENCE – A SUMMARY

 Before leaving your child on his own, you must be 100 per cent confident that he is in a safe and secure environment.

 Always explain what you are doing, and make the independent times short to start off with, but be consistent and repeat them several times a day. After three consecutive days of the new routine, your child will become more accepting of this new experience.

 Remember that most children can only manage short bursts alone:

6 months–1 year	5–15 minutes
1–3 years	10–20 minutes
3–6 years	15–30 minutes

Before long, you may find that your child is requesting independent space for himself. When this happens, it means he has learned an important life lesson – and you have earned yourself some well-deserved 'me time'.

In this chapter we have looked at the components a young child needs in his day to day life in order to feel secure and happy: enough sleep, three meals and some healthy snacks, independent play as well as structured playtime with you.

Is this what your child's life is like? If so, I'm sure you have worked hard to achieve it. It's not always so straightforward, though. In the next chapter, we will look at what you can do when problems arise with your child's routine, for whatever reason, and I will explain the principles of my three-step plan for turning around even the most ingrained bad habits. Bear with me if you want to see big changes for the better in your family life.

CHAPTER 2

The principles behind the three-day plans

Children can easily slip into bad habits, such as kicking up a fuss at bedtime, refusing to eat meals you put in front of them or rebelling against being strapped into pushchairs or car seats. A lot of the time they are testing their boundaries, which is a perfectly natural and healthy thing for them to do, so the first thing I'd like to say is "Don't blame yourself." Rather than looking back and trying to find causes for any difficult behaviours, we are going to look forwards and find solutions – and we'll do it in just three short days.

They won't be easy days. If the habit is deeply ingrained, your child might fight noisily to maintain it and he might get very upset when you put your foot down. But put your foot down you must, for the sake of the whole family and most of all to help your child grow up healthy, happy and ready to thrive in a school environment.

The three-day plans for sleeping, eating and good behaviour follow certain basic rules, which are adapted slightly for different age groups. You should follow the central principles to the letter but some of the details of the plans can be adapted to fit in with your family routines and preferences, your personal parenting style and the character of your child.

WHAT TYPE OF PARENT ARE YOU?

When I visit new clients, I usually start by asking them some questions about their approach to life management, and their parenting style in particular. Different types of parent take different approaches to child-care, depending on their individual characters and the way they've been brought up themselves. If I understand their parenting style, I can be aware of it as we work through the three-day plan and I can help them to use their strengths while compensating for any weak points.

It's not that I am judging them.

For the purposes of this book, I've identified three different parenting styles:

There is no right and wrong way of parenting, and no right and wrong type of parent. It's very important to understand that.

🦋 Orderly and organised

🦋 Mindful and attentive

🦋 Relaxed and adaptable

I expect you will know at a glance which one you resemble most closely. Read the advice for your particular style, and just bear it in mind as you start to think about implementing a three-day plan with your own child or children.

THE ORDERLY AND ORGANISED PARENT

You are the type of person who likes to follow procedures and guide-lines, someone who takes control of their life and prefers everything to be in its correct place. You put all appointments in a diary and keep lists of tasks that you tick off as they are completed. The fact that you thrive on order and structure in your day will mean that you run a very organised ship when caring for your child(ren).

As we've discussed in Chapter 1, children take great satisfaction in routine. Knowing what is going to happen and when is a comfort and a reassurance – but children are not always predictable and sometimes routine has to alter. It could be that you will find it difficult to alter your routines to fit in with the three-day plans, but you can get back into your comfort zone by reading the plan carefully and making all the preparations you can in advance: buy any tools you will need, stock the fridge with all the food you will need for the three days and clear the decks of any work or other distractions.

If you are over-authoritarian in the way that you lay down rules, you might sometimes make your child feel powerless. Remember that you don't need to approach the changes in this book in a serious, authoritarian way. Present the plan to your child as an exciting process, something that you will all do together as a family. Tell your child that you need his help because it is not something that you can do alone, but that the benefits will help the whole family. Make your child feel important not powerless.

THE MINDFUL AND ATTENTIVE PARENT

You may be a first-time parent, who frequently feels uncertain about parenting – which is a totally natural way to feel. You have probably read a huge number of parenting books but still the questions are circling in your mind. You like to hear other people's opinions and do your own research before reaching any decision and probably tend not to simply follow your own instincts. You prefer to be sure of your course before taking action.

Sometimes you worry unnecessarily because it is in your nature to be cautious. Such worry can be exhausting, especially after one of those unproductive days when you feel you've taken one step forward and three back. This can be a problem if your children pick up on your anxiety and become anxious themselves. When I go into family homes I can sometimes sense parents' hesitancy or doubt – and if I can sense it then their child most definitely can as well. If you doubt yourself, your child will be less likely to believe in himself.

Before starting a three-day plan, make sure you organise a support team for yourself. This should include your partner, the child's grandparents and/or any other carers who look after him on a regular basis – but it can also include some friends on the end of the phone who are there just for you, to reinforce your own self-belief and tell you that you're doing a great job! Feel their belief in you, take it on board, and then it will flow naturally into your child. That way the whole task gets so much easier.

THE RELAXED AND ADAPTABLE PARENT

You are a laid-back character who likes to take life in your stride. You are very aware of the world around you but can sometimes get distracted from the task in hand as you stop to smell the roses along the way. I visualise you as a parent who has many projects on the go at the same time and knows that all jobs will eventually be complete – you just don't know when. You don't like deadlines and prefer to live life in 'holiday' mode. You are great at adapting to new environments and situations and very little will cause you to get stressed – other than time-keeping!

Having a calm and relaxed approach to parenting is very healthy – but being too relaxed can sometimes cause your child to take control and that's when life can become challenging. Over-relaxed parents may not give their children the clear boundaries they need and in this situation even a young child will often slip into the role of 'leader'. But children cannot create their own realistic boundaries. They have to be shown right from wrong at this age.

The three-day plans may be harder for you than for any other parent type because you need to follow them to the letter for three days. The only way you will manage this is if you clear any other commitments from your calendar, take time off work, strike out any social engagements and give your child your complete focus. It will be worth it.

WHAT'S YOUR CHILD'S STYLE?

The three-day plans can also be adapted to accord with your child's nature and the way he or she responds to the world. There are, of course, hundreds of different types of children but the ones I see tend to be the fiercely independent ones who are striving for control in the household. Placid, easy-going, eager-to-please children are much less likely to need a three-day plan. So if you're reading this book, I'm guessing you have an independent child.

I have found over my years of guiding parents and children that when it comes to getting their own way, children have three main styles:

- The Negotiator
- The Fighter
- The Drama Queen/King

Once again, I expect you know at a glance which category your child falls into.

Read the appropriate section below for some tips on coaxing your independent child into completing the three-day plan they need.

> If you study your child's behaviour for long enough you will see yourself … or your partner … or both!

THE NEGOTIATOR

No matter how much you give, this child always wants just that little bit more! Even before they can talk, if you place one thing in front of them they will let you know by pointing and straining that they want something else. They won't shout; in fact, they may flash you a gummy smile to win you over. But if it means that he is only eating his favourite food at every meal, then you are giving him too much control.

When Negotiators learn to talk, they will use their word skills to get their own way.

> "I need to have three stories at bedtime because I love all these three stories and I can't choose between them. I need them all."

You can guarantee that if you give in and read them three stories, tomorrow they will want four. Sticking to your word is fundamentally important when dealing with a Negotiator.

Here's my suggestion. Hold up one hand with the fingers closed in a fist, and on the other hand hold up two fingers, then say:

> "You choose: two books or no books."

It may take a while but you need to stick to your guns with a Negotiator or they will end up running the household. Don't let them wear you down with their charm, no matter how hard it may be at times. (You'll find more on dealing with this type on page 226 in Chapter 5.)

THE FIGHTER

This little one sees life as a challenge and is determined to get his own way. If he senses defeat, he is likely to shout, scream and even lash out. As a parent it can be tempting to give him what he wants to avoid the outburst but this is taking the easy option and will almost certainly lead to problems in the long term.

You will know if you have a Fighter on your hands even when he is still a baby. Maybe he shouts whenever he is strapped into a high-chair or car seat. He knows it is going to happen anyway, but still he wants to fight it all the way. At mealtimes, he may suddenly try to sweep all bowls and finger food to the floor, as a protest. All you can do is stay calm and choose your battles. Don't fight fire with fire. Choose one behaviour to focus on at a time, and follow a three-day plan until you are able to change it.

If your child has a temper, it is important to let him vent his anger. Once he is able to walk, he needs to be taught to remove himself from the social situation when he gets angry, find a place to let off steam and calm himself down. Once calm you can then reason with him and the day continues.

In rugby a player will be sent to the 'sin bin', while a football player will get a red card. It is no different with children: angry behaviour needs to be isolated. You'll find out more about this in the Behaviour section of this chapter, on page 52.

THE DRAMA QUEEN/KING

If something is said that she doesn't like, this child will start to whinge and whine, and the tears will flow relatively quickly. If you still don't back down in the face of her big sad eyes, the noise levels will increase rapidly. Younger children may throw themselves to the floor face down, as if abandoned, or turn on the waterworks. With older children there may be a dramatic departure and the slamming of a door with screams of "It isn't fair!"

It is important that you remain consistent and don't allow this manipulative behaviour to cause you to waver and give in. If you scoop up a Drama Queen and place her on your hip, she has won! Don't let her pull on your heart strings, no matter how convincing the dramatic performance. All actresses need an audience and if she doesn't have one, she'll stop soon enough.

If the behaviour becomes unbearable you need to guide your child to her own space to calm herself down. Once she has released her emotions, then you can both continue with the day. Sulking is best ignored, because if you focus on negative tendencies, they will last longer. Leave her alone as much as possible until the mood changes. (There's more on whingeing and whining on page 227 in Chapter 5.)

❦

My three-day plans are suitable for all different types of children. Just make sure that you don't let their tactics divert you from the task in hand, which is encouraging them to learn behaviours that will help them to grow up as healthy, balanced, sociable and successful adults.

THE MIND GAME

I've seen all kinds of challenging behaviour over the years I've been working as a Bespoke Nanny. It can start as early as six months old and continue right into the school years and beyond. If your child consistently challenges your authority, you'll feel demoralised and the whole family will be affected. It's important that you know you are not alone as you sit on the sofa with your cup of tea reading these words. Every family reaches this point at some stage.

It's easy to give in to a few seemingly harmless things – such as bringing your child into your bed so you can get an extra hour's sleep; letting him leave his green vegetables, reckoning you'll reintroduce them after his next birthday; turning a blind eye to his 'little white lies' – but before long you'll reach a point when you find that your child is dictating the way the whole family lives, and you will know in your heart of hearts that you need to take action. Exasperation and exhaustion will make the decision for you!

My three-day plans will help you to turn around even the most recalcitrant offender if you stick to them consistently. There can be no compromises, though. You, your child and the rest of the family must follow the rules exactly for the system to work. And it *does* work, if you give it a chance.

I don't think anyone can go through life without praise and reward, most importantly children and parents. We all need to know what we are working towards. When you follow one of my programmes, it means changing your child's routine, a routine the child was probably quite happy with. They need to have a reason to change, and this is where the reward system comes in. It's one of the key principles of the three-day plans.

My reward system does not involve new toys and material possessions. It involves the one thing your child wants more than anything in the world – your time. Time together as a family. Quality time together is a fundamental part of creating a happy family life.

In order to motivate your child to change his routine, you need to give him an incentive and, if he is old enough, this can be something you discuss together. Find rewards that will engage him, something he will consider worth working towards. Here are some examples that you could offer to a child who is over eighteen months old:

- A treasure hunt
- A bike ride around the park
- A special TV programme
- An ice cream in a café
- One-to-one story time with Daddy
- A board-game challenge
- A trip to the swimming baths
- Building a den in the woods
- Baking with Mummy
- Digging in the garden

The main driving forces that you will use to guide your child towards good behaviour are praise and rewards.

- Playing a ball game
- A song and a dance together
- An amazing art project

If you are working on a three-day programme with a child under the age of eighteen months, they won't understand rewards but will respond to warm praise that is communicated through positive body language and speech.

> "I am so proud of you for making such a great choice. Well done! You have made Mummy very happy."

Back up your words with lots of cuddles and kisses, and perhaps some special story time sitting on your knee, and most young children will find that an incentive to behave well.

There is a very fine line between rewarding and bribing, though. Every parent is tempted to bribe a child sometimes, especially when they are in a hurry and are too stressed to take time to resolve the situation otherwise:

> "If you get into your pushchair now like a good boy, we'll buy an ice cream on the way home."

It's easy to see how this could become a problem, though. The smart child is going to put two and two together and deduce that if he resists being put in his pushchair every time, then it's an easy way to get an ice cream.

The main difference between bribes and rewards is that a bribe is mentioned before the event, and a reward is mentioned after. An example of the way a reward is presented might be:

> "You've been so good today that we will have a treasure hunt when we get home, as a special treat."

The day before you start a three-day plan, you and your child can sit down and make a list of all the things that might be good as rewards.

Let your child suggest things that he would particularly like. Explain that when Mummy and Daddy are particularly pleased with him, you will all pick a reward together.

Once the programme has started, you can use rewards to provide encouragement and congratulate him on his progress:

> "Well done. Mummy and Daddy are so pleased. You are making changes and becoming a grown-up boy. Let's go to our reward list and you can choose whatever you like!"

He doesn't get to decide when a reward is due but he has a say in what goes on the reward list, and he can make the decision to behave well.

As well as the special reward they get for good behaviour, you will devise some form of guidance tool: a visual symbol of achievement so that your child can chart their progress. Once again this is age-appropriate, but it might involve putting stickers on a poster, putting marbles in a jar or adding magnets to a magnet sculpture. You will have to buy any materials necessary for this in advance, so it can start on the first morning you implement a three-day plan.

Children need to see the reason for an action. They need to see praise and reward.

PRAISING AND REWARDING YOURSELF AS WELL

Parenting is a tough job, especially when you are trying to implement a new routine, so I always advise that parents praise and reward themselves as well as their children. It helps to keep your morale high and your determination strong.

First of all, when your child takes a small step in the right direction, find yourself a mirror, take a look in it and wink, then whisper "You did that!" It may sound silly, but try it.

At the end of the day, find your solace. This may be a glass of wine, a chocolate bar, a bubble bath – or all three! Make sure you praise yourself each night of the three-day programme.

Write yourself a reward list and ask your partner to do the same. Once the new regime has been implemented, choose the reward you both want, and make sure your child knows what you are doing. Explain to him that there are rewards all the way through life, and not just when you are a child.

Examples of rewards you might choose? How about:

- A day at a spa
- A day on the golf course
- A night out for dinner (babysitter organised)
- A trip to the theatre or cinema
- A long lie-in on a Sunday morning
- Time in the garden reading the weekend newspapers

All the family need praise and rewards, so if older siblings are involved in helping to implement a three-day plan, make sure they get something they'd like as well.

PREPARING FOR YOUR FAMILY CHALLENGE

In this book I have covered four main family challenges that require a new regime to be implemented: problems with sleeping, eating, behaviour and potty training. Remember that you should always deal with sleeping problems first and move onto the others after sleeping is sorted out. Make sure you follow the correct three-day plan for your child's age group.

I am a great believer in the number three, so I suggest that you read through the plan three times and make sure you understand it fully before implementing it in your home. You'll need to make a number of preparations before you start.

The first thing you must ensure is that everyone involved in the situation is aware and singing from the same song sheet. By this I mean that your partner and any other babysitters or childminders must understand the plan and agree to help you follow the steps. There should always be one main person – you! – who is implementing the plan but you will need moral support along the way and at the very least others shouldn't undermine your methods or change the rules if they are in charge when you are not around.

If you have older children they need to be made aware of the situation. Explain what you are doing and what you hope to achieve:

> "Mummy and Daddy have decided to help [Johnny] make a change and [stay in his own bed/eat his food/behave nicely]."

Secondly, make sure that your home is organised as you want it, that there is plenty of food in the fridge, and that your tasks and phone calls have all been made, so that for the next three days you can be fully focused on the matter in hand. If you work, I advise taking time off for three days, or doing the plan over a long weekend or during the holidays. This does not mean that you are going to be housebound or that you can't visit friends or go to the shops. It does mean that you need to clear your mind of any distractions in order to concentrate fully on the three-day programme.

After these preparations have been made, you should sit down and talk to your child about what is going to happen. Even little ones as young as a year old will understand the gist of what you are saying. I recommend telling your child either the day before, or on the morning of Day One. Sit with him at the breakfast table first thing in the morning, when he is not distracted by any toys or television screens or other people, and explain that you are going on an exciting journey to make a change that will make the whole family happier.

Planning ahead and being organised will make you feel more in control. Give yourself a pat on the back when you're all ready.

Children understand what we are saying to them long before they utter first words themselves. The one tactic that *never* works is trickery. Be honest with your child and talk to him as an equal. Obviously you will need to simplify your language, but your child will gain an understanding.

Listen to yourself while you're explaining to your child that you think it is time to make a change. When you hear the words come out of your own mouth and look into your child's eyes, you will begin to believe in yourself and realise that you are capable of guiding your child to make this change. It really is going to happen.

The ethos behind my three-day pro-grammes is not about telling your child how to behave. You are guiding them to make the right choices and when they understand the importance of making these choices they will make the change for themselves – and feel very proud for doing so. The work to be done is a family effort and not for you alone. And when you succeed, it will be a family achievement.

I'm now going to run through the basic principles behind each of the plans. You should read these sections carefully so that you understand the general rules before refer-ring to the correct parts of Chapters 3 to 6 for your own specific plan.

> Never underestimate your child's ability to understand you.

BASICS OF THE THREE-DAY SLEEPING PLAN

The fundamental reason why some children don't sleep as you want them to is because they are unsure how to settle themselves to sleep – both at the start of the settling process and also when they wake at night or in the early hours of the morning. I have devised this plan to help children who can't settle themselves to sleep at any stage of the day or night without you rocking them to sleep, taking them into your own bed or otherwise doing the difficult bits for them.

If your child senses for one moment that you are going to return to your old habits he will continue to shout. And the moment you return to your old ways, your child will have won. When your child senses your confidence and true belief in this new routine, he will follow your lead. Your confidence will cause your child to trust and believe you. Keep it up for three consecutive days and you won't believe your eyes!

The timing of sleep is very important when you are implementing a three-day plan for sleeping. Don't be tempted to keep your child up late so they are over-tired, which will disrupt their routine and make it even more difficult to settle them. During the day, don't let them sleep past 10am or 3pm, as this will interfere with their next sleep. Always follow the timings suggested in the plans for your child's age group, even if it means you have to waken a child who is sleeping peacefully. (Yes, I know that goes against every parental instinct, but bear with me!)

Before you start the plan, I need you to truly believe in your heart of hearts that your child is capable of settling himself.

To start the plan, you'll need:

- The child's bedroom to be as dark as possible (get black-out curtains, or use my tin-foil trick from page 4.)

- The room should be at a pleasant temperature – neither too hot nor too cold – and I recommend using a sleep sack for children under two (see pages 4–5).

- A guidance tool of your choice (there will be age-appropriate suggestions in the specific plan you follow).

- A digital clock or timer.

- Timing sheets and a pen.

These last two items are a vital part of the sleeping plan. This is the way it works.

You'll need several sheets of paper with four columns on them topped by the following column headings:

TIMER START	TIMER STOP	LENGTH OF SHOUT	LENGTH OF PAUSE

You can either print them out on your computer, or write the column headings by hand on the top of the pages of a notebook. What you are going to do is put your child down to sleep according to a settled routine of stories, milk, teeth brushing, kisses and cuddles, then a few loving words before you leave the room. After that, you will stand or sit in an adjoining room, out of sight but within earshot, and time the length of their protests, and the length of the pauses between protests, to help you decide when you need to go in and resettle your child and when he is starting to settle by himself.

If he wakens during the night, or too early in the morning, you will resettle him briefly then leave him, timing the protests as before. This is the only way your child will learn how to settle himself into sleep. If you apply the rules consistently he will pick it up very quickly.

There are some terms you will need to understand.

THE SHOUT

If you usually stay with your child until he falls asleep, he is going to react with confusion followed by frustration when you stop doing so. The noise he is making is not crying but shouting. He is not upset. In your head, try to put a little voice to the shouts. He is saying:

> "What on earth is going on, Mummy? You usually rock me to sleep. Why don't you come back and rock me? What am I supposed to do now? How do I go to sleep? Tell me. Tell me! Tell me!"

This will make it easier for you to deal with as you sit or stand outside the bedroom with your timer and timing sheets. Whatever you do, you mustn't give in and go back into the room at this stage. Just keep the timer on and listen for any pauses in the shouting.

THE THINKING PAUSE

Understanding the Thinking Pause is a fundamentally important part of the sleep programme. At first your child will simply shout, because he doesn't understand what you are asking of him. As the shout timings become shorter and the pauses between shouts get longer, it is a clear sign that your child is thinking about what to do next. He is starting to accept that he needs to do something alone. He knows why he is in his cot or bed. He will shout out in frustration again then think some more. In life, thinking will often lead to doing. Give your child space to think and he will eventually progress to getting to sleep by himself. Every time he takes a pause, even if just for a couple of seconds, write it on your chart and start the timer when he begins shouting again.

THE CRESCENDO CALL

When your child is shouting loudly, he hasn't paused for some time and the shout is becoming a high-pitched scream, you need to enter the room and restart the settling process. It will be hard for a child to settle himself when he has reached this stage so you will have to intervene. You need to lift a young child from his cot very briefly, and then once he has calmed down, place him back in his sleeping position and repeat the same settling process for 30 seconds at the most. With an older child you can tuck him in again, but don't offer any kisses, cuddles or soothing words. He should not be rewarded for Crescendo Calling.

I have often seen the timing process fail in a sleep programme because a parent thinks their child is Crescendo Calling when they are not. If you enter your child's room too often, you are continually interrupting his Thinking Pause. This will prolong the lesson he is learning about how to settle himself to sleep.

BEFORE YOU START A SLEEPING PLAN...

You should be able to answer 'yes' to the following questions:

- Is your child 100 per cent healthy?
- Are you feeling mentally and physically strong enough to remain positive even if you are sleep-deprived?
- Have you cleared three days in your diary?
- Have you got all the materials you need for the timing sheets, guidance tool and rewards?

🦋 Have you got a support network in place? If you don't have a live-in partner to back you up, you should at least have a friend on the end of the phone, who is aware of the three-day plan and ready to provide moral support.

🦋 Is the fridge fully stocked with the family's favourite foods? That will give you one less thing to worry about.

Now turn to page 64 if your child is aged six to eighteen months, page 115 if they are eighteen months to three years, and page 174 if they are three to six years. And look forward to the night that is coming soon when you will get eight hours' sleep yourself!

BASICS OF THE THREE-DAY EATING PLAN

You have read all the books, you understand about the nutrients the body requires for healthy growth and you know you should be encouraging your child to eat a variety of foods of different flavours – but he just won't have it. He spits out each mouthful or zips his lips firmly together so you can't get a spoonful inside and meals turn into a running battle each time. Older children might decide they are only going to eat chips and ice cream and refuse anything else.

It's very distressing for parents who fear their child's growth might be stunted or they might develop malnutrition, but be reassured that it's very unlikely to come to that – especially now you have taken a huge step in the right direction by deciding to make changes. Know that you are not alone. I have helped many dozens of families who have concerns about their child's diet.

If you follow this plan to the letter you should see some fundamental changes after three days, but first you and your partner need to be 100 per cent sure that this is what you want to do. You both need to read and understand the plan because after the three days, the programme is going to continue and become part of your lives.

Sit down as a family and discuss the eating plan. Its goal is that everyone in the house will eventually be eating the same meals and you, the cook, will only have to prepare one dinner every night. I've met mothers who make separate dinners for each child because little George doesn't like potatoes, Henry won't eat tomatoes and Sarah wants pasta for every meal. This is plainly ridiculous and gives children entirely the wrong signals.

During the three-day programme meals need to be eaten at home and ideally with both parents present at the dinner table. I know this is difficult for busy couples but you could start the programme over a weekend or when you have taken some leave from work. If only one parent can be present I advise that the other at least tries to arrive home for the evening meal at 5pm on the third day. Remember that this is for the sake of your child and it is about making a fundamental change to enhance the lives of every family member.

> Your role in life is not to fulfil your child's every command!

As with the sleeping and behaviour plans, one parent will 'take the lead' while the other follows. If you both direct your child, it could send mixed messages. The most important thing for the 'following parent' is that they sit at the meal table and eat a similar meal to the one your child is eating (although we'll spare you the vegetable 'mush' given to young babies).

HOW DOES IT WORK?

The idea is that you plan menus in advance, choosing meals that both adults and children can enjoy, even if the children need theirs mashed or liquidised. Make up charts showing what will be served for lunches and dinners. Breakfast will probably be toast, cereal and fruit, so you don't need to include them. Here's an example that would work for a three- to six-year-old:

	LUNCH	DINNER
FRIDAY	BOILED EGG & TOAST FINGERS	SAUSAGE CASSEROLE & MASH WITH SWEETCORN AND BROCCOLI
SATURDAY	GRILLED CHEESE & HAM SANDWICHES	PASTA DISH WITH SALAD
SUNDAY	ROAST CHICKEN & VEGETABLES	SAVOURY PANCAKES

When it is time to prepare the meal, ask your child to help you, giving tasks according to his age and abilities and letting him taste as he goes along, if he wants to. You then sit down to eat.

The key principle on the three-day plan is that your child will be given a small portion of the food on offer – and there are no alternatives.

If he doesn't eat any of the main course, he can have some fruit for dessert but don't try to fill him up with yoghurts, cakes or ice cream. He won't starve.

Every day you serve two between-meal snacks at times that are far enough away from meal times not to affect your child's appetite, but these snacks should not be huge, so that by the time he sits down to his next meal, he is hungry. And then you offer the food that you have decided the family is going to eat.

There are no arguments about food at table, no fuss. Simply offer the food, comment on how tasty it is and, if it is not eaten, take it away again. I'll give you detailed step-by-step instructions in the plan according to your child's age. The first day might be very difficult if your child's fussy eating has been going on for a while. The second day should be a little easier, and by the third day he should be eating at least some of what is on his plate at every meal.

As with the sleeping plan, you will use praise and reward, with some kind of guidance tool such as a sticker chart or jar for marbles on which you can mark progress, and rewards for any achievements. You should try to give a reward for something every day – even if it is just sitting nicely at table.

If you are thinking this will never work with your own fussy eater – try it. It really does work if you stick to the plan exactly and don't weaken by offering chunks of bread if they won't eat the main course and claim to be starving. You're going to have to be tough at first, but it's not long before children cotton on.

WHAT WILL YOU NEED?

Before you start, you should have planned your menus for the next three days and bought all the food you will need. It is important that you build on what your child already knows rather than introducing loads of new foods in one fell swoop. If they have a sweet tooth I recommend buying plenty of fruits (a range, not just ones you know she likes already) and also the sweet vegetables (carrots, sweet potato, squash and pumpkin). Keep some of her favourites but make it clear she will have to eat other foods as well. Here's what you'll need:

- A fridge full of food (refer to the meal plans in the appropriate chapter for ideas).

- Plenty of finger foods and healthy snacks (there are suggestions in the individual plans).

- Attractive bowls, plates, cutlery and bibs, according to the child's age.

- A handheld blender for blitzing up adult meals for the younger ones.

- Containers in which to freeze portions of food.

- A guidance tool of your choice.

As with the sleeping plan, choose a time when your child is completely healthy and you and your partner have the space to focus on the plan without getting distracted by work or other stresses.

The age ranges for the eating plans can be flexible. If your child is taking to weaning quite slowly, don't challenge him to eat chunky, chewy foods before he is ready. Introduce new foods slowly, following the stages I've described on pages 80–85 of Chapter 3. Once he can cope with a range of textures, you'll find suggestions that he can progress to, and then an eating plan for children up to eighteen months. In my experience, if your child has older siblings he is likely to want to eat the same meals as the older ones so he may be ready for the eighteen months to three years eating plan (see page 128) soon after the age of one, and ready to go on the three to six years plan (see page 190) before his third birthday. You know your own child best, so read the plans and see what you think he is ready for.

BASICS OF THE THREE-DAY BEHAVIOUR PLAN

Before the age of one year, a child does not really need to be disciplined. It's only after they are crawling and getting themselves into potentially dangerous situations that you need to be sure that when you say 'Wait!' they will stop what they are doing. After they start crawling, children realise they have a degree of independence and some problem behaviours can start.

- Between the ages of one and two, you might find they refuse to share toys, don't want to be strapped into their high-chair or buggy, and they may bite or hit.

- Between the ages of two or three, problems can include running off in public places, ignoring your simple instructions, spitting, tantrums, refusing to say 'sorry', and generally struggling to assert their independence.

- Between the ages of three and six, you might find you have problems with sibling squabbles, swearing, sulking, shouting and hitting, poor table manners, and an ongoing negotiation of every last detail of life, which can drive you to distraction.

I have three basic systems for helping children to choose to behave correctly: the Guidance System, the Consequence System and Zero Tolerance. I'll describe the basics below but you'll find the details of how to implement them in the chapter relating to your child's age.

THE GUIDANCE SYSTEM

Every child is an individual. They are unique. Together you and your partner created a being like no other. The most effective method of discipline will take into account their individual character. I recommend using a basic framework, as follows, which you can tweak according to the nature of the child.

- *Guide* child away
- *Direct* towards another toy or activity

🦋 *Ensure* they are engaged

🦋 *Praise*

🦋 *State* next activity in the day

🦋 *Leave* child to play.

Here's an example of the framework, which has been 'tweaked' to suit a two-year-old boy who loves trains.

GUIDE

🦋 Ask your child not to do something: *"George, I don't want you to do that. Come on, take my hand."*

DIRECT

🦋 Hold your child's hand and guide him towards a toy that will engage him.

ENSURE ENGAGEMENT

🦋 Sit down with him for a moment: *"Isn't this is a fantastic train track? How many carriages do you think we can pull with the blue engine?"*

🦋 Attach the carriages and let your child pull the engine.

PRAISE

🦋 *"Well done. These engines are lucky to have you as their driver."*

🦋 Stand up.

STATE NEXT ACTIVITY

🦋 *"Now, I am going to finish the [washing/cooking/my email] and then it will be time to [have lunch/go to the park]."*

LEAVE

🦋 Walk away. Don't linger. *"Brilliant work, train driver George!"*

What if the guide/direct/ensure/praise system doesn't work and your child continues to disobey? This is when you need to take action to make the message clear. In my experience, if a child says 'no' the first time you ask them to do something, he will carry on saying 'no' the second, third, fourth and fifth time as well, so there's no point repeating yourself. My advice is to make it clear to the child that he has a choice, and believe that he will follow your guidance.

Here's an example. Let's say you have a house rule of 'no jumping on the sofa' and your child starts jumping on the sofa. You try to direct him towards a jigsaw puzzle but it doesn't work. In that case, you need to remove your child from the sofa and sit him down on the carpet away from the sofa, saying something firm:

> "We do not jump on the sofa in this house. Mummy and Daddy do not jump on the sofa."

Then you offer the choice:

> "Either you can sit there or you can come and build this lovely Thomas the Tank Engine puzzle with Daddy."

Don't wait for your child to respond. Start to build the puzzle in front of him and before long the sofa will have been forgotten and he will start to help you.

My mother is an amazing parent but I have to admit that I wasn't easy. I was the child who would continue to test my boundaries until a consequence was required. I can remember her saying, well into my teenage years, "Why, Kathryn, do you always have to learn the hard way?"

Now that I am a professional nanny, and have studied and helped so many families, I can answer that question. Some people in life are strong achievers and they don't stop until they get what they think is right for them. The successful businessman pushed and strived to succeed and get where he is today. Children who 'test their boundaries' need clear strong guidance to steer them towards their success ... and equally need strong guidance to teach them right from wrong. They are the ones with inquisitive minds and may well be top business people in the future, but for now they need to learn to behave in a way that will be appropriate when they come to socialise with other adults and children.

THE CONSEQUENCE SYSTEM

The Guidance System should work well with children aged between one and two years but as they get older, they'll test their boundaries more and this is when your systems may need to become firmer. The Consequence System is usually implemented once children are over two years of age but if your child is advanced you may need to do it earlier.

Everyone needs a space where they can go and think. Personally, I run a bath and lock myself away, or I disappear on my bike. The people close to me know that this is my Thought Space. You owe it to your child to give him his own space where he can go and think. This is a place where he can digest what is being asked of him. The important thing is that you find a space where you can confidently leave your child without distractions such as television or older siblings. He must feel that this is his time to question and assess his behaviour. Your Thought Space could be:

The consequence of continued bad behaviour is that he will be taken to a place that you will refer to as his Thought Space.

- A bean bag in the hallway
- The bottom stair
- A chair in a safe corner
- A sofa in a quiet room
- If he is over three, he can be sent to his bedroom

Children over the age of two are usually fully aware when they are doing something wrong. Here's how the Consequence System would work in the case of a three-year-old girl who insists on jumping on her parents' bed, despite being fully aware that she is not allowed to.

- Firm instruction
- Warning

🦋 Guide from situation

🦋 Offer alternative

🦋 Thought Space

🦋 Apology

🦋 Move on

FIRM INSTRUCTION

🦋 *"We don't jump on beds in this house. Get down NOW."*

WARNING

🦋 *"One … two … three."*

GUIDE FROM SITUATION

🦋 Take your child's hand (lift if necessary) and remove from the bed. *"Right. Enough is enough. Come with me!"*

🦋 Walk her to her Thought Space and sit her down.

OFFER ALTERNATIVE

🦋 *"You can come and [do some lovely artwork/help me to bake a cake/other engaging activity] or you can sit here. You choose what you want to do. I am going to [set out the art materials/ baking ingredients/get things ready]."*

🦋 If she says she wants to come with you at this stage, bend down to her level and make eye contact. *"What did I ask you not to do?"* If she gives you the right answer, ask her to say sorry and then you can both go and do the promised activity.

🦋 If she is not ready to say sorry, you must get up without any further hesitation and leave her on the Thought Space.

🦋 If she tries to follow you, return her to the Thought Space without a word.

THOUGHT SPACE

🦋 Your child might be shouting, screaming or crying. It is very important that you let her behave in this way. Do not suppress your child's emotions. Let her vent her frustration. She will calm down when she is ready.

🦋 Ensure that she remains in her Thought Space until she calms down. If she gets up, simply return her to her space. Do not relent. This system works.

APOLOGY

🦋 Once your child is sitting calmly on the step and you know she understands why she was put there, say *"OK, now I think it might be time to go and do something nice together."*

🦋 If the shouting begins again, simply walk away, saying *"I will come back when you are ready."*

🦋 Once ready, bend down to her eye level and ask her to look at you.

🦋 Say something like this: *"Let's have a hug to say sorry. You really don't need to behave like that. You are a wonderful girl so let's have wonderful behaviour. Are you ready to do some [art/baking/ whatever the activity was] now?"*

I've had parents ask me if there isn't a danger the child will behave badly in order to be offered the chance of appealing activities, but in my experience children aren't this calculating. If you did suspect your child of trying to manipulate the system you could

> Strong defiance is often due to lack of boundaries. Make sure the boundaries are clear to your child.

offer plainer activities, but it is important to give them a positive option and allow them to make the right choice by themselves.

ZERO TOLERANCE SYSTEM

In every household there will be behaviours that are unacceptable under any circumstances. These should be agreed between you, your partner and any other carers, and you must react every time your child displays these behaviours. Here's my list of behaviours that I think should invoke the Zero Tolerance System:

- Biting
- Hitting
- Spitting
- Stealing
- Lying
- Spiteful words
- Deliberately damaging or breaking things

The Zero Tolerance procedure is as follows:

- Tell
- Act
- Apology
- Explain
- Move on

Let's imagine an example in which a two-year-old boy has had a toy taken from him by his older sister, so he decides to bite her. Admittedly she was wrong to take his toy but the immediate Zero Tolerance act must be dealt with.

First of all, ensure that the child who has been bitten is OK. Pacify her with a book or a toy and let her know that you are going to come and play with her once you have dealt with the child who bit.

TELL

- *"We never bite people. You need to go to your Thought Space straight away."*

ACT

🦋 Take your child straight to the Thought Space, saying *"Do not move until you are ready to come and apologise."*

🦋 Now focus on the injured party.

🦋 If the child who bit leaves his Thought Space, he should be taken back to it. He may shout and scream in frustration, or start to show signs of guilt by crying. An apology is compulsory with Zero Tolerance behaviour, but you must wait for him to calm down first.

APOLOGY

🦋 Once your child is quiet in his Thought Space, you can approach and ask if he is ready to come and hug his sister.

🦋 Take his hand and help him to do this. It is difficult to admit when you are wrong so give him the guidance he needs. You can all hug together as a family.

EXPLAIN

🦋 *"Nobody in this house is a biter. We only bite food. We never hurt people."*

MOVE ON

🦋 *"Let's go and [suggest a fun activity such as playing with a ball] now we are all happy again!"*

🦋 If your child refuses to apologise and just remains in his Thought Space, you need to be firm and make him fully aware of the upset he has caused. *"You are not saying sorry even though I have asked you. This has gone on long enough now. You can come off the step when you are ready but you will not [remove some privilege that the child was looking forward to, such as watching television later]."*

🦋 This is likely to cause your child to apologise quickly but at this stage it is too late. He must go without the activity he wants. He needs to feel upset so that next time he will remember and apologise more promptly.

🦋 If he starts to shout and scream again, place him back in his Thought Space and walk away, saying *"Maybe next time when I ask you to apologise for something you will do it."*

Eventually the shouting will cease and you can guide him to an activity and start afresh.

A word of warning: never say you are going to remove privileges unless you are fully prepared to follow through. In an airport recently, I heard a father say to his son (aged six or seven years), "If you don't stop doing that now we are not going to get on the plane and go on holiday!"

The boy's reply was "As if!"

My thoughts entirely.

DEALING WITH DIFFERENT TYPES OF CHILD

Your child needs to learn what will happen in the three stages of discipline I have outlined and at first it can be a steep learning curve for you both. You will need to use your intuition about which system is appropriate as you go along, but I give more specific guidance in the chapters relating to your child's age. If you get it slightly wrong, don't worry; just learn from the error and correct it next time.

Your child will fight the system to the best of his ability, pushing his boundaries to see how serious you are about this discipline. He'll try his best to guide you back to the way things were before, especially if you have one of the three independent types I described in Chapter 1.

The Negotiator may try to convince you that his way is right but you need to stand your ground and believe in what you are doing. Don't start a big discussion. Terminate the argument before it starts by saying "This is not something that is up for discussion." Change the subject or simply walk away, telling your child what you are off to do. If your child has a valid point to make and you find yourself agreeing with it, say "Your point is a good one. I think you are right and I am willing to do it your way this time, but not every time. Do you understand?" Make sure they say 'yes'. Don't make a habit of giving in to Negotiators, though. It's not good for them!

The Fighter is likely to spend the first part of the three-day plan shouting at full volume and rebelling in any way he can think of. If you stick to your guns and respond in the same way each time, he will soon start to understand that his 'fighting character' is no longer getting him what he wants. Remember that you need physical and emotional strength to deal with this. You are likely to have to return the Fighter to his Thought Space several times before he stays there. Initially it will be exhausting – but in the end it will be worth it.

You don't want to set so many boundaries that you spend the first day continually taking your child to the Thought Space. You can build on boundaries over the three days. Don't overload your child with information on Day One.

In the past, the Drama Queen has managed to get what she wants by throwing herself on the floor and being melodramatic. The best way of changing this behaviour is to ignore the stage show. A performance without an audience is boring. Leave her in her Thought Space to weep crocodile tears until she is ready to apologise and rejoin the household.

Whatever child type you are working with, you will have to retrain your own thought processes and go against your instincts.

- Don't react immediately
- Stay calm
- Think boundaries
- Think system
- React with firm clear guidance
- Reap the reward afterwards!

Pick your boundaries carefully and be realistic with your expectations.

THE IMPORTANCE OF CONSISTENCY

You will need to repeat the system three times in exactly the same way before your child starts to understand what is happening. Eventually, if you do the same thing every single time, he will get there and know what to expect. Over time he may even use the system of his own accord. I have known children take themselves to their Thought

Space after doing something naughty. It is at this stage you realise they are learning self-discipline. They have realised that anger and frustration are socially unacceptable so it is best to take yourself away for a moment to calm down and return when you are ready.

They will only reach this stage, however, if you are totally consistent in your application of the rules. I cannot stress enough the importance of consistency. The boundaries and Zero Tolerance factors must be clear. If you don't want your child to open the kitchen cupboards make it a firm rule. Children do not understand flexibility. A rule is a rule.

If you send mixed messages your child will start to create the rules themselves and before you know it, you'll realise that life in your household is running on your child's terms.

Of course, if you can predict situations that might cause a child frustration and circumvent them, you will save yourself a lot of trouble. At the end of Chapters 3, 4 and 5, we'll look at some key battlegrounds you may encounter with children of these ages. See page 97 for advice on children aged six to eighteen months old; page 143 for those aged eighteen months to three years; and page 205 for three to six years.

NOW YOU'RE READY TO START YOUR PLAN

You will see from the plans that I am the queen of bullet points! So here's what you have to do in a nutshell.

- Choose the plan you are going to follow.
- Read the plan and discuss it with your partner or any other adults who are going to help.
- Re-read the plan so it is clear in your mind.
- Prepare everything you will need.
- Believe it is going to work.
- Implement the plan.
- Remain consistent.
- See family life change before your eyes!

Discipline is not easy … but it is compulsory!

CHAPTER 3

Three-day plans for children aged six to eighteen months

By the age of six months, your baby will be becoming a human being with a recognisable personality and his own likes and dislikes. This may first show itself when you start weaning, and he gobbles up some foods while refusing others. He will have favourite toys, probably including one that he likes to sleep with, and he will enjoy time rolling around on the carpet and interacting with you.

At around seven months he will want to see the world from a different perspective instead of just lying on his playmat and he will now be rolling from back to front and enjoy sitting up with a little bit of support. By nine or ten months he may start being able to propel himself from one spot to another, either by crawling, rolling or just using sheer force of will. Then walking will come next, and by eighteen months he is no longer a baby but a toddler. He may be chatting away in baby language and showing all sorts of signs of asserting his independence.

In an ideal world, your little one will be sleeping through the night and having one or two decent naps a day, as well as eating a wide range of foods, but we all know that we don't live in an ideal world – so that's where my three-day plans come in. Don't hesitate to use them on little ones. The sooner good habits are instilled, the easier it is for everyone – including your child.

THE SLEEP PLAN FOR CHILDREN AGED SIX TO EIGHTEEN MONTHS

By the age of six months, a baby should be able to sleep through the night from 7pm to at least 6am. He will still need around three hours' worth of naps during the day as well, but these will gradually reduce down to one nap of one to two hours by the age of eighteen months. So long as you have calmed him, following an established routine, you should be able to put him down in his cot while he is sleepy but still awake, and leave him to settle himself to sleep, and if he wakes briefly in the night, he should be able to get himself back to sleep again so long as there is nothing wrong (such as a strange noise somewhere or if he is feeling ill).

Is your child not doing this? Do you have to rock him to sleep every time? Does he complain about being left alone? You will need to guide him so he understands what he has to do. That's what the three-day sleep plan is designed for.

Before starting the plan, make sure his bedroom is conducive to sound sleep. It should be kept cool, with black-out curtains or tin foil on the windows (see page 4). If you are not already using a sleep sack (see pages 4–5), why not give it a try? Babies like the security of being wrapped up in them.

If your child falls asleep easily at first but wakens at the wrong times, try to work out what might be disturbing him.

Could it be the noise when the central heating comes on? Is he too hot or too cold? Are older siblings making a noise in an adjoining bedroom? Is anything startling him? Could he be hungry? Or has he just got into a pattern that needs to be readjusted?

Once you have ruled out any other obvious causes, the chances are that he has got himself into a pattern that is not beneficial to himself or you. But don't worry, because his sleep patterns can be reprogrammed reasonably quickly.

Before you start the plan, remember that you need a digital timer and a chart on which to note your progress (see page 45). At six months, your baby is too young for a guidance tool but once he is over a year old, you may find that he follows the logic behind a simple tool such as adding marbles to a jar when he has slept right through the night.

During the plan, you are going to follow a daily routine, and to start with it should be followed exactly. If you are the parent leading the plan, you will need to clear your other commitments to ensure that you can do this. It needs to be you putting him down every time for the three days, not you in the morning, a childminder in the afternoon and the child's other parent at night. Don't start the plan until you have a period when you can achieve this. The routine will be as follows:

6–7am	Waken and give milk (if he is still having morning milk)
7–8am	Solid breakfast. Dress, brush hair and teeth
8–10am	About two hours after waking, children aged six to twelve months may need a cat nap of 45 minutes to an hour, but they should not sleep beyond 10am
10–11.30am	Morning activity
11.30–12.30pm	Preparing and then eating lunch
12.30–3pm	Afternoon nap of one to two and a half hours during this period. They should not sleep beyond 3pm
3–5pm	Afternoon activity
5–5.30pm	Teatime
6–6.20pm	Bath-time
6.20–6.35pm	Down-time
6.35–6.50pm	Story and milk
6.50–6.55pm	Brush teeth
7pm	Bedtime

Even if your child is in a completely different routine at the moment, I suggest you use this one, which is designed so that he will feel naturally tired the moment you put him down in his cot, but not over-tired, which could make him grizzly and difficult to settle. I've been using it for many years now and I know it works.

Are you ready to start changing your child's sleeping patterns? You'll find step-by-step instructions below to take you through each part of the day.

PLAN DAY ONE

The new routine starts straight away, and that means that I don't want you to offer a milk feed if your child wakens before 6am. This is the earliest hour at which he can have some milk. (If he is twelve months or over, you may have stopped this morning feed anyway.)

From about six months, you will be weaning your child, so serve a solid breakfast between 7 and 8am. (You'll find advice on weaning on pages 80–85.)

If your child is aged six to twelve months, he will most likely need a morning nap around two hours after wakening, so if he was up at 6am that means an 8am nap. If your child is between thirteen and eighteen months you can continue your day after breakfast, but you may find he needs his lunch at 11.30am and his afternoon sleep at 12 noon.

If he is having a morning nap, this will be the first time you will ask him to settle himself to sleep. It will be confusing for him if he is used to falling asleep in your arms, but follow the routine below with confidence and he will pick up what is required of him before too long.

MORNING NAP

❧ Change your child's nappy. Wipe his hands and face to remove any traces of breakfast.

❧ Place him in his sleep sack (if you use one).

❧ Return to the nursery or bedroom and pull down the blind.

❧ Hold him in your arms and talk to him for 30 seconds (not any longer). Say something like this: *"Mummy can see that you are feeling tired. You are now in your lovely bedroom, with your beautiful [list three things, such as an aeroplane light, cuddly bunny/zoo picture]. You have a little rest, while Mummy is going [for a shower/to tidy the kitchen/to talk on the telephone]. Then we will start our lovely day together."*

🦋 Place your child in his cot in his sleep position.

🦋 Rub his back or stroke his face, something personal to you. Say: *"Well done, you good boy. Mummy loves you. Sleep tight."*

🦋 Turn and leave the room. Don't look back. *"Well done, little man, sleep tight."*

🦋 Close the door or pull it shut.

🦋 The shouting will probably start immediately. Start timing the shouts and the pauses, using your timing sheet and digital timer.

🦋 If your child shouts continuously for five minutes without pausing and the pitch is getting higher, this is a Crescendo Call and you should enter the room.

🦋 Pick up your child and reassure him: *"You can do this, young man. It is time for a little rest."*

🦋 Place him back in the cot in his sleeping position.

🦋 Rub his back, stroke his hair or use the same gesture you did before. *"Good boy, that's right. Mummy loves you."*

🦋 Leave the room still talking: *"Well done, little man. Sleep tight. You can do this."*

🦋 Start the timer when the shouting begins and listen for the Thinking Pauses.

🦋 Within twenty minutes you should see a pattern forming, maybe something like this:

TIMER START	TIMER STOP	LENGTH OF SHOUT	LENGTH OF PAUSE
8.40	8.45	5 MINS (CRESCENDO)	VISIT TO RE-SETTLE
8.46	8.50	4 MINS	2 SECONDS
8.50	8.55	5 MINS	2 SECONDS
8.55	9.00	5 MINS	3 SECONDS

🦋 The goal is that you will only go back to re-settle your child once. He may shout a lot but give him the time he needs to learn. Don't keep entering the room and trying to hurry him to settle or he won't work it out for himself.

🌿 If the Thinking Pauses don't seem to be getting longer after 30 minutes, dress your child, place him in the pram in a sleeping position and take him for walk.

🌿 Let your child sleep for 45 minutes to an hour at most. Don't let him sleep beyond 10.30am.

This was your child's first attempt at settling himself to sleep. The lesson has begun … and you are a great teacher.

Have a fun morning together and a delicious lunch, then the next challenge will be when you put your child down for his afternoon nap. Once again, follow the step-by-step instructions.

AFTERNOON SLEEP

Ideally you want to have your child fed and ready for his nap between 12 and 1pm. If you miss this opportunity he may become over-tired and it will be much harder for him to settle himself, so aim to start lunch between 11.30am and 12 noon.

🌿 Start settling him to sleep no later than 1pm, following exactly the same procedure as you did for the morning nap.

🌿 As soon as you leave the bedroom, start the timer and note the shout and pause times.

🌿 Only enter the room after this if there is a Crescendo Call, and try to keep your visits to a minimum. Each time you re-visit, you will frustrate your child and make him shout even more. Watch for the Thinking Pauses getting more frequent because this is the sign that your child is on the way to understanding that he needs to settle himself to sleep. Again, you should see a pattern forming, for example:

TIMER START	TIMER STOP	LENGTH OF SHOUT	LENGTH OF PAUSE
12.30	12.35	5 MINS (CRESCENDO)	VISIT TO RE-SETTLE
12.36	12.41	5 MINS	2 SECONDS
12.41	12.46	5 MINS	1 SECOND
12.46	12.51	5 MINS (CRESCENDO)	VISIT TO RE-SETTLE
12.52	12.56	4 MINS	2 SECONDS
12.56	1.01	5 MINS	3 SECONDS
1.01	1.04	3 MINS	4 SECONDS
1.04	1.09	5 MINS	5 SECONDS
1.09	1.13	4 MINS	15 SECONDS

🦋 Continue noting the times until your child settles himself to sleep. This may take an hour or more but you need to jump the first hurdle and this is it.

You may find this distressing if you have always leapt to soothe your child at the first sign of protest, but remember that he is shouting words to you. He is not upset. He is trying to work out what you want him to do. I want you to jump this hurdle before the daytime sleep rather than the night one. It is easier on you both, because you are more alert during the day.

🦋 Your child *will* eventually settle himself to sleep, as long as you give him enough thinking time. Do not visit him unless he hits Crescendo.

🦋 Once he is quiet, don't go into the nursery straight away. Leave him for at least twenty minutes before you take a quiet peek.

🦋 When you see him sleeping, hug yourself. You've taught your child the skill of self-settling. Now relax and reward yourself.

You are aiming for your child to sleep for between one and two and a half hours. If he wakes before an hour has passed:

🦋 Leave him for three minutes.

🦋 If he is shouting (not murmuring), enter the room and re-settle him for ten seconds but don't lift him.

🦋 Start the timings sheet.

🦋 If he is unable to settle after 40 minutes of 'shout, pause, shout, pause', get him up and start your afternoon slowly.

Your child has still done well. He settled himself to sleep. Tomorrow you need to work on lengthening the sleep time in the same way as we have done today.

If your child manages to sleep for an hour he has done very well indeed. Don't persevere in trying to resettle him if it is close to 3pm. You don't want him to sleep past this time in the afternoon. In fact, if he is still asleep at 3pm, you should go into the nursery and gently waken him ready for his afternoon activities. This way he will have a full four hours to get tired before you try to put him down again.

NIGHT-TIME SLEEP

It is vital not to rush the end of the day. Leave plenty of time between teatime and bedtime for a relaxing routine. I find that serving tea at 5pm and finishing around 5.30pm gives plenty of time before heading to the bathroom for a bath at 6pm. Make sure the bath water is warm enough to relax the muscles but not too hot, as this could make your child feel dizzy and nauseous.

After the bath there should be some 'down-time' spent with gentle play, listening to music or watching some television. However, if you decide to use the television as a down-time tool, make sure the programme is calming and not overly stimulating. Now for books, bottle or beaker, and bed.

If you still have to hold your child's bottle for him, I suggest he has his stories before his milk. The child who can hold his own bottle or beaker can drink his milk sitting on your lap while you read to him. After the milk has been drunk, teeth need to be brushed swiftly.

Now into bed, at 7pm. The room needs to be dark and if you have a night-light, make sure it is positioned low in the room and is not shining directly into the cot. Place your child in his sleep sack and give him a hug. I now suggest you do one of three things. Either:

🦋 Sing your child a soothing and relaxing song while he is in your arms. 'Twinkle, Twinkle Little Star', 'Over the Rainbow' and 'Sing a Rainbow' are all good.

🦋 Talk briefly about the day:*"We have had such a lovely day. We have been to our music class, had a yummy pasta lunch, visited the park, been to the shops and we had a nice bath and now it is time for a lovely sleep in your beautiful room."*

🦋 Or talk briefly about what you are going to do the next day: *"We are going to have a lovely day tomorrow. We'll go to the shops in your pushchair, then we might go and feed the ducks. After lunch we have friends coming to visit us for tea and we might play outside if the sun is shining. Now it is time to have a sleep in your wonderful cot."*

Whichever you choose of these three options must be repeated on the coming nights so the child gets to know the routine.

🦋 Now place your child in his cot (under the covers, if used) in his sleep position and repeat the same sequence you used when settling him for naps earlier.

🦋 Rub his back or stroke his face, something personal to you, saying *"Well done, you good boy. Mummy loves you. Sleep tight."*

🦋 Leave the room still talking: *"Well done, little man, sleep tight."* Close the door.

🦋 Start the timer and write timings down, listening for the Thinking Pause. Return to the room only if your child has shouted continually for five minutes without pause.

🦋 If you have to go in, pick up your child and reassure him. *"You can do this, young man. It is time for a little rest."*

🦋 Place him back into the cot in his sleeping position. Rub his back or stroke his hair, exactly as you did before. *"Good boy, that's right. Mummy loves you."*

🦋 Leave the room still talking: *"Well done, little man, sleep tight. You can do this."*

🦋 Start the timer. Listen for the Thinking Pause.

🦋 If your child continues to shout solidly for five more minutes without a pause, re-enter the room and simply put him in his sleeping position. Do not lift him out of his cot. *"Good boy."* And leave the room.

🦋 When the shout starts, restart the timer and note the time.

I know it's hard but stay strong and focus on the timings table.

Try not to go back any more than twice. If you continue to enter the room you are sending your child a mixed message. You entering makes him think you are going to do something, such as lift him out of the cot. After two visits, aim to let him settle himself.

Remember what your child is saying: *"I am trying my best, Mummy. I know I need to settle to sleep. I will do it. Just let me shout a little longer. I will get there. I can do it. This is all so new."*

It may feel as though your child is taking forever to settle but please, please stick with it.

🦋 Put words to your child's shouts.

🦋 Understand that he is *not* in distress.

🦋 He can and *will* settle himself to sleep.

🦋 He is still learning.

🦋 This is only his first night.

🦋 He will eventually settle himself.

Once the Thinking Pauses are increasing and the shout times are decreasing, your child is heading in the right direction.

NIGHT WAKENINGS

If your child wakens in the night you need to remember that he settled himself for the first time this evening. He has just learned the skill but he still needs some practice.

🦋 Let him shout out initially for five minutes. He might be able to settle himself without you getting up.

❧ If he shouts for more than five minutes, you will need to go to his room and settle him, but don't turn on the light. Check he hasn't soiled his nappy and that he doesn't feel too hot or too cold. Hold him for just twenty seconds then put him down in his sleeping position and go back outside the room.

❧ If he is still shouting, start your digital timer and continue with the timings chart. Listen for the Thinking Pause.

❧ Only re-enter at Crescendo stage and repeat the twenty-second re-settle plan. You may need to pick your child up but keep it to twenty seconds. If you cuddle him for longer, you will send a mixed message to your child and undo the good work you have already done. Think of it as him testing his new skill. He is also testing you. You know what is best – a full night's sleep – and this is what the two of you are working towards.

The first night is the toughest, but if you remain consistent it will only take three days of your life before the pattern has changed and everyone is sleeping.

Believe it …
believe it …
believe it.

PLAN DAY TWO

Today you will take a step further. Now you will no longer lift your child out of his cot when you enter the room to re-settle him. Your aim is only to visit him once after putting him down to sleep. Otherwise, the routine is the same as for Day One.

When your child wakens at 6am or later, praise him and let him know how proud you are of him. He has taken the first step towards learning to settle himself to sleep and if you remain consistent he will get better at it today. I advise that you don't let your child sleep past 7am, even if he had a disturbed night. You don't want to start altering the daily routine. A long lie in bed in the morning can affect the lunchtime nap.

You may have had a long night yourself but if you managed to use the timings sheet and your child eventually settled himself to sleep without you, then it was a great night!

You might find that your child is particularly tired this morning and requires an early nap. Watch for signs of tiredness and when you notice them, follow the routine.

- Change child's nappy. Wipe hands and face after breakfast.

- Place child in sleep sack (if you use one).

- Return to the nursery. Pull down the blind.

- Hold your child in your arms and talk to him for 30 seconds (not any longer).

- Place your child in his cot (under the covers, if used) in his sleep position.

- Rub his back or stroke his face, something personal to you.

- Leave the room still talking. Close the door.

- If he begins shouting, start the timings chart.

- Enter once to settle him after 5 minutes if there has not been a pause and the shouts are Crescendo but don't lift him out of the cot.

- Rub back, stroke hair or whatever you did before.

- Leave the room still talking.

- Start the timings chart. Only re-enter the bedroom if there is a Crescendo Call.

- Don't resort to the pram today. Keep timing until your child settles himself.

- Remember that he should not sleep beyond 10.30am.

At this stage I hope you will notice a few little changes. You are in tune with the system and understand how it works. The Thinking Pauses are easier to identify and they are getting longer sooner. Even if it's still hard, you are over the first hurdle.

LUNCHTIME SLEEP

Have lunch between 12 and 12.30pm and start settling your child to sleep no later than 1pm, using exactly the same routine as for the morning nap.

You are aiming for your child to sleep between one and two and a half hours. If he wakes before an hour has passed:

- Leave him for five minutes.
- If he is shouting (not murmuring) enter the room and re-settle for ten seconds without lifting him.
- Start the timings sheet.
- If he is unable to settle after 40 minutes of 'shout, pause, shout, pause', get him up and start your afternoon slowly, perhaps reading a book together.

Your child has still done well. He settled himself to sleep. Tomorrow you need to work on lengthening the sleep time in the same way as today.

If your child manages to sleep for an hour, he has done very well.

Don't persevere if it is close to 3pm. You don't want him to sleep past this time.

NIGHT-TIME SLEEP

Stick to the routine of tea, bath, down time, milk and stories, brush teeth, bed at 7pm. Your child will remember what comes next, even though this is only the second day of the plan. He knows what he has to do now.

- Place your child in his sleep sack and give him a hug. Sing a song or talk about today or tomorrow. Place him in his cot.
- Rub his back or stroke his face, something personal to you. *"Well done, you good boy. Mummy loves you. Sleep tight."*
- Leave the room still talking: *"Well done, little man, sleep tight."* Close door.

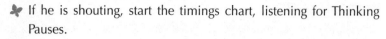

- If he is shouting, start the timings chart, listening for Thinking Pauses.

- If there is a continuous five-minute shout, go in and re-settle for twenty seconds only, without lifting him. Have the confidence that you are only going to re-settle once. You need your child to sense your confidence and belief.

- Continue the timings chart until your child has gone to sleep.

NIGHT WAKENINGS

If your child wakens in the night …

- Leave him to shout for five minutes.

- Enter the room and re-settle in a calm fashion, without turning on the light.

- If he is still shouting, start the timings sheet.

- Only go back if there is a Crescendo Call.

No matter how many times your child wakes up, repeat exactly the same pattern. He needs to know that no matter what he does, you will react in the same way. There is nothing he can do that will make you pick him up for cuddles, take him to your bed, give him some milk or put the light on and start playing. He must not be rewarded for wakening in the night. He has to go back to sleep. By now, the message should be getting across so don't undermine it by giving in even once.

PLAN DAY THREE

I hope you will have seen significant changes over the last two days. You may be feeling tired but you have taken steps to change a pattern of behaviour and you have remained firm, guiding your child towards a good night's sleep.

Your child should now understand the settling routine. Today you will continue as before, only entering the bedroom if there is a Crescendo Call.

🦋 The morning nap, roughly two hours after wakening, should last around 45 minutes to an hour for a child aged six to twelve months. Waken your child if he is still asleep at 10.30am.

🦋 Put your six- to eighteen-month-old child down for an afternoon nap after lunch, between 12 and 1, and let him sleep for between one and two and a half hours. Waken him if he is still asleep at 3pm.

He may still be shouting himself to sleep after you put him down. This is normal. No child falls asleep immediately and some need a quick chat to themselves before they sleep. Let your child settle himself in the best way he knows. Do not interfere by entering the nursery.

At night, follow exactly the same routine, with the same song or chat, the same gestures of affection and the same words as you leave the room. Start the timings chart if he is shouting and listen for the Thinking Pause. Compare your chart with the chart for Day One and I am sure you will see that the periods of shouting are shorter now and the pauses are longer. He should settle more quickly because he knows now that there is no alternative to settling. This is what he has to do.

When your child falls asleep, reward yourself. You've done an amazing job getting through the three days of the plan. You didn't take the easy option.

Continue with the routine, the timings and the chart until it is no longer necessary because your child knows exactly what will happen each time he is put down to sleep. He knows that if he closes his eyes, sleep will come and that it is not scary or difficult to settle yourself. When he wakes up again, he will no longer feel sleepy and will be full of energy and ready to play. He knows that although you say goodnight and leave him on his own, you are still nearby, and he will be safe and secure until he wakes.

> You stuck with the challenge, and now you are reaping the rewards: unbroken sleep.

FREQUENTLY ASKED QUESTIONS

My fifteen-month-old girl still seems to need a morning nap. Is that alright?
If your child appears tired after being awake for two hours in the morning, it's fine for her to have a nap. Cut it back by five minutes a time to 45 minutes long, and then 30 minutes, and gradually wean her off her morning nap over the next three months so that she doesn't need one by the age of eighteen months.

What should I do if my child stands up in his cot while I am trying to settle him to sleep?
If your child has never settled himself to sleep before, he is very likely to stand up at first. Place him in his sleeping position, say "Sleep well" and "Goodnight" and walk away without looking back. Follow the timings chart and don't re-enter the room unless there is a Crescendo Call. If you have to re-settle him, lie him down again then walk out of the room without watching to see whether he stands up immediately. He may eventually lie down by himself, but if he goes quiet and is still standing after fifteen minutes, go into the room and lie him down without a word.

I'm not sure I can distinguish a Crescendo Call from a shout. It all sounds pretty Crescendo to me!
There are shouts of protest, shouts of bewilderment and uncertainty, and these are fine, but when the pitch of the shout rises to a scream and remains at a high-pitched level, your child has reached a stage of frustration that she will not be able to come down from on her own. A Crescendo Call is continual without any pauses (except to breathe). Some children need to Crescendo Call for several minutes before they calm down and consider settling to sleep.

How many times should I visit my son to re-settle him? I keep having to enter the room and still he won't settle.
I recommend that you try not to enter the bedroom more than twice after putting your son down for the night. The more you enter, the more frustrated he will become. He is tired and deep down he *wants* to go to sleep but you keep interrupting him. Don't let him sense that

if he shouts in a particular way you will come into the room or he'll keep doing it. Let the gaps between your visits get longer and longer each time and when you do have to settle him, only spend twenty seconds doing so.

Do I have to use the timer and timings charts after I've finished the three-day plan?
If you don't need a visual aid to reassure yourself that you are not entering the nursery too regularly and you can hear the regular pauses, that's fine. Carry on with your evening, just listening in case there is a Crescendo Call. Use a baby monitor instead of sitting in the room next door and it will give you much more freedom to get on with your own tasks – or to relax and put your feet up.

What should I do if she soils her nappy during the settling process?
Quietly and quickly change the nappy in the bedroom. Don't leave the room. Don't chat or engage in any playfulness. As soon as the nappy is changed, start the settling process once more. Place her in her cot, say goodnight, tell her what a clever girl she is and leave the room, closing the door behind you.

What happens if my child gets ill during the three-day programme?
If your child has a bad cold, a cough, a temperature or is under the weather in any other way, I would stop the programme and return to it when she is in good health again. It is hard to learn something new if you are battling illness.

If your child just has a slight cold or runny nose, she should be alright to continue with the plan.

Can I vary the new routine after the three days are completed?
I suggest you continue following the same schedule for the next seven to ten days. After that, you can change the times slightly or go out for a day trip so that day-time sleeps have to be in a buggy rather than a cot. But ideally you want to remain consistent as much as possible. It's alright to alter the routine slightly for one day then go back to normal, but don't keep changing routines or your child will get confused.

When can someone else start to settle my child to sleep?
The moment you feel confident and comfortable with the routine, you can show someone else what to do. I recommend that you do it yourself for five consecutive nights before bringing anyone else in.

❧

Don't forget to reward yourself when you've finished the three-day plan. You may think this is a gimmick but it's psychologically very important. Treat yourself to a night out, a new outfit, a spa afternoon, a long lie-in, or anything else you fancy.

Re-setting a child's sleep routine can be hugely draining on the parent responsible, causing sleep deprivation and stress, but once you have broken the old routine and embraced the new, you'll see all kinds of benefits. Your child's behaviour should improve when they have good solid sleeps, and they'll have more energy and enthusiasm when awake. A happy child means a happy parent too. All this for just three days of hard work! I'm sure that once you have established new sleep patterns you will never look back again.

THE EATING PLAN FOR CHILDREN AGED SIX TO EIGHTEEN MONTHS

When your child is around six months of age, you should be starting to wean her onto solid foods, and the way you approach this can make all the difference to her eating habits in future years. If you are anxious as you offer new foods, perhaps worrying that she will choke, develop an allergy or that it will upset her stomach, then your baby will pick up on this anxiety and mirror it. However, if you are calm and relaxed, she will make positive associations with mealtimes. Don't create drama around the meal table. If your child senses that you will react to certain behaviours, such as the refusal of food, she may start to do this simply to get a reaction. All children like an audience!

There are no hard and fast rules about the exact stage at which weaning should start. Big babies may need to be weaned sooner than small ones. You'll notice that your baby doesn't seem to be full up after a milk feed and that she becomes fascinated by watching you eat. At this point she is ready for weaning stage one. Even if you haven't noticed these signs, it's worth starting solids after she reaches six months to see how she reacts. Most babies are excited by the lovely new flavours and the sensation of fullness in their tummies.

Don't give up milk feeds though – not yet. Between the ages of six and twelve months your child needs 500ml of milk a day. Milk contains calcium, which is vitally important for strengthening bones, and protein which they need for growth and development. This milk is usually given in morning and evening milk feeds (at 6–7am and 7pm). If your child is only just six months, you may still give a feed when she wakens from her afternoon nap.

From stage two of weaning, additional dairy will be consumed in yoghurts, cheese sauces and milky desserts. Don't give her a milk feed close to mealtimes, though, or you will line her stomach, meaning she is not so hungry for solid food.

Once your child is over a year in age she will only require 350ml of milk a day. This is often given in cereal and foods, with one feed at the end of the day (7pm). Continue offering an evening milk feed until you have reached the stage when you want her to sleep through the night without a nappy (see Chapter 6 for more on this). After that, you don't want her settling down to sleep with a full bladder.

Before you start weaning, you need to buy a secure high-chair which will allow your child to sit up comfortably. I recommend strapping her into the chair to prevent her slipping and, as time passes, climbing out!

Here are the three stages – but bear in mind that the months in which they are reached are not set in stone.

STAGE ONE: SIX TO SEVEN MONTHS

Start by offering little tastes of baby rice mixed with some milk, feeding her from a plastic spoon. Once she is happy to take that and is used to the sensation of swallowing the unfamiliar texture, you can add in new tastes – but only introduce one new puréed food at a time to let her get used to it. Try:

- ❧ Steamed apple
- ❧ Steamed pear
- ❧ Potato
- ❧ Sweet root vegetables: carrot, swede, sweet potato, butternut squash

Initially you will only offer one meal with solids per day but soon you can give a lunch around 12 noon and tea around 5.30pm.

Every few days, you can introduce more fruits and vegetables – all puréed – and maybe begin to mix two or three flavours together.

STAGE TWO: SEVEN TO NINE MONTHS

Once your child is happy to accept puréed fruits and vegetables, it's time to add some protein. First proteins to introduce are: chicken, fish, lentils and red meat – all still puréed in your blender, or served as good-quality shop-bought baby foods. Another source of protein that can be offered at this stage are foods containing cows' milk, such as white sauces and milk-based desserts.

At first, protein meals should be given at lunchtime so that they can be digested by the end of the day. Continue giving one protein meal a day for seven to ten days before introducing protein at teatime.

Around this stage you can start giving a solid breakfast, such as baby rice and fruit, an early lunch at 11.30–12 and tea at 5–5.30pm before evening milk at 6.30–7pm. A milk feed may also be given at 2.30–3pm when your child wakens from her sleep, but as time passes, this can be phased out.

Meals will now contain more texture, forcing your child to 'chew' before swallowing, and you can also start giving her finger foods. It is amazing how a child without teeth can gnaw her way through a piece of apple or French bread. Strengthening her gums and helping their teeth come through are two strong reasons why I recommend a variety of finger foods, but it is also a great way to introduce your child to the concept of feeding herself.

When your child starts teething, she is likely to want to have some control over what goes into her mouth because her gums will be sensitive and a solid spoon touching them could cause a little pain and discomfort. Be especially gentle when spoon-feeding and give appropriate finger foods for her to suck on. These must be chopped into pieces that are large enough to hold, while still leaving a bit exposed to go in the mouth. A quarter of peeled pear is about the right size.

There are many things you can offer to children as finger foods:

CHUNK OF FRESH BREAD	¼ RED PEPPER	SOLID CARROT STICK (LIGHTLY STEAMED)	CELERY STICK
BREADSTICK	TOAST FINGER	¼ APPLE OR PEAR	SOLID STICK CUCUMBER
OATCAKE OR RICE CAKE	COOLED, STEAMED BROCCOLI FLORET	LARGE PIECES COOKED PASTA	HALF A BANANA

Place a couple of options on the tray in front of your child for her to choose between. You can then spoon a few mouthfuls of puréed food into her mouth while she is absorbed in picking up her finger food.

There will come a natural stage when a child no longer wants to be spoon-fed. This varies from child to child but is usually between eight and sixteen months. At this stage you can start teaching her how to hold a spoon herself, while providing more of her diet in the form of finger foods she can pick up.

It is at the stage when they introduce finger foods that many parents will be concerned about choking. The fact is that children have to 'gag' on certain textures before learning the importance of chewing. It's important that you remain calm and don't panic if your child makes a sudden gagging noise and the food comes back up. They gag the food from their throat back into their mouth. This does not distress them and it is not the same as choking. However, don't offer small foods such as cherry tomatoes and grapes without cutting them in half. These could get stuck in the windpipe if swallowed whole. Don't leave the room while your child is eating, just in case this happens – but don't worry unduly about it either.

STAGE THREE: NINE TO TWELVE MONTHS

At this stage your child is capable of eating three meals a day, as well as having either two or three milk feeds. The amount of solids consumed will be increasing while the milk feeds get smaller. You can offer a variety of flavours and textures, and should aim to make your child's meal similar to what you are eating yourself, at least in part (although you should avoid giving her eggs, soft cheeses, salt, honey or nuts). The ultimate goal you are working towards is that all the family eat the same meals.

Your child now has teeth and is showing interest in feeding herself with her hands and occasionally a spoon.

When I am called in to family homes to help children who are refusing to eat at this age, I often find that the bland flavours of baby food are no longer interesting the child. Once she starts weaning, she will very quickly require actual meals rather than simple puréed vegetables. The weaning stages can pass very quickly, particularly if you have chosen to wean your child later rather than earlier.

Obviously if your child has a specific diet or is under medical guidance, you may have to limit the foods offered, or adapt them to suit. But otherwise, it's time to start getting her used to the meals you like to eat as a family.

STAGE FOUR: TWELVE TO EIGHTEEN MONTHS

If you are still giving your child milk in the morning when she wakens, I would leave between 30 and 60 minutes before introducing a solid breakfast so that she is hungry. Breakfast can be a variety of things but most children have cereal or toast. Make sure you choose cereals that are low in sugar, and don't put sweet spreads on the toast. Offer some fruit for sweetness. Pancakes, French toast or well-cooked scrambled egg on toast are all great breakfasts for a child over twelve months.

Here are some suggestions of dishes you could try for lunch and dinner – but cook them without salt, sugar or soft cheeses:

	LUNCH	DINNER
MONDAY	CHICKEN, SWEET POTATO AND PEAS	SAVOURY PANCAKES
TUESDAY	SPAGHETTI BOLOGNAISE	SUGAR-FREE BEANS ON TOAST
WEDNESDAY	PASTA AND VEGETABLE SAUCE	CHEESE, HAM & SPINACH OMELETTE
THURSDAY	COD, MASHED POTATO AND PEAS	PUMPKIN SOUP AND FRENCH BREAD
FRIDAY	BROCCOLI AND CAULIFLOWER CHEESE	MINI SANDWICHES
SATURDAY	BEEF STEW WITH GREEN BEANS	PIZZA, CRUDITÉS AND HUMMUS
SUNDAY	ROAST CHICKEN AND VEGETABLES	CHEESE & HAM TOASTED SANDWICHES

Dessert options could include:

- Puréed fruits and yoghurt
- Custard
- Rice pudding
- Fruit smoothie
- Fruit crumble
- Fruit jelly

You might be looking at this menu and thinking "My child would never eat that." It may be that they don't like food with lumps in it, or they only like sweet things, or they scream in horror if you try to introduce anything new. That's exactly why we have a three-day plan. I am going to show you how to change your child's approach to food until she is willing to try new foods without protest and able to eat more or less what you and the rest of the family eat.

PREPARING FOR THE THREE-DAY EATING PLAN

Problems can set in at any stage of weaning. If it's still early days and your child is rejecting solid foods altogether, it may be that you have started too early and should stick to milk feeds for another few weeks. However, if she starts wakening at night and demanding feeds, then a liquid diet is no longer enough. Most children will accept baby rice mixed with their normal milk without problems, and you just need to build from there. You really should have started weaning by seven months.

The eating plan in this section is aimed at children aged nine to eighteen months who will not accept a range of flavours but want to stick with the same familiar favourites every time. You need to teach them to eat a wide range of nutrients if they are to grow up healthy, and the work starts here.

As the amount of variation increases you can place favourites on alternate days. It's best if there is an element of familiarity about the new meals. For example, if your child will eat pasta, vary the pasta type and change the sauce; if your child eats beef burgers add meatballs or bolognaise to the menu plan; if he has a sweet tooth, make dishes with sweet potato and pumpkin squash.

Create a meal plan for a week so you can shop in advance. It may seem a lot of work but the secret is to cook in batches and freeze the food. You can label it and bring it out of the freezer the following week and the week after. We are aiming to follow the same weekly menu plan for two weeks so that your child becomes familiar with certain meals. If you cook larger quantities than you will need, you can label and freeze the leftovers so that you soon have a well-stocked freezer.

I recommend that you cook enough for four portions of two to three tablespoonfuls each at a time. You will be adding finger foods to this, as well as steamed vegetables and sometimes some rice, pasta or bread, so two to three tablespoonfuls is fine as a single portion.

Prepare the two meals for Day One of the plan the day before you start and keep them in the fridge, while freezing the other portions. During your

To prepare for the plan, make up your own menu in which you alternate meals that you know your child likes with ones she has refused in the past or hasn't yet tried.

When you cook for children over nine months, don't purée the food to a smooth consistency. Keep some texture and leave some of the food in its original form, such as a stick of carrot, some peas, a piece of chicken.

child's daytime sleeps on Day One, you can cook the meals for Day Two, and on Day Two you can cook the meals for Day Three. Keep batch cooking whenever you have time until you have enough mini meals in the freezer to last you for a couple of weeks. This way, you can heat and serve meals calmly without getting flustered about running late. It all helps to create a relaxed atmosphere at mealtimes.

Choose a time when you don't have many other commitments because you will have to eat all meals at home for the duration of the plan.

Print out some sheets to fill in, as follows:

DAY ONE	MEAL AND DESSERT	NUMBER OF SPOONFULS	FINGER FOODS EATEN
BREAKFAST			
MORNING SNACK			
LUNCH			
AFTERNOON SNACK			
DINNER			

Make sure you have the Day One meals prepared. And now you are all ready to start!

PLAN DAY ONE

Give your child some milk around ten to fifteen minutes after wakening then leave an hour before offering her breakfast. Lay everything you need on the table so you don't have to keep getting up. Porridge is a good breakfast that provides slow-releasing carbohydrates for energy through the morning. Serve it with some fruit purée. If your child shows little interest in the porridge, place a piece of toast in front of her, which she will pick up when she is ready. You can also offer chunks of fruit.

If your child is still showing little interest in breakfast, the chances are she is not hungry. Finish your own breakfast but place your child's food in front of her where she can see it. Talk to her as you are eating your food. Whether she eats or not, she should remain in her high-chair and watch you eating. You are showing her, by example, the importance of eating food. This is your first achievement of the day.

Remember this process involves little steps. Write on the Day One sheet what she has eaten for breakfast.

After breakfast, get your child dressed and let her play until it's time for the morning nap (if she still has one). Use nap times to cook the two meals you will be offering for lunch and dinner the following day and to freeze batches of meals.

After her nap, try to go outside for some fresh air. Allow your child to exercise while you are out rather than simply sitting in the buggy. You want her to build up an appetite.

If you would like to offer a mid-morning snack, your child should finish it no later than 10.30am. The snack should be small (it is not a meal). Fruit is an ideal offering, or a rice cake, oatcake, small piece of flapjack (reduced sugar and nut-free) or simply a breadstick (reduced salt).

Ensure that you return to the house for 11.45am and that you are ready to eat together at midday. If your child is very restless and doesn't appear hungry, lunch could be stretched to 12.30pm. Just be aware that you don't want her to become over-tired or she will not be interested in eating. Choose the window of opportunity carefully.

LUNCH

Have everything you need at the table for both of your lunches.

- A bowl of your child's food with two plastic spoons
- A bottle or beaker of water
- A plate of finger foods
- Your meal and drink
- Wipes for the end of the meal

Make sure that some of your lunch is similar, if not exactly the same, as your child's. Ensure that she is sitting safely and comfortably in her chair and is wearing a bib to protect her clothing.

Place both spoons in your child's meal and tip the bowl so that she can see the contents then spoon a mouthful into her mouth. Don't overload the spoon. If she turns away, give her her own spoon and place some food on it for her. While she is focusing on this, bring the spoon you are holding towards her mouth. Try to get some food on her lips because she will lick her lips and hopefully get a taste for what is being offered.

Continue to spoon food into her mouth but take it slowly. If you manage six to ten small spoonfuls, you are doing extremely well. If there is still resistance, place a piece of the food in its whole form onto her tray, such as a carrot and a few peas. Children over a year old may like to have finger foods on their tray from the start. If she is at a stage when she wants to be independent and doesn't want you feeding her at all, simply place a small portion of food in front of her and give her a spoon.

Don't focus on what your child is eating. Simply chat generally and continue eating your own food. Talk about the afternoon you are going to have. Don't keep reminding her to eat. She knows her food is there and will take some when she is ready. Be patient and calm.

If your child gags when trying an unfamiliar food, don't over-react or startle her. Simply say *"That's it, well done. How about some water and then we can carry on with lunch?"* Give her some water (you may need to hold it up to her mouth) then continue with your lunch.

Leave dessert out of sight while you are eating the main meal. Go to the fridge to retrieve it only when you have finished your meal and your child has stopped eating. Remember that dessert should mirror the size of main course eaten. Don't be tempted to give your child extra dessert if she hasn't eaten much of the main meal. If she hasn't taken any of it at all, simply offer some fruit.

Always leave an hour and a half between finishing a snack and serving the next meal, to ensure that your child is hungry.

It can be worth offering the main meal again after dessert. Sometimes it will be taken but, if not, just clear the table. If at the end of the main course you notice your child is sleepy you can always settle her to sleep and offer dessert when she wakens.

While she has her afternoon sleep, write down what has been eaten.

After the sleep offer a snack such as a rice cake, an oatcake, a breadstick or some fruit, as well as a beaker of water. If milk is still being given at this time a solid snack is not required, but I recommend that the quantity is kept low: 120ml or one breast only if breastfeeding.

The afternoon snack should be finished no later than 3.30pm.

After the afternoon snack I advise an afternoon of activity and ideally some fresh air before dinnertime. Make sure that you have returned home by 4.45pm.

DINNER

Prepare the finger food and warm the meal. Ensure everything is placed on the table as close to 5pm as possible.

Follow the same routine as at lunch. Your child needs to see consistency.

- Start by introducing the puréed food on a spoon.

- Give your child her own spoonful of food to hold.

- Introduce a finger food (only one) and try to spoon in some food while your child is distracted by the finger food.

- Introduce three types of finger food to her tray.

- Drink your own drink and eat a little of the same food as your child.

- Don't appear anxious and concerned, as your child will pick up your anxiety.

- Keep the main course on the table when you introduce the dessert.

- Offer the main meal again after the dessert. Only offer twice, no more.

- Complete the meal and note the amount eaten.

Stay relaxed. Even if your child doesn't eat a great deal she still has her evening milk to drink before bed. This will line her stomach and satisfy her for a solid night's sleep. Continue with the evening routine of bath, book, milk and bed.

Tomorrow is another day. You have managed the first day perfectly if you have:

- Produced meals on time
- Offered puréed, textured or whole foods, according to your child's age
- Offered some finger foods
- Offered plenty of water
- Eaten at the same time as your child
- Kept calm
- Recorded the intake of food
- Kept snacks small.

Now have a relaxing evening. Your child has eaten enough for the day and is capable of sleeping through the night. Switch off and have some 'adult time'. Well done – you have got through Day One!

PLAN DAY TWO

Offer milk ten to fifteen minutes after wakening, then serve a solid breakfast an hour later. Any sooner and your child will not be hungry. Have the breakfast all laid out on the table so that once you are both sitting down you don't need to stand up and disrupt the meal.

Place some cereal on the spoon (depending on her age this could be baby rice, Weetabix or porridge) and give the spoon to your child to hold. As she is taking it from you, slip a spoonful of cereal in her mouth. Wait until her mouth opens as she thinks about what to do with the spoonful she is holding before you feed her, and don't push the spoon too far into her mouth, which will cause her to gag. She's won't choke on cereal, so don't worry; it tends to be solid foods such as grapes and baby tomatoes that cause actual choking. Once she's had that spoonful of cereal, she will be familiar with the taste and texture.

Place some finger food on the high-chair tray. While she is concentrating on it, try to feed the cereal again. If it is not accepted, leave her with the finger food while you continue to eat your breakfast.

Keep watching for a window of opportunity. Your child might suddenly show interest in what is in her bowl. If this occurs, load a spoon and give it to her to hold, then swoop a spoonful from the other spoon into her mouth.

Some children like to sit at the table for a while before they begin to eat. Don't pressure them. You simply need to be patient and leave plenty of time for meals. If your child doesn't eat the cereal and you have finished your own meal, get up and start the day's routine. If she has a morning nap, use the time to prepare the two meals for later in the day, and freeze batches for a later date. After she wakes, dress her, brush her teeth then try to head outside for exercise and fresh air to help build up an appetite.

Remember: if you are offering a snack mid-morning, make sure it is finished by 10.30am. A snack should be no more than a small cracker or biscuit or a piece of fruit.

LUNCH

This will be the fifth meal you have given your child since beginning this programme so she should be familiar with the routine now.

- Make sure you have everything you need on the table, except the dessert.

- Remember that you should eat some food that is the same as your child's.

- Continue with the method of putting some food onto a spoon and placing it in your child's hand. While she is focusing on this, start to spoon food into her mouth.

- Offer praise for any achievements and remain positive and enthusiastic throughout. Remember that your child is watching your facial expressions and body language. If you are anxious your child will sense this and is more likely to refuse food.

- Introduce finger foods one at a time. Too many placed in front of your child is overwhelming and it is at this stage that food can end up decorating the floor!

- If your child stops eating simply give her a couple of finger foods and her water beaker while you continue eating.

🦋 Keep the dessert small and simple and don't give a bigger dessert if she hasn't eaten her main course. A small yoghurt a day is a good idea.

> There is a great sense of achievement as a parent when you feel organised.

After lunch, when your child goes for her nap, fill in the food diary.

Make the afternoon snack small and healthy, and ensure it is finished by 3.30pm.

During the afternoon I suggest more fresh air and exercise, but make sure that you return home by 5pm for dinner.

DINNER

This is the final meal of the second day. By now I am sure that you are starting to relax and accept that if your child does not eat much it is not the end of the world. She will have milk at bedtime so you can be assured that she will not go hungry.

At the end of the day complete the food diary and accept that if you remain relaxed and calm, so will your child. Weaning can be a slow process and it involves a great deal of patience. Children need to introduce new foods to their digestive system slowly and in small quantities. They will take it at their own pace and shouldn't be hurried or they will pick up a sense of anxiety that they will associate with food in the future.

PLAN DAY THREE

I am sure that the routine is now clear in your head and you are starting to see a pattern forming. For your child to manage to eat six to eight teaspoonfuls of food at a meal, including finger foods, is a fantastic achievement. Follow this with some fruit and they will have had enough. The main thing is that you are instilling eating habits in your child that she will take with her through life. Diet needs to be varied. She can't have her favourite at every meal.

I spent some time living in Australia and while I was there I helped a family with five children. A large part of my role was the cooking for the family. Each evening they sat down to eat as a family and on one particular day one of the children started to moan about the meal that was placed in front of him.

The mother allowed the boy to continue with his verbal protest and once he had finished she said: *"Now listen. There are seven of us in the family and seven days in a week. If you get your favourite meal one day of the week you are lucky! The other six days you are to be grateful and eat up!"*

She was right. Besides, if you have your favourite meal every day it becomes the norm and no longer special.

This is the final day of the three-day programme but you should continue following the basic rules after this. Here's a reminder:

- Morning milk: ten to fifteen minutes after waking up (not before 6am).

- Breakfast: 60 minutes after morning milk.

> Finger foods build independence and co-ordination and help to strengthen gums.

- If you have time during the morning, prepare and cook meals for the coming weeks. You will now have meals stacking up in your freezer, which can be rotated over the next twelve days without you having to do any extra cooking. These meals will become familiar to your child and as they recognise them they will relax and slowly increase the amount they eat.

- Morning snack to be finished no later than 10.30am.

- Lunch 12–12.30pm. Introduce finger foods at every meal.

- Afternoon sleep for your child while you fill in the food diary.

- Afternoon snack if you wish to offer one (or a small milk feed of 120ml or one breast maximum). Finished by 3.30pm at the latest.

- Dinner 5–5.30pm. Remember that if only a small amount of this meal is eaten your child still has their evening milk to drink. They will not go hungry!

In my experience, children enjoy one meal in the day more than the other. By this I mean that they will eat well at lunchtime or dinnertime but rarely at both. I have also found that, particularly with boys, they may eat extremely well one day and then run on almost empty the following day. Our appetite is not always consistent. We sometimes eat more one day than the next, and we still function. Children are the same.

So you have reached the end of the three days and you have managed to keep your diary to refer back to. I suggest that you continue serving the meals from your freezer for the next twelve days before batch cooking any more. At that stage, you can cook for three consecutive days and mix in some new meal ideas with the old familiar ones. That way your child will recognise some foods and experience new flavours at other meals. She will undoubtedly have favourites – we all do – but the important thing is that you continue to educate her palette with new flavours and textures. You are instilling in her the importance of trying new foods with confidence. A varied diet enhances life.

Continue on this path and you will see wonderful results. You only need to take little steps at a time.

FREQUENTLY ASKED QUESTIONS

I'm trying to wean my six-month-old baby but he spits out the baby rice and steamed fruit I give him. What should I do?
I advise that you offer baby rice for three consecutive days but if he refuses it, wait between a week and ten days before introducing it again. He may simply not be ready. Alternatively you could try other baby cereals and fruits but I would not persist beyond three days. He will soon get the idea and should be accepting some solids by the age of seven months.

My child has a habit of throwing food onto the floor. What should I do?
If food is thrown on the floor, stay calm and continue eating your own meal. Don't react straight away. When she starts to shout, place the food back on the plate and put it in front of her but arm's length away, saying: "I am going to put it here if it is going to end up on the floor. Tell me when you want it. I am busy eating my lunch."

Wait for your child to reach towards the plate or bowl before you offer it to her again. If it is refused, simply offer some dessert (fruit).

The important thing is that she sees you eating and notices that you are remaining calm. She did not get the reaction she wanted. After a while she will start to realise that it is pointless to throw food.

What if my child screams through the meal?
If your child is between six and twelve months, she will get tired of screaming before long. I suggest she remains in her chair watching you eat for five minutes and if the noise continues I would take her to her cot for a sleep and offer lunch when she awakes. If your child is between twelve and eighteen months old, you can ask her to stop making a noise. Use the Guidance System described on page 97, in the Behaviour section of this chapter.

How much water should my child be drinking?
In my opinion, Tommee Tippee free-flow beakers are best for children who are just learning to drink. Place one on the high-chair tray at every mealtime so that your child can drink as much as she chooses. You can also offer watery fruits such as grapes (halved), mango, melon and cucumber. All of these have a high water content. Your child will also get hydration from her milk feeds, so she is very unlikely to get dehydrated. Offer drinks of water more frequently on very hot days.

All children progress at different rates, and this is as true with eating as it is with walking and talking. Some children speed ahead while others are more wary and take their time.

The main message is to stay calm and keep introducing new foods and flavours while also including old favourites on the menu. Make a conscious effort not to get stuck in a pattern of producing the same three meals over and over, because eventually your child will get bored with them and then you'll have a whole new challenge on your hands.

Ideally, your child will be prepared to eat at least six or seven different meals by the age of eighteen months.

Meeting around the meal table, discussing the day and making plans for the future is a healthy part of family life. Keep with it. No matter how fussy an eater your child may be now, remember that she will probably turn into a teenager who eats you out of house and home one day!

THE BEHAVIOUR PLAN FOR CHILDREN AGED UP TO EIGHTEEN MONTHS

The first year of a child's life seems to flash past in an instant and before you know it they are crawling, then gliding around the house from one piece of furniture to the next. It is usually at this stage that you realise you are having to guide your child, ensuring that he does not touch certain things in the home. Every room needs to be made safe with cupboard locks, electric socket covers and stair gates, and he needs to learn to obey when he hears a firm instruction, whether it's you telling him not to touch something hot or not to hit another child.

Your child still doesn't know right from wrong and he definitely doesn't know his boundaries or the 'house rules' but it is your responsibility to start teaching them. My systems may not work immediately. The first time you implement a new system, your child is likely to challenge it. It will take at least three consecutive days in which you act in exactly the same way before your child will start to fully accept the system. Once a system is understood, he will begin to think before he acts. This is the first step towards learning self-discipline.

The main tool you will use for a child under eighteen months is the Guidance System. You'll find full details of it on pages 52–55, but here's a quick summary.

- Firm instruction
- Guide the child towards another toy or activity
- Ensure he is engaged
- Praise him

✿ State the next activity in the day

✿ Leave the child to play.

Now we are going to look at how you might implement this system in some common situations your young child might encounter that could provoke misbehaviour. Read down the list below and select the one that you find most challenging in your own child's behaviour.

✿ Refusing to share

✿ Being unwilling to play alone

✿ Refusing to get in the buggy or car seat

✿ Refusing to hold hands when walking

✿ Not listening to the word 'no'

✿ Continually shouting

In order to address the chosen behaviour with a three-day plan, you will need to create situations in which the problem might arise. For example, if your child is bad at sharing toys, organise play dates for each of the three days. Invite friends you feel relaxed and comfortable with and explain the systems you are going to be implementing. If your child resists getting into his buggy or car seat, arrange a couple of outings a day in which you will be able to implement the new system.

Don't shy away from asking your child not to do something in case they start shouting. Learn to say what you want and to follow it through. After three days of behaviour retraining during which you press your child's buttons and guide him to the behaviour you want, he should get the message loud and clear.

REFUSING TO SHARE

Sharing is not an easy concept for many children. It can be hard to accept that when other children enter your home you have to let them play with your toys and hope that they do not break any or take them away. For a child, their toys are part of their identity. They are their belongings, their world.

I advise using the word 'swapping' rather than talking about 'giving' when children come for a play date. You might think that a child aged twelve to eighteen months wouldn't understand the word 'swapping' but children will build an understanding of all of the language you use with them. This is no different. The sooner you show your child how to exchange toys, the better.

> "We are swapping toys today with our friends. When they come, they will bring something for you to look at and you can show them your toys."

Make it clear that your child's toys will not leave the house.

> "They are always safe here and when your friends leave they will help put all of your toys away in their safe places."

Most children have some special toys that they couldn't contemplate sharing, so these should be put away in a safe place before the other children arrive. It's fair enough to want to keep some things to yourself. I expect you feel this way about some of your own possessions.

As you play with your child, encourage them to share their toys with you. Pick one for yourself and play with it. If your child tries to take it from you simply say "Mummy is playing with this. You are playing with the car. We can swap in a moment." Your child may shout and moan but you are teaching him the importance of sharing. Wait for a few moments and then swap the toys. "Well done, that is called sharing." This is a process I would advise a parent to practise on a daily basis if you sense that your child is having difficulty sharing, for example if they always seem to want the toy that someone else is holding.

It's a difficult situation when you have invited a friend for coffee expecting that the children will play nicely together – and they don't. It is not until children are two and a half or three years old that they actually begin to play together. Between the ages of one and two the play is simply parallel. This means that they will play alongside one another but they do not interact. In fact, the only time you are likely to see interaction is when one child wants to take something from the other.

Let's imagine a scenario in which two children aged eighteen months old are playing alongside one another, when one takes a toy from the other child's hands. Here's how to implement the behaviour plan:

FIRM INSTRUCTION

❧ *"Now, let's give that back straight away."*

❧ Take the toy and pass it to the other child.

GUIDE

❧ *"Why don't you play with your farmyard?"*

❧ Hold your child's hand and take him to the farm.

ENSURE

❧ Sit for a minute to build the yard together then place some animals in it.

PRAISE

❧ *"Now you have a fantastic farmyard to play with and we can give some animals to [other child's name] to put in the field."*

❧ Give three or four animals to the other child.

❧ *"I think this farmyard is going to be just perfect. Well done for sharing the animals and playing so nicely."*

STATE NEXT ACTIVITY

❧ *"I am going back to the kitchen to chat to [name of friend]."*

LEAVE

❧ *"You are brilliant farmers. Well done to you both."*

BEING UNWILLING TO PLAY ALONE

All children reach a stage in their development when they suffer from separation anxiety and don't like it if their main carer leaves the room. This can occur any time between nine months and three years of age but is most common between nine and eighteen months.

It's important not to pander to clinginess. Don't always pick your child up the moment he demands it. Bend down to his level and pacify him this way rather than picking him up and resting him on your hip, or you'll simply have problems when you try to put him down again to get on with your day. The more you pander to this behaviour, the longer it will continue. You need to teach your child to play on his own, while reassuring him that you will always return before long.

Let's imagine a fourteen-month-old child who plays happily while her mother is engaging with her but starts to shout the moment her mother gets up to leave. Here's the procedure:

FIRM INSTRUCTION
❧ *"Now [child's name], don't make that silly noise."*

GUIDE
❧ Crouch and touch her toys.

❧ *"Look at these wonderful toys. All the lovely animals."*

ENSURE
❧ *"I think the elephant is going to hug the giraffe and talk to the giraffe."*

❧ Show your child the animals hugging.

PRAISE
❧ *"You look after the animals like a very good zookeeper. Well done."*

❧ Stand up ready to walk away. Feel strong. Do not doubt your child's ability to play alone.

STATE NEXT ACTIVITY

❦ *"I am going to load the washing machine and prepare dinner. Then I will come and see you and all the animals."*

LEAVE

❦ Walk away, saying *"Well done, zookeeper. You are great!"*

As you leave, your child may moan and whine. Continue to leave the room and repeat that you will not be long. Get on with another job while listening carefully to your child's vocal performance. Don't let the moan and whine become a scream, but don't rush to soothe her immediately. Remember that the more you carry out this process, the faster your child will learn. Aim to do it at least three times daily.

If your child is mobile and tries to follow you around rather than play alone, I would let her do so, as long as she is not hindering you in any way. Let her help you around the house. However, if she is moaning and whining, create a play area in the room you are in or the room next door. Continue to guide her to her toys. She will eventually realise that playing is far more interesting than trailing around after Mummy or Daddy.

It's ideal if you have a separate playroom for your child's toys, which you can make completely safe, and seal with a gate across the doorway. That way you can leave her for a moment knowing she can't come to any harm, and she will have a chance to get used to playing on her own. If you don't have a room you can dedicate to this purpose, maybe you could think of a way to cordon off part of a room.

Every time your child plays alone, even if it is for a very short period, praise her for her efforts as soon as you come back into the room again.

> "You clever girl. Look what you have done. You've been playing with all your lovely toys. I am very pleased with you."

REFUSING TO GET INTO THE BUGGY OR CAR SEAT

Many children protest when it's time for them to be strapped into a chair. They will arch their backs trying to resist and some yell till they are red in the face. This is most common between the ages of seven months and three years, as children strive to show their independence and test the boundaries. I have found that it is not such a challenge getting them into the pushchair when you are leaving home to go somewhere. It is when you are out having fun and it's time to get home that problems occur.

The first rule is to give your child a five-minute warning before you have to leave an activity that they are enjoying. With young children who don't understand the concept of time, I tell them three more things we can do before returning home.

I also find it useful to have a little bag full of toys and items that you would not usually give your child to play with. This 'bag of tricks' can be kept in the base of the buggy or inside the car and only played with when your child is seated and strapped into her chair.

Give your child the entire bag. This activity is about discovery and choice. For girls it is seen as an imitation of Mummy and her handbag! Items in the bag could include:

- An old lip-gloss

- A matchbox car

- A small picture book

- A clothes peg

- A bendy toy

- A stress ball

- An old watch

- A bunch of old keys

- An old mobile phone

Choose small items that will be seen as a 'treat' and rotate the contents of the bag regularly. Don't wait until the interest is exhausted.

Here's an example of how this might work when you are trying to get your child to leave the park:

FIRM INSTRUCTION

🦋 *"OK [child's name], we are going to be heading home in five minutes and I will need you to jump in the buggy."*

GUIDE

🦋 Walk with your child to an activity, such as the slide.

🦋 *"Let's go down the slide, ride on the see-saw and have a swing before home time."*

🦋 Walk to the see-saw: *"Up and down we go, then lastly to the swing."*

ENSURE

🦋 Walk to the swing. Ensure that they know this is the last activity before home time.

🦋 *"Lovely swinging and then we are going to have some lunch."*

PRAISE

🦋 *"Well done [child's name]. Let's run to the buggy and find your special buggy bag."*

🦋 Take hand and lead towards the buggy. Do this quickly, without hesitation. Scoop her up if you need to and then place her close to the buggy.

🦋 *"Let's get our 'bag of tricks' out. What do we have here?"*

🦋 Look inside the bag and remove something and give it to your child.

🦋 While she is engaged place her in the buggy.

🦋 *"Look at that, it's Daddy's old watch. Can you hear it say tick, tock, tick tock?"*

🦋 Smile to distract from the buggy.

STATE NEXT ACTIVITY

🦋 *"Now, you look after Daddy's watch and let's get home for lunch."*

LEAVE

🦋 *"You got into the buggy like a good girl. Well done."*

If this doesn't work and your child still refuses to get in the buggy, let her walk for a bit until she gets tired. You may have to leave the park earlier if you think your child will prefer to walk before getting in the buggy.

When she gets tired of walking, don't pick her up. Find a distracting toy in the bag of tricks and place her in the buggy while she is looking at it. If she refuses to walk along holding hands with you, though, you may need to refer to the next section first!

REFUSING TO HOLD HANDS WHEN WALKING

When children get their first taste of walking independently rather than being pushed in a buggy, you may find they make frequent bids for freedom. It's difficult hanging on to a tiny hand while pushing a buggy and perhaps clutching a shopping bag as well, so you need their co-operation. They need to learn that they must hold Mummy's or Daddy's hand while they are out in a busy street. There must be no argument and no running away.

The system I use for changing this behaviour is simple but effective. When you first implement it, it will take you a long time to cover even a small distance, so choose days when you have no urgent deadlines.

As you leave the house, bend down to your child's level and say *"We are going to hold hands while we are walking along. You look after Mummy and Mummy will look after you."*

The moment your child lets go of your hand, sit him down on the pavement. Say:

"Walking, we hold hands. No hands, we sit down."

When your child stands up, ready to continue, he has to take your hand or you sit him down again. He must realise that you are going nowhere unless he is holding your hand.

When you reach a park or open space, the rule is different and you need to explain this. *"Now, there are no cars and the park is safe for running. Let's have fun."*

During the three-day plan, try to go out twice a day and sit him down every time he refuses to hold your hand. By the end of the third day, he should have got the message!

NOT LISTENING TO THE WORD 'NO'

None of us likes to hear the word 'no' and children are no different. My advice is that you try to avoid using it if at all possible. When your child is behaving in a way you do not like, I suggest you stop for a moment and consider what you could say instead.

For example, if your child is approaching the oven or fireplace, instead of saying 'No!' you could say *"Don't touch. Very hot. No touching."*

If he is about to touch something sharp, say *"Don't touch. Ouch! It hurts."*

You could walk around the house making your child aware of the dangers, and explaining that if he touches certain things it will hurt him. "Ouch!" Make sure this is done seriously and is not seen as a game, though.

Save the word 'no' for emergency situations only, and it will be much more effective. If your child is about to run out into speeding traffic, a shout of 'No!' might be essential to stop him. I find that when I use it, once in a blue moon, the child tends to stop in his tracks and burst into tears. If I used it more frequently, it would be much less effective.

After the tears, give the explanation: *"Look how fast the cars are going. We don't want a car bumping into you."* Clap your hands loudly. *"It would really hurt."*

For other types of behaviour you want your child to stop doing, give a simple instruction in your clear, firm voice (the one you've been practising in front of the mirror).

"I have had enough of that."

"Stop that right now."

"Come here right now."

"Come away from there now."

"Don't do that."

"Enough of that."

"Stop right there, young man"

These phrases are more effective than the word 'no'. The key is in the tone and firmness of your voice. Here's a quick bullet point guide:

- Bend down to your child's level
- Make eye contact
- Be firm with your instruction
- Guide him away from the situation
- Ensure he is distracted from the incident
- Explain your reason for being firm if necessary
- Smile to indicate the incident is now over
- State next activity
- Move on. This means that the incident does not need to be mentioned again.

This is something you will have to practise every time there is an undesirable behaviour to tackle, but it should get easier when your child becomes familiar with your firm voice. At this age, most children want to please.

CONTINUALLY SHOUTING

It must be most frustrating when you don't have the words to explain yourself. A couple of years ago I visited Morocco and found myself in a village in the Atlas Mountains where not a single person spoke English. The frustration was enormous, and as I tried my best in sign language to get myself a bottle of water I spared a moment to think about how children feel.

A child from as young as a year old can understand all that you are saying to him but he is unable to respond with words. The frustration is expressed in a range of ways as he tries to get what he needs or wants. One method he might use is shouting, or crying, but he needs to be taught that this is the wrong way to go about things. You can't go through life shouting to get your own way. If your child tends to do this, it's time to teach him some anger management techniques!

The type of shouting can vary. For some children it is more of a whine or whimper; with others it sounds like genuine crying, and yet more simply yell at the top of their lungs. Whatever the noise, it is frustrating and exhausting for you both. You need to guide your child to express himself differently. Once again, you start by using the Guidance System, but if this doesn't work you can take it a step further by offering them a choice.

FIRM INSTRUCTION

🦋 Bend down and hold your child's arms and make eye contact.

🦋 *"Mummy doesn't want this silly noise any more. It is not nice."*

GUIDE

🦋 Distract your child with something from the bag of tricks if you are out, or a toy if you are at home.

🦋 *"Let's have a teddy bears' picnic and we can give all the teddies a nice snack."*

CHOICE

🦋 If the noise continues, you will give your child a choice. He can shout all he wants but only in one particular place in the house.

🦋 In a calm voice say *"Come with me for a minute. I need to show you something."*

🦋 Walk your child silently to the bottom stair, a bean bag or a little chair in the hall.

🦋 *"Now. If you want to shout or make that silly noise you can come and do it here."*

🦋 Be calm as you say this. It is not a punishment. It is a choice your child can make, and children as young as twelve months understand that.

❧ Sit your child down then crouch in front of him and look in his eyes.

❧ *"Shouting is here."* Tap the chair or step.

❧ *"No shouting in there."* Point to the kitchen.

❧ *"No shouting in there."* Point to the sitting room.

❧ Repeat for each room on that floor of the house.

❧ *"This is where we shout."* Tap the chair again.

❧ If your child is still shouting, place him on the chair or step and say: *"You shout there and I will come and see you when it is all finished and quiet."*

❧ Walk away.

❧ If he follows, still shouting, return him to the chair. Sit him on or next to it.

❧ *"Shouting here, [child's name]."* Turn and walk away.

This process needs to continue until your child understands that from this moment on if he decides to shout in the house he is going to have to go to this place to do it. The process could take up to an hour but you must persevere.

❧ When he calms down and is quiet, bend in front of him.

❧ *"That's it. All the shouting is finished. Thank you, shouting chair/ step/bag. Let's hug to say sorry for that shouting. Then we can go and play."*

❧ Sit and play together.

This may have been exhausting but your child will remember the system and when he next shouts you can ask him: "Do you need to go to the shout chair/bag?" If the shouting continues, you can take him to the chair and start the process once again.

Follow the same principle through. After doing this for three consecutive days your child will understand that if he starts to shout, this is what will happen. Consistency is the key.

FREQUENTLY ASKED QUESTIONS

If other children bring their toys to our house, my child instantly snatches them away. What should I do?

Sit on the floor with both children and ask the owner of the toy if your child can have a look at it. If he agrees, sit with your child while he takes a look and when he has finished ask if you can take the toy and put it in a safe place until the owner goes home.

If the owner does not want to share, say "Let's give it to your mummy for when you go home." Take it away and immediately distract the children by instigating a new activity (see page 98).

How soon should I encourage my child to tidy away her toys?

When your child is around nine months, you can start explaining what you are doing as you tidy the toys away: "I am putting your toys all in their box nicely."

Hand your child a toy and say: "You put it in the box. Well done. Tidy up time."

They will soon relate the phrase 'tidy up time' to placing toys in the box.

At this age I would simply tidy up together, maybe asking her to throw the occasional toy into the box. At this age you are leading by example and will still have to do most of it yourself but it's worth starting to talk about tidying and letting them watch you do it.

My daughter refuses to go to my partner and if I leave the room she will just scream for me until I come back.

Your child is shouting and your partner should follow the system explained on page 107:

- Firm instruction

- Guide

- Choice

You should remain out of sight while this is done. If you come back into the room, you are giving the impression that screaming works as a tactic. Put the system in place, apply it consistently and you will see a difference before long.

My child often starts shouting when we are out in the buggy, which is deeply embarrassing. What should I do?

Shopping with children is always a challenge because for them it can be a dull experience. I help many parents with this dilemma and I always advise that you give your child a bag of tricks to explore and don't shop for longer than 30 minutes without stopping for a break when your child can get out of the buggy and run around. Most indoor shopping centres have child-friendly open spaces and high streets will often have a park nearby.

Let him run around then return him to the buggy with a drink and a snack. You may then get away with a further fifteen minutes of shopping before your child simply wants to return home. With young children, a 45-minute shopping trip might be the limit. Any further shopping may have to be done on the Internet!

My fifteen-month-old little girl has started biting me and she giggles when I tell her off. I'm worried she will bite other children. What should I do?

Biting is a Zero Tolerance behaviour, even at her young age, and you will have to react firmly and consistently every time she does it. Follow the Guidance System with a choice used for shouting (see page 107) and make it clear to your little girl that she will always have to go to the stair/chair/bean bag every time she bites. Any other carers who look after her should do exactly the same thing. She should soon get the message that the consequences of biting are not fun. Remain consistent so she gets the same reaction every single time.

How do I implement the Guidance System with a choice when I'm out of the house?

If you are in a park, choose a bench. In a shopping centre, find a quiet seat. In someone else's home, use their bottom step or a chair in their hallway, then follow exactly the same procedure as you would at home.

If you are implementing a three-day plan to deal with a particular behaviour, warn your child in advance that if she shouts/bites/

throws/pushes, she will have to sit on that bench. Don't worry about any passers-by who may be watching. If anything, they will be impressed that you are acting firmly and not ignoring bad behaviour. Set a good example!

If you follow the basic steps of the Guidance System – firm instruction, guide to another activity, ensure they are content with the activity, praise them for behaving nicely, state next activity and move to your task, leaving your child happily playing – you will have laid the groundwork for a polite, well-behaved child. Add on the 'choice' if you feel it is necessary.

The sooner you implement these systems, the less work you will have as your child gets older. Lay the groundwork that will help him to understand right from wrong while respecting you and listening to what you ask of him, and he will have a headstart when he gets to school and has to listen to his teachers. You are planting the seeds of self-discipline and showing him the basics of good behaviour. If you can do this while your child is still only little, you have the makings of a fantastic parent!

CHAPTER 4

Three-day plans for children aged eighteen months to three years

When your child reaches eighteen months old, she is no longer baby-like. She is toddling around, chatting in her own language, and has become a little person with her own views and opinions. She is determined and busy testing her boundaries – and yours.

This determination continues into her pre-school years as her character develops and by the time your child reaches three years of age her character will be fully formed. You won't change this basic nature but if you are able to tune into it and work with her, you can still guide her to make the correct decisions in life.

Between the ages of eighteen months and three years, children try to take control of key areas of their lives, whether it's sleeping, eating or behaviour. The difficulty arises in judging when to allow them to have control and when they need firm direction from you. It's important that your child feels she is able to make some decisions; this is a first step towards the independence she will need when starting school and other activities outside the home. However, you can't let your child control the lives of the rest of the household and particularly your own.

Tantrums are the classic reaction when a child is told she can't have her own way. It's a protest, with which she hopes to get you to change your mind, and if you reinforce the behaviour by giving in, you'll encourage her to try again next time. Tantrums may occur more frequently when there is a change in your child's life, such as the arrival of a new sibling, parents separating, one parent working away from home and returning at irregular intervals, or when she is starting nursery school.

Whether you are aware of an underlying emotional reason for the tantrum or not, it still needs to be managed and disciplined.

At this age, your child will understand virtually everything you say to her, but may become extremely frustrated when you are unable to understand what she is trying to communicate to you. With the best will in

Change is scary, and children often don't know how else to express their fear so tantrums result.

the world, you won't always pick up her stumbling language. I suggest that when this happens you bend down to her level, look her straight in the eye and ask her to take a deep breath and blow. Do this together several times so that you are blowing in each others' faces and laughing, then say *"Mummy is not sure what you are saying. Can you show me what it is?"* Remember that she is still learning the language and needs help, just as you would in a foreign country where no one spoke English.

As we've seen before, one of the main things children need to feel secure is a daily routine. They are creatures of regularity and pattern. Below is the type of routine I recommend for this age group.

7am	Wake up in own cot or bed
7.30am	Breakfast
8am	Dressed and teeth brushed
9–11.30am	Morning activity
12–1pm	Lunchtime
1–2pm	A sleep of between 60 and 90 minutes
2.30–3pm	Afternoon snack
3–5pm	Afternoon activity
5.30pm	Teatime
6pm	Bath-time
6.30pm	TV then stories and milk (if still having)
7–7.30pm	Bedtime

There will be times when the routine is altered – on holiday, for example, or when on day trips – but in general children need to return to their routine when they are in their own home. It's quite understandable that they like to know the sequence of events. Imagine not knowing when you were next going to eat or what time your working day was going to end. The feeling would eventually be very unsettling.

Even if your child has been sleeping and eating well as a baby, the changes in her life as she grows can disrupt the pattern. As she progresses from a cot to her own bed, it becomes possible for her to get out of bed by herself if she wakes in the night and most likely she will want to come and find you. She will be eating a more varied diet and encountering other children at play dates, some of whom will be well-behaved and some who won't. When she is being toilet trained, she might waken in the night feeling disorientated and needing a wee. All of these developments are stressful and can lead to challenging behaviour, but my three-day plans will help you to guide her back towards a healthy routine.

Remember: if you have more than one issue to address, always deal with sleeping first and after that choose the one that is causing most disruption to the family.

THE SLEEP PLAN FOR CHILDREN AGED EIGHTEEN MONTHS TO THREE YEARS

If your child has got into bad habits – refusing to go to sleep unless you lie down with him, waking in the night and insisting on coming into your bed, or even refusing to go to bed at all – the sooner you do something about it, the better. Toddlers need between eleven and fourteen hours sleep in a 24-hour period in order to thrive.

At this age, he will resist fiercely changes to an established routine he likes, such as coming into your bed whenever he stirs in the night, and it may take longer than three days to change these habits, but change them you must.

First of all, don't rush to transfer him from a cot to a big bed. Some parents do this too soon, perhaps because a new baby has come along and needs the cot. If your child seems happy in his cot, I recommend leaving him there until he is two and a half or even three years old.

However, if he starts climbing out of the cot, or showing signs of doing so, you will have to make the change sooner so as to prevent accidents. It is a good idea to put a gate across the bedroom door if a child under the age of two is able to get out of bed themselves, so that they don't wander out in the night and fall down the stairs.

Before starting a sleep plan, make sure your child's bedroom is as dark as possible (put foil on the window if need be – see page 4), at a cool but pleasant temperature, and that there are no noises or distractions that might cause him to wake in the night. If you use a glowing night-light, position it below the child's eye level as he lies in bed.

The sleep plan should be implemented by the same carer every night until the new routine is established, and it should be carried out in exactly the same way. The equipment you will need is:

- A digital clock or timer
- A timings sheet and a pen
- Paper, pens, scissors, stickers and glue to make a visual reward chart

Make sure that your child is completely healthy and that you have a quiet diary for the next five days. It's a good idea to stock the fridge with the family's favourite foods and enlist a support network – either your partner, a family member or a friend on the end of the phone who's aware of what you are doing.

PLAN DAY ONE

You and your child are going to do the sleep plan together, so you need to explain it to him. In the morning after breakfast, sit at the kitchen table with the art materials laid out and introduce the plan to your child, saying something like this.

"Now I want us to do something very special this week. We have a task we need to do together. You know that we have been finding it difficult to go to bed at night and/or stay in our bed until morning? Well, this lady has written a book to guide us to stay in our bed and it looks really fun. The first thing we have to do is make a colourful chart with five days of the week written on it! What colour card shall we start with?"

Draw five circles on your card and write a day of the week in each one. If you like, you can decorate around the edge of the card by gluing on television characters cut out of a children's magazine. Alternatively, the chart could be a train with five coaches, or a flower with five petals or five fishes swimming in the ocean. Let your child choose, according to what he likes. Make this chart personal so that he feels proud of the finished object.

When you have finished, take the chart upstairs to the bedroom and stick it on the wall in a place where your child can see it when he is lying in bed at night. It might need to be close to the glow light. Now comes the second explanation:

"We need to stick this on your wall for everyone to see what a marvellous job you have done with your chart. Tonight at bedtime we are going to see if we can go to bed like a good boy. We will have our bath and two stories and then we will snuggle into bed. When you stay in bed and settle to sleep you will get a sticker on your chart and if you stay in bed until morning you will get another sticker. Let's try to put stickers in all of the [circles/petals/carriages] and then we get a reward. A prize!"

Point at the chart saying the days of the week. Do not make the chart more than five days long and don't show him the stickers at this stage. They will be a surprise in the morning.

"Now what shall we have for a reward/prize?"

The thing children of this age love the most is time spent with their parents. Ask your child what he would like, and provide some prompts if necessary, such as:

- Playing football with Daddy in the park

- Going to a café for cake with Mummy and Daddy

- Picnics

- Snuggling on the sofa with Mummy for stories

- Baking cakes with Mummy

- Swimming together as a family.

> The rewards should be activities rather than material possessions and he can have one on each of the next seven days if he earns them. (And you'll try to make sure he does.)

Write the rewards he wants on a separate piece of paper or card and stick them on a wall in the kitchen. If a reward has been earned at night, it will be chosen each morning after breakfast and carried out that day so make sure all the rewards are realistic. This is not a situation in which you want to be saying 'no' to your child.

You may find that a child of just eighteen months is happy with the stickers alone. It may be too complex to introduce rewards as well. Make a decision based on your knowledge of your child. Older children from two and a half onwards will definitely respond to the reward system.

Make sure he understands the system. If he goes to sleep in his own bed/stays in his own bed, he will be rewarded with:

- A hug

- A sticker

- And a reward (if you are doing this).

AFTERNOON NAP

Continue with the rest of your day and don't talk about the sleep plan until it's time for his afternoon nap. If he goes to sleep by himself and sleeps for more than an hour, tell him he can have a sticker on his chart after he wakes up. (If he no longer has an afternoon nap, just continue with your normal afternoon activity and don't mention the sleep plan until bath-time tonight.) Here's the afternoon nap procedure:

❧ Guide your child to his bed and talk about what you will do later.

❧ *"I hope that it's sunny later and we can go out and play ball outside. You be a good boy and close your eyes and when you wake up we will put a sticker on your lovely new chart."*

❧ Turn around and leave the room, pulling the door closed.

❧ If your child starts to shout straight away, start the timer and listen for a pause in the shouting. When the pause comes, mark the time on the chart and the length of pause. Don't go back in unless there is a Crescendo Call – a continuous call that lasts for five minutes without a pause and in a rising pitch (see page 47).

❧ If you have to go back in and your child is standing up or has got out of bed, put him back in his bed, stroke his hair or rub his back for ten seconds to calm him, then say *"Good boy, I know you can do this. Have a little sleep and I will see you soon."*

❧ Leave the room and start your timings again. If after 30 minutes he is still not going to sleep, put him in the buggy and take him out for a walk somewhere. With any luck he will doze off for a while. He doesn't get any stickers for this, though, but don't mention it.

❧ If your child does go to sleep in his own bed and wakens after an hour, produce some attractive stickers that he has never seen before and let him stick the first one on his wall chart. Praise him, saying *"You are such a clever boy for sleeping in your own bed. Tonight, if you manage to sleep here, you will get even more stickers. Isn't that exciting? Well done you for learning something new."*

The ideal way to spend the afternoon is doing something out in the fresh air. He should get out of the buggy and run around for a while. This will tire your child, but be careful not to make him over-tired.

BEDTIME ROUTINE
❧ Teatime needs to be at home between 5pm and 6pm.

❧ Bath-time should be from 6–6.30pm. While your child is calmly playing in the bath, remind him of the bedtime routine and the stickers he will earn.

❧ *"Remember the chart we made this morning and placed on your wall? We want to see the lovely stickers in the morning. Now we are going to put our pyjamas on after our bath. After that we are going to come upstairs to brush our teeth and have two lovely stories. Then you are going to snuggle down in your bed and have a wonderful sleep until breakfast time. You are such a good boy. I know you can do this. Let's put on our pyjamas."*

❧ Brush his teeth and visit the loo, or change his nappy if he is still in nappies.

❧ Read two stories in the comfort of the bedroom, then before you tuck your child under the covers, make sure there is nothing he can ask for. Any preferred comforter should be there, and there should be a drink by the bedside if he usually asks for one.

❧ As you tuck your child into bed, talk about the next day:*"I hope that the sun shines tomorrow and we will go to the park. We can take a picnic and feed the ducks. We might even be able to have an ice cream. Now you be a wonderful boy and tomorrow we will put stickers on your chart."*

❧ If your child starts to shout the moment you try to put him in bed, simply give him a big hug and say into his ear *"You are such a clever boy, I know that you can do this. Come on, let's snuggle you under these covers."* If your child refuses point blank to get into bed let him lie on the floor.

❧ Turn around and leave the room. Pull the door closed.

❧ Your child is likely to shout because this routine is new and he is unsure what to do. The moment you leave the bedroom, start the timer and mark the time on your chart. Find somewhere to sit, either in the next room or further down the corridor, but make sure your child can't see or hear you. Children are more likely to perform if they have an audience!

❧ Time your child for ten minutes and unless he is playing with his toys or destroying the bedroom, do not go back in. If your child has not paused in his shouting for ten minutes and the calls are Crescendo, you need to go back in.

🦋 Place your child in his bed and stroke his hair or rub his back for ten seconds to calm him a little. *"Now I know you can do this. You are such a good boy. Mummy loves you very much. Settle down now. I will see you in the morning at breakfast time."*

🦋 Stand up and leave the room. Make up your mind that you will not enter the room again until your child is asleep. He needs his own space to realise what is happening and from now on, every time you enter his bedroom you are likely to escalate the situation. Remember: your child is trying to learn something new. Give him the space to learn.

🦋 Fill in your timings chart and you will notice that the protesting will gradually start to fade and the thinking time will lengthen. Your child is doing well, as are you. Believe in him.

TIMER START	TIMER STOP	PROTEST TIME	THINKING TIME	CALM TIME
7.10PM	7.20PM	10 MINS	2 SECS	
7.20PM	7.30PM	10 MINS	2 SECS	
7.30PM	7.38PM	8 MINS	5 SECS	
7.38PM	7.45PM	7 MINS	10 SECS	

🦋 Once your child's thinking time has gone above ten seconds, this is what I call 'calm time' and he is on his way to settling himself to sleep. This may take a while on the first night, but persevere.

Whatever you do, don't give up after the first night, no matter how difficult you find it. It will work in the end, and it has to be done.

NIGHT WAKENINGS
Be prepared for disturbed sleep on the first night of the plan and you will be pleasantly surprised if he sleeps through. Most children will test the system by wakening when they enter a period of light sleep.

🦋 If your child wakes in the night and gets out of bed, return him to his room, saying *"What has happened here? You have left your lovely bed. Now it is the middle of the night. Let's get you back."*

☙ Guide your child by placing your hand on his back. Try not to lift him. Let him walk back to his room. Guide him to his bed and praise him: *"Well done, you are being lovely and quiet. You are such a good boy. Now let's tuck you in."*

☙ If your child refuses to get into his bed, continue with the praise. *"I know you can do this. You are a good boy. Get into your lovely bed when you are ready."* Then leave the room.

☙ Return to the timings chart if your child starts to protest. Fill in the chart using the timer and be aware of the times changing. The thinking time will lengthen eventually. Everyone has to sleep some time!

You may be exhausted and sleep-deprived but congratulate yourself for making a good start along the route to creating a healthy sleeper. If you stick to the plan, you will make big changes in just two more days. Believe, believe, believe!

PLAN DAY TWO

Your child has spent the night in his own bedroom – something he may never have done before. This deserves a sticker and you need to let him know why he is getting that sticker.

> "You are learning something new. I am so proud of you because you stayed in your room. Well done. Let's choose a special sticker."

If your child got out of bed in the night but returned to his bed quietly when you guided him, this earns another sticker. Your child needs to feel rewarded so that he continues with his efforts. Please remain positive the entire time. Keep reminding yourself that he is learning something new.

When you go into the kitchen for breakfast, take a look at the rewards on the wall and choose the one for today. *"I have looked at the rewards and I would like us to do some baking today and take our cakes to the park."*

If your child says he wants to pick the reward, be positive and say *"If you manage to keep quiet at bedtime tonight and you don't do lots of shouting, you can choose tomorrow."*

Don't let your child negotiate. You have made the decision. Carry on with your day, remembering to give the reward. Don't mention the sleep plan during the day or talk about it with anyone else when your child is within earshot.

Follow the same routine as yesterday if he has an afternoon nap, and then exactly the same procedure in the run-up to bedtime.

- Tonight at bath-time talk again about the bedtime routine and keep it exactly the same as yesterday. Stay positive.

- Watch TV (if this is part of your normal routine), brush teeth, visit the loo (if necessary), and then read two stories in the comfort of the bedroom.

- Now settle your child into his bed and chat about the next day. Make this chat no longer than 30 seconds. If he refuses to get into bed, you can chat as he sits on his chair or rug. If he is shouting, hold him close and talk quietly into his ear: *"I know you can do this. Remember that we will choose stickers and rewards. Quieten down now, you clever boy."*

- Leave the room and start the timer. Make sure that your child cannot see you from his room.

- If you have to enter after the first ten minutes, be calm but firm with your child. He knows what the system involves. It is no longer a new concept. Say in a clear, firm voice (not a shout): *"Now come on, young man, you know what this is all about. How about you jump into that lovely bed and quieten down? I love you so much."*

- Give him a hug or kiss and then leave the room. Don't enter again unless there is a Crescendo scream with rising pitch and no pauses for five minutes.

TIMER START	TIMER STOP	PROTEST TIME	THINKING TIME	CALM TIME
7.10PM	7.20PM	10 MINS	2 SECS	
7.20PM	7.25PM	5 MINS	3 SECS	
7.25PM	7.30PM	5 MINS	10 SECS	
7.30PM	7.37PM	7 MINS		20 SECS
7.37PM	7.41PM	4 MINS		30 SECS
7.42PM	7.46PM	4 MINS		30 SECS

If you have applied the system consistently you should be feeling more confident with it by now. Compare the Day Two chart with the Day One chart and you may see that your child has made a little bit of progress. Make a mental note. This improvement is due to your teaching. Well done!

If your child wakens in the night remain consistent with your guidance. If he has left his room, turn him around and walk him back to it with your hand on his shoulder. Talk to him as you do this: *"Well done, nice and quietly, back to your wonderful room."* Start the timings chart if you need to. You'll get there!

PLAN DAY THREE

A day shouldn't really start before 6am, and 7am is better. If he wakens too early, guide him back to bed using the same procedure as for night wakenings.

When it's time to get up, first of all place at least one sticker on the chart, then there should be hugs all round and a great big 'well done'. Even if your child still protested at bedtime and during the night, you should be able to see some signs of understanding. He knows the programme and realises that you are not going to change it. Once this happens, the protests will get shorter and eventually disappear altogether – usually within a week.

Consistency and a positive approach are the most important factors.

Let him choose his reward over breakfast then continue with the day as normal. If he goes to sleep in his own bed and sleeps for over an hour in the afternoon, that earns one sticker. At bedtime, do things in exactly the same order: bath, TV, teeth, toilet, stories. By now you will have the routine down to a fine art and your child will sense that this is the way that bedtime is now going to be from now on.

On Day Three you shouldn't need to enter the room again after you have said your initial goodnight. Only go in if your child's shout develops into a Crescendo scream. In this case spend 30 seconds with him to calm him down and remind him it is night-time. Tell him he is very clever to be able to settle himself to sleep.

Continue to keep the timings charts for as long as the shouting continues. Compare this night with the first night. There are bound to be signs of improvement, which show that your child is heading in the right direction.

You should be very proud of both yourself and your child. You have introduced something totally new into your family life and have remained consistent and positive, even when feeling tired.

On Day Four, find some time to praise and reward yourself.

- Buy yourself flowers or a glossy magazine – or both!

- Order something for yourself on the Internet.

- Ask your partner to make a special dinner.

You have spent 72 hours totally dedicated to changing your child's life for the better. Be proud of yourself. You have been guiding him to make the right choices.

After the three-day programme, it's a good idea to continue using a stickers and rewards system for six or seven consecutive nights until the routine is lodged in memory. Try to avoid travelling anywhere or spending nights away from home. Your child needs to sleep in his own bedroom for at least ten consecutive nights.

By that time, you will feel relaxed and confident about bedtime and the shouting will be a distant memory.

When you do venture on holiday or for a weekend away you may adopt a slightly different routine. This is OK as long as you explain to your child that when you get home you will be going back to normal.

If you think your child is having difficulty at any time, I suggest devising another reward system to get him back on track.

FREQUENTLY ASKED QUESTIONS

My child keeps getting out of bed and coming downstairs. She is not shouting. What do we do?

Your child is testing you in the silent way. I suggest that you give her the same treatment and simply turn her around and walk her back up the stairs without talking. If she refuses to walk, turn her face away from you and hold her under her arms and walk her up the stairs. Try to intercept her before she reaches the kitchen, sitting room or wherever you are. Keep doing exactly the same thing every time and you will get results in the end.

When I put my child to bed she tells me she is not tired. What do I say?

"You don't have to fall asleep straight away. This is your own special time to relax in your bed and think about the lovely things we have done today."

Give her something to think about and tuck her under her covers. "Think lovely thoughts and they will turn into happy dreams. See you at breakfast time."

My child is quiet in his room but I can hear him playing with his toys. Should I leave him?

No, absolutely not. Enter the room and tell him that now is not the time to play. Toys need to rest as well as children! Tuck him into bed and make him aware that if he continues to play then you will remove the toys from his room. You must follow this through. If he begins playing again, enter the room and remove the toys. Say "You can do this. Time to relax in bed. The toys will be here for you to play with tomorrow. See you at breakfast time. Sleep tight." Leave the room and if he is shouting, start the timings chart.

My child will not physically get into bed. The shouting starts straight after stories are read.

Sit your child on the edge of his bed or on the floor as close to the bed as possible. Say "It is now time to relax and then fall to sleep. Your bed is the best place to relax and sleep. You can sleep on the floor if you wish or in your bed. It is your choice. I am sleeping in my bed tonight. Now sleep tight and I will see you in the morning."

Kiss your child on the head and walk out of the room, leaving him where he is. If he starts to shout, leave him for ten minutes then go back into the room if he is still not in bed. "I think all the shouting is finished. Your body wants to lie down. Let's try this wonderful bed." Walk together to the bed and guide your child in. If he still refuses, leave him where he wants to be. Let him make the decision.

As your child is drifting off to sleep, enter his room again and calmly tell him that the floor gets very cold in the night. Guide him into his bed, lifting him if necessary. "Now you will sleep wonderfully in your lovely bed. See you at breakfast time." Try to do this before he has actually nodded off. If you lift him in his sleep he is likely to wake in the night and shout because he has woken up somewhere different from where he fell asleep. You can bet he'll remember!

When I leave the bedroom, my child starts throwing things around the room. What should I do?
Enter the room and say "Right. This is not on. Let's get into bed. I want to tell you something." Guide him by taking his hand and placing him in bed. "Now, you are such a good boy. You know you don't throw things. This is a time to relax and think about all the lovely toys you are going to play with tomorrow. If you throw anything else I will have to remove it from your room. You will end up with only a bed in here. Your toys want to stay in your room so relax here in bed and I will see you at breakfast."

Keep your word. If anything more is thrown remove it from the room and keep it out of sight for the next 24 hours. After that, you will have to judge whether to return it or not.

If things have not gone well during the night, should I not give my child a sticker and a reward?
The stickers should always be given and you should praise your child

for his efforts. Say that you know he is trying hard. Give a reward each day as well, but after a particularly challenging night you might only choose a small reward. Don't tell your child that's what you are doing. It's not a punishment. You may not feel like a big reward after getting up and down like a yo-yo all night, so save the bigger rewards for when he manages to do better.

When do I stop the stickers and rewards?
I have found that after seven consecutive nights the routine is firmly established and the stickers are not so important to your child. Leave the chart on the wall as a visual reminder that you talk about from time to time. The incentive system is no longer required, though.

THE EATING PLAN FOR CHILDREN AGED EIGHTEEN MONTHS TO THREE YEARS

By eighteen months old, children are likely to challenge what they eat. Even if they've been eating a variety of foods up to that point, they can become fussy almost overnight. The fact is that they like familiarity, especially at mealtimes. They want to recognise the food placed in front of them and have a clear memory of what it tastes like. That's why they want their favourites every time and are less prepared to try anything new.

Over the twenty years I've been helping families I've found that most children would be more than happy to survive on two or three different meal choices – but this would not provide all the nutrients they need for good health, so you can't give in to it. I totally understand why some parents do just feed their child meals they know they will eat because it's horrible to think of them going hungry, but it's vital for their health that they learn at this age to eat a balanced diet. And the only way they will do that is if you serve them nutritious meals and don't offer any alternatives if they won't eat them.

By eighteen months old, children have teeth and are capable of eating the same foods as you and your partner. When I go to work in a family home I sit down with the parents and ask them what meals they like to cook and what they enjoy eating. The aim is that eventually they will all eat together as a family.

I suggest that you sit down with your partner and anyone else who lives in the house one evening and list all of the meals that you like to eat at home. Also include in the list the meals your child likes to eat, even if they're as simple as fish fingers and chips. Choose meals that your child will be able to help you prepare, as this is an integral part of the three-day plan.

From this list create a weekly meal plan containing the meals you like and those your child enjoys. Highly spiced foods may need to be made milder or avoided for the time being. Make sure there is always one meal a day that you know your child likes and one new one. In the new ones, it's a good idea to include an element that you know your child will eat. For example, if you are offering beef stir-fry as a new dish on the Wednesday, serve it with something familiar like noodles that you know she will normally eat. If the beef is not eaten – even if the noodles are not eaten – fruit and yoghurt will follow, and possibly milk at bedtime, so your child will not wake in the night hungry.

Here's a sample meal plan:

	LUNCH	DINNER
MONDAY	CHEESE & HAM OMELETTE	MILD CHICKEN CURRY & RICE
TUESDAY	TOASTED SANDWICHES	FISH PIE WITH GREEN BEANS
WEDNESDAY	PIZZA	BEEF STIR-FRY WITH NOODLES
THURSDAY	JACKET POTATO WITH BAKED BEANS	SAUSAGE CASSEROLE & MASH WITH CARROTS
FRIDAY	BOILED EGG & TOAST FINGERS	STEAK & CHIPS WITH PEAS
SATURDAY	TUNA & CUCUMBER SANDWICHES	PASTA DISH
SUNDAY	ROAST CHICKEN & VEGETABLES	SAVOURY PANCAKES

During this three-day programme I advise that dessert is offered after a main meal and consists of a healthy option of fruit and yoghurt, jelly, a home-made flapjack, an egg custard or a small piece of apple tart. Save heavy puddings with custard or chocolate puddings for special occasions.

Avoid giving your child a drink just before her meal, which could reduce her appetite. She can have a drink with her meal of water, diluted fruit juice or very weak cordial. Avoid fizzy drinks, which are loaded with sugar and E numbers, and milk, which will line the stomach and make your child feel full.

It's good for children to get used to eating out, so if you enjoy eating in restaurants take your child along. Order a couple of starters before the main and share these together as a 'tasting platter'. Don't let the waiter bring a bread basket, though, or you can be sure that's what your child will fill up on!

Every family has their own unique way of living and there is no 'right' or 'wrong' way. You need to find a realistic meal plan that will work for your family, while introducing your child to the basics of a healthy diet.

Offering substitutes defeats the purpose of the meal plan and sends a mixed message to your child: "Eat it if you like but if not I will give you something you prefer." In the three-day plan there are no options.

Before you start the plan, make sure you have the following:

> The key principle of the three-day plan is that the child does not get an alternative if she refuses the meal on offer.

🦋 A meal plan for a week

🦋 All ingredients in the fridge, freezer and cupboards

🦋 A comfortable chair at the table, which your child cannot get down from without your help. Make sure she is high enough to see what is going on. I favour Tripp-Trapp chairs, but choose what suits your child.

🦋 Wipe-able bibs for the younger age group.

🦋 Wipes for cleaning hands and faces at the end of the meal.

🦋 A cup your child feels confident drinking from.

🦋 Praise and reward materials (see below).

Choose your moment for starting the plan. It's important that you, your partner and any other caregivers give a consistent message, that you all understand the eating plan and that you won't back down in the face of your child's protests. You will be the main person guiding the plan, but you will need support from everyone else.

Choose a period when you are going to be based at home for at least ten days. If your child usually has lunch at nursery school, begin the plan during school holidays so that your child will be used to it by the time she goes back.

It's important that you keep calm and believe it is going to work, even if your child doesn't accept any new meals for the first few days. You may need to keep trying, and keep calm. Don't let the dinner table become a battleground.

> If you send your child mixed messages she will not know what is being asked of her.

PLAN DAY ONE

During breakfast on Day One, sit and eat alongside your child and explain to her the changes that are going to be made. Tailor the explanation to suit your child's ability to comprehend. Here's an example:

> "Daddy and I have been talking and we have decided that we are going to make some exciting changes in the house. We are going to sit together and eat as a family and I would like you to help me with the cooking. What do you think of that?"

Pause to answer any questions.

Continue with:

> "I would like us to make a lovely picture and every time we sit up at the table and eat our meal we are going to put a sticker on our chart and hunt for a prize! Doesn't that sound like fun? Let's finish our breakfast and then create a lovely picture for our stickers."

Older children love the hunt for a prize, while younger ones may simply be happy with the sticker principle. You know your child so decide on the reward system that suits her best.

MAKING THE STICKER PICTURE

Take a large piece of card or paper and draw around a small cup to create fourteen circles on it. These circles will symbolise plates and there are two for each of the coming seven days. (Breakfast is not included in the plan because all children have something they will eat at breakfast, whether that's cereal, toast, pancakes, eggs, bacon or yoghurt and fruit with a glass of fruit juice. However, if breakfast is also a challenge in your household you could choose to include it in the plan.) Let your child help to draw the circles, if she can, then she can colour or paint them.

Above each circle, write the day and the meal: Monday lunch, Monday dinner, Tuesday lunch, Tuesday dinner, and so forth.

Now explain that we put two stickers on each plate after a mealtime.

- One for good manners and staying on your chair.

- One for eating some of the food on your plate like a good girl/boy.

Stick the picture on the wall where it can easily be seen from the table.

Now announce: *"I'll show you the stickers after lunchtime today. This is going to be great fun."*

Your child may continue to ask about stickers but simply distract her by talking about the next stage in your day.

PLANNING THE TREASURE HUNT

You will only have a treasure hunt if your child has earned two stickers at a meal. Give your child an empty cup or a jar and tell her that there is treasure in the [garden/living room/a room of your choice], and that she has to go and find it and put it in the jar. Explain that once she has filled up all the plates on the picture with stickers, the jar will be full of treasure.

For the treasure, you could choose:

- Tiny rubber animals

- Miniature cars

- Shiny gem stones

❧ Large marbles

❧ Pretty beads to make a necklace

The importance of the treasure is that it is something 'precious' that will captivate your child's imagination, something she does not generally get so that she feels important and responsible.

Ask your child to sit in her chair at the table and close her eyes. She can count to ten if she is able. This is when you need to go and hide one of the pieces of treasure.

You will need to supervise the treasure hunt and make sure she puts the treasure in the jar immediately after finding it. The jar is then placed somewhere high up for the family to see but not to touch until the next treasure hunt.

Explain that *"Treasure needs to be kept in a very safe place. We do not want to lose it. We are trying to fill up the jar."* Say: *"Let's hope we put stickers on our next plate and then we will be hunting again!"*

If your child wants to play with the jar, move quickly on to the next activity. Lead the way with confidence and your child will follow. Do not back down and give her the jar. If you need to, tell her you will look at it together later.

COOKING TOGETHER

During the three-day programme and further into the week, I advise that you and your child cook together in the mornings after you have had breakfast. Have her standing close to you and involve her as much as possible. Never underestimate her ability in the kitchen. A child aged two to three years is capable of tearing lettuce leaves for a salad, throwing vegetables into their water, rolling pastry and stirring sauces (off the heat). By helping you with the cooking she will take ownership and pride in what she has helped make. This may make her more likely to eat the meal.

I advise that you spend part of both the morning and the afternoon outside so the fresh air builds your child's appetite. It is important that she feels hungry at each mealtime.

SNACKS

Your child may need a mid-morning and a mid-afternoon snack. Make sure it is given over 90 minutes before the next meal, so if lunch is at 12 noon the snack needs to be finished by 10.30am. A snack only needs to be small – something the size of one digestive biscuit is enough! Select from the following:

- Dried fruit selection
- A piece of fruit
- A breadstick
- A biscuit (only one)
- A rice/oatcake
- Cucumber sticks with hummus
- A cracker with cheese
- A small yoghurt
- A home-made juice lolly

Never give a snack less than 90 minutes before a meal. If your child says she is hungry, move the mealtime forward a little bit rather than offer something 'to keep her going'.

LUNCH

Lunch should be served between 12 and 1.30pm. If your child still has an afternoon nap, you will want her to go down by 2pm. Give a five-minute warning before lunchtime so the announcement does not come as a total surprise. Encourage your child to wash her hands with you and then to sit up at the table in her 'comfy seat'.

- When you serve your child's portion, give her a maximum of two tablespoons of food. Sit down together and explain what you are having for lunch (unless she already knows because you prepared it together).

❧ *"This is what Mummy and Daddy had for dinner last night. It is beef with noodles. I love it. Let's try some together and then we can take a look at our stickers and pop them on our plate!"* Speak with an assertive yet calm tone. It is crucial that your child does not pick up any sense of anxiety from you.

❧ Start to eat your own food and talk about the afternoon activities or something you know will interest your child. If she likes Peppa Pig, Fireman Sam or the Octonauts, slip in the fact that they are probably having their lunch at the moment.

❧ Now place a small amount of food onto your child's spoon or fork. *"When you are ready, you can have a little taste. Just a little one."*

❧ Continue to eat your own meal and, after you have finished, ask your child again if she is going to taste the lovely flavour. Don't praise your child as she lifts the spoon to eat or she may get 'stage fright' and stop. Nobody likes to feel that they are being watched as they eat.

❧ After a few moments, offer praise. Don't over-exaggerate. *"Well done, you tried the noodles. Next time we have them I am sure you will eat a little bit more. They're nice, aren't they? The more you eat, the stronger your body will get!"*

❧ If she refuses to eat, simply slide the plate to the middle of the table and announce that you are going to have a 'little dessert'. Now offer dessert of yoghurt and fruit. Your child needs the vitamins and minerals which can be found in fruit and dairy-based products.

❧ Don't fall into the trap of giving a large dessert because she has not eaten her main meal. Small main = small dessert.

❧ After dessert ask one last time if your child would like to taste the noodles. If the answer is 'no' then leave it be. She will have the opportunity to eat a snack in a couple of hours.

When your child has asked to leave the table you need to go together to the 'plate picture' and place a sticker on the chart as appropriate. If she hasn't tried the meal on offer but has remained at the table, reward her with one sticker. If she sat nicely and tried the food as well, she gets two stickers and you can have a treasure hunt, but don't mention it if she hasn't earned two.

Head outside for some fresh air and exercise to build up an appetite. The afternoon snack should be given no later than 3.15pm to be finished by 3.30pm. Follow the snack suggestions above.

DINNER

I suggest dinner is served between 5 and 6pm when your child is hungry but not over-tired. Don't serve dinner too late. Follow the same procedure as at lunchtime.

> Children do not want to be the focus of attention when they are trying something new.

- ❧ Give a five-minute warning.

- ❧ Wash hands together.

- ❧ Sit your child at the table.

- ❧ Serve the meal and sit down together.

- ❧ Praise your child if she made this meal with you. Say how you enjoyed cooking together.

- ❧ Start eating your meal slowly (you don't want to be finished before your child has taken her first mouthful).

- ❧ Place food on your child's spoon and fork, saying *"Take a taste when you are ready. You are a good girl."*

- ❧ Continue eating and talking about the day's events. Converse with your partner or other siblings if they are present.

- ❧ Keep calm and do not hurry your meal.

- ❧ Prompt for the second time. *"I am sure your body will love this dinner. It will help you get bigger and stronger."*

- ❧ Serve a healthy dessert and leave the main meal on the table.

- ❧ After dessert ask one final time if she would like to try the main meal.

- Encourage your child to ask to leave the table at the end of the meal.

- Go to the plate picture to place one or two stickers, depending on whether she tried her dinner and sat nicely at the table.

- Offer lots of praise for the day's efforts.

- Have a treasure hunt if she earned two stickers.

As you put her to bed, remind your child how proud you are of her and gently make her aware that you will do some fun cooking tomorrow and get some more stickers.

If your child claims she is hungry simply tell her that she has had plenty to eat today and finish the day with some milk. Say that her body needs to sleep now and when it wakes up in the morning it will be very excited about breakfast time. Move swiftly onto story time/ song time and saying goodnight. Don't worry too much about her going hungry because she doesn't need any energy when she is asleep and she will be offered breakfast in the morning.

Well done! Day One has come to a close. You have started implementing a new system and I am sure that both you and your child are exhausted as you have had to absorb so much information and make changes to your routine. Tomorrow will run more smoothly. You have leapt the first hurdle!

Write down everything your child has eaten and record how many stickers she has been awarded. When you look back in a few days' time you will see how much progress you have made. Now put your feet up and relax!

PLAN DAY TWO

The reward system is now clear in your mind and also in your child's. It is important that you continue with the same routine today so that your child will start to accept that this is a permanent change in your lives.

Most children will eat breakfast, and after that you will be offering one meal that she likes already and one that is new, as well as two small healthy snacks and milk before bedtime.

Don't have unrealistic expectations. Just stick to the routine and your child will eat what she needs, when she needs it. Your day might look something like this.

Please relax and accept that your child is not going hungry.

7–8am	Breakfast of cereal/toast/eggs Yoghurt and fruit A glass of fruit juice
8.30–10am	Cooking the main meal of the day together Morning snack
10–11.30am	Morning activity involving some time outdoors This could simply be playing in the garden or going to the park
12–1pm	Lunchtime, in which you offer the food in exactly the same way as you did on Day One: start eating your own meal, put a little on your child's spoon or fork, continue talking about your day, prompt twice, then serve a healthy dessert, leaving the main course on the table in case she goes back to it Stickers and treasure (if applicable)
1.30–3pm	Sleep or quiet time at home Afternoon snack
3–5pm	Outside activity, if possible
5–6pm	Dinnertime, in which you offer the food in exactly the same way as you did on Day One Stickers and treasure (if applicable)
6–6.30pm	Bath-time Followed by milk (if this applies)
6.45–7pm	Story time Praise for the day's achievements and a brief discussion of stickers and mealtimes

It takes longer for some children than others, but your child will get there in the end if you stay strong. Believe that you can do it!

PLAN DAY THREE

By Day Three most children will accept that their mealtime routine has changed. They are often exhausted by the alteration and this can be reflected in their behaviour. Your child may start to challenge you and protest but you must stand your ground. This change is good for your child and your entire family.

Today, you will cook together again after you have eaten breakfast but this time make a meal that you are going to invite guests to share. Invite a friend of your child's for dinner and make a meal you know that the friend is willing to eat. Cook a lovely dessert together to serve after dinner.

As you are cooking, talk about how your body likes new foods and enjoys gobbling them up. Make a funny gobbling noise to make your child laugh.

After cooking and baking have a mini snack and a run around outside to build up an appetite for lunch.

LUNCH

Remember to stay calm and don't worry if a certain food is untouched. There is likely to be something on the plate your child will eat and, if not, there will be a healthy dessert to follow. Follow the routine:

- Warning of meal to arrive in five minutes
- Hand washing
- Sit down together and serve
- Start your own meal slowly
- Encourage once
- Eat and talk about the day's events
- Place food on your child's spoon and fork
- Encourage again
- Continue eating and finish your meal

- Encourage once more
- Serve healthy dessert
- Ask your child to ask permission to leave the table
- Place sticker(s) on the chart
- Proceed with treasure hunt if necessary.

> Never ask your child if she is going to eat something because there's a 99 per cent chance she will say NO!

Encourage no more than three times at the table.

After lunch and an afternoon nap it is time for your social afternoon. Offer your child a snack and then start the afternoon in the fresh air.

Arrange for your guests to arrive around 4pm and let the children play together. Show your friend the 'plate picture' you have been making. You can also mention the treasure hunt and show the jar. Tell the children that if they do well at dinnertime there will be a treasure hunt before it is time for your friends to return home.

Wrap two small 'party bag' presents and hide them in the garden or in your child's bedroom so they are ready the moment dessert is finished. With any luck, peer pressure will nudge your child to eat the same meal as her friend, but if not you can still reward her for sitting nicely at the table or eating some part of the meal. Try to make sure the treasure is at least part-earned.

At the end of the play date, your child is likely to be exhausted – as are you. It has been a three-day learning curve for the entire family and together you have made a change. Think of this change as being life-long. We need to embrace new things throughout our lives and it's a good idea to start in the secure environment of your dinner table at home.

WHAT HAPPENS NEXT?

After three days, your child may not be a perfect eater but she will realise that the changes you have made are here to stay. A new pattern has formed and if you stick to it rigidly, you will notice her accepting it and perhaps even forgetting to object. You've taken back control of mealtimes and that's the way it has to stay until she is mature enough to choose a balanced diet for herself.

You will generally find that a reward system will work for a maximum of ten days before the novelty starts to wear thin. This is when you need to re-address the situation. After two weeks the menu will also start to feel boring, so it needs some alterations and additions.

Sit down with your partner and other family members to choose some new meals. If your child is old enough, she could be encouraged to look through cookery books and suggest savoury dishes she would like to try. Stay away from the chocolate and cake pages, though!

Print out a new menu plan for the coming week and attach it to a wall in the kitchen where everyone can see it.

After ten days, continue mealtimes without any reward system. Praise your child but don't fuss and never try to force her to eat. Sitting at the table is an achievement and any food eaten is a bonus.

After two weeks without a reward system, you may want to introduce another. Think about what your child really enjoys and devise something that will engage her. I once visited a family home where they were slowly constructing a Lego kit together. When a new food was tried they went into the room where the Lego was scattered over the table and they worked for ten minutes a time for each meal tried and tasted. This developed the child's sense of achievement. His efforts were developing in front of his eyes by the use of Lego.

Find a reward tool unique to your child – or just start a fresh treasure hunt with new rewards if you think her eating habits need another boost.

FREQUENTLY ASKED QUESTIONS

My child simply refuses to come to the table and sit down. What should I do?
Give your child a five-minute warning before meals. Set a timer so that when it goes off, he knows it is time. Visit the loo and wash your hands together. While washing hands say "Now you have a choice: sitting at the table or sitting on the stair in the hallway. It is not a time to play with toys. Stair or chair – you choose."

You now have to implement this and continue returning him to the stair until he is ready to come and sit up at the table. This may take a period of time but you need to break the habit of him not coming to the table. Leap this hurdle. Remain strong.

How long can I leave my child without eating?
The way I've designed the meal plan should ensure that she will eat at least once a day and most children like some element of breakfast as well so that means twice. Don't panic if she refuses any meal completely. She will just build a bigger appetite for the next one a few hours later. Remember that your child needs to be hungry in order to eat so don't try to compensate by offering bigger between-meal snacks. Children aren't capable of completely starving themselves. She is not going to come to immediate harm from missing meals. If she still hasn't eaten anything after two days, you might have to take action, but I'm confident this won't happen if you follow the three-day plan exactly.

My child pushes the plate away and sits quietly refusing to eat. Suggestions?
Continue to eat your meal and talk about topics other than food. The important point is not to react. The plate has been pushed for your benefit. He wants to see your reaction so keep calm and eat your own meal. Ignore him for ten minutes or so then place the plate close to him again and say "I am going to get myself a little more. Why don't you try it and see what it feels like in your mouth?"

Don't watch him. Sit and finish your meal. If he doesn't want to eat he can have a small dessert and one sticker for sitting beautifully at the table. Remember: tomorrow is another day!

My child puts the food in his mouth, chews it and then spits it out. What do you advise?
Don't react dramatically. Stay calm and carry on eating. Say "If you swallowed your food your body would grow stronger. Your body is not happy with you. Swallowing food leads to a big treasure hunt, not a little one." If he manages a meal without spitting food out, you could perhaps offer two pieces of treasure instead of one.

Your child is clearly happy to eat. He is simply testing you, so don't rise to the bait!

My child is eating a huge breakfast and nothing else. What should I do?
Everyone has their own favourite meal and your child's is obviously breakfast. His body is craving energy to help power him through the day and he's tucking it away. He needs to try more of a range of foods, though, so reduce the size of the breakfast you serve and eliminate all snacks. Eventually your child will get hungry and start to nibble at least part of the lunches and dinners placed in front of him. Remain strong, calm and consistent. He will get there. Trust him.

THE BEHAVIOUR PLAN FOR CHILDREN AGED EIGHTEEN MONTHS TO THREE YEARS

This is the stage when children are questioning the world around them – and that includes you! They may start refusing to follow your instructions and answer your suggestions with one word – 'No!' It's a challenging time.

You might be able to recognise characteristics inherited from yourself or your partner. Your child may be outgoing and confident when confronting new situations or he may be cautious and hesitant. He may be a thinker, who takes time to assess new things before acting, or a leader who tries to boss others around. Whatever your child's character, you won't change it so you need to work with him rather than against him.

A key element when spending time with a child of this age is always to think one step ahead of them. It's a good idea to map out a plan for the day in your mind, listing the chores that need to be done alongside activities you would like to do with your child.

NEED TO DO	WANT TO DO
COLLECT DRY CLEANING	VISIT FRIENDS FOR TEA
SEND THREE EMAILS	ARTS/CRAFTS WITH YOUR CHILD
IRONING	READ THE NEWSPAPER FOR 15 MINUTES
MAKE EVENING MEAL	

Now map in your mind the order in which these tasks are going to be done. Some people like to write out the plan, while others just make a 'mind map'. Either way, this kind of plan will help you to stay one step ahead of your child.

Take your child's interests into consideration and structure the day so that there is plenty to suit him. If he loves art, always have a good supply of materials for him to entertain himself at the table while you continue with your tasks. If he loves ball games, try to find time for one daily. Some children like to help with the housework and cooking.

The key is to stop and think. "What is the best way to entertain my child while I complete the task I need to do?" Set up the activity and stimulate him with it for five minutes and then get on with your own work. You may need to have the next activity idea in your head for when the present activity comes to a natural end.

ENGAGE

🌿 Introduce your child to an activity.

STIMULATE

🌿 Play with him to start the activity.

STEP BACK

🌿 Let him discover through his own play.

IT'S ALL IN THE VOICE!

Even if your child is not speaking much at eighteen months old, he will understand what you are saying to him. You can speak to him as you would to a five-year-old child. You don't need to simplify what is being said or talk in a baby fashion. Your tone of voice should be the same as if you were speaking with an adult. If your child senses that you are treating him below his ability, this is how he will behave.

There are times – many – when your child needs firm direction. This will involve altering your voice slightly so that he knows this is the voice that requires a response. Many women need to lower their voice when giving an instruction. Children respond to a deep firm voice. This is why many children respond quicker when they hear their father's voice than their mother's.

Your child is perfectly capable of following simple instructions but he will sense very quickly whether you believe that he will actually do it. If you believe, it's likely he will follow the instruction. If you don't, he probably won't.

Imagine you are asking a child to come to the table because it is time for lunch. If you ask him again and again while you stand over him, he is not likely to do it. He can sense that you are becoming frustrated because you have asked several times and he knows that you will eventually react and either leave him to continue playing or pick him up and take him to the table.

The way to deal with this is to say, in your clear firm voice: *"We need to have our lunch now because we have a busy afternoon. I am going to put the food on the plates and sit at the table. I will see you in the kitchen in a minute."*

Walk away from where he is playing and start to serve the lunch. So long as he hasn't just had a snack and is genuinely hungry, he will eventually toddle into the kitchen.

If your child hears uncertainty they will not do what is asked of them. They will see it as unnecessary – after all, Mummy didn't seem too sure!

It is important that you don't hesitate or murmur or mumble when asking him to do something. Be precise and direct.

PREPARING FOR THE THREE-DAY PLAN

In this section, I have created a three-day plan to address some different types of problem behaviour. If you implement the plan into your daily life you will see dramatic change by the time you reach Day Four. The key, as always, is to remain consistent and for everyone caring for your child to follow the system in the same way as you. It guides your child to alter his behaviour and make the right choices and it will benefit the entire family.

You are about to undergo a change in your family life and it is important that you dedicate all of your energy to it for three days. Make sure that you have some support yourself. If possible, ensure your partner will be at home every evening and is willing to let you discuss the stages in the day. If this is not possible, I advise you have a friend or family member you can talk to each evening during the three days.

Aim to keep your diary clear of appointments so that you can focus on behaviour in the home and also on outings to the park and shops.

If there are several different types of behaviour you want to address, make a list of them in order of importance. Start with the one that is most disruptive to family life. By writing the list you will see what the challenges are and as you implement systems you can begin to tick them off!

Aim to have the fridge full and the meals organised for both children and adults. You need plenty of energy for the days ahead so you must eat well and unwind each evening.

Structure the next three days in a way that will benefit you most, by organising activities that in the past you have found challenging. These might include a visit to the shops or to a friend, making a phone call or sending an email, or a play date in your home.

It is fundamentally important that you implement a reward system. This needs to be something visual that will engage your child. Here are some suggestions:

- A tower is built with Lego brick by brick
- A marble is placed in a jar
- Stickers are placed on a drawing
- A story is read from a favourite storybook.

On Day One at breakfast time, you will explain this system to your child. Keep the explanation simple. You might find that he doesn't clearly understand but once you start putting systems into place and praising him all will become clear.

This is not simply a bribe to make your child behave. It is a tool that needs to be on display to keep you both focused on the positive element of good behaviour rather than continually talking to your child about 'bad behaviour'.

THE SHOUT SPOT

If life is not going the way they want, most children aged between two and three years of age will shout. Some people call this 'having a tantrum'. Personally, I don't like the idea of parents suppressing their child's emotions. We must allow a child to shout and this is why I recommend you have a Shout Spot in your home.

The two main systems we will be using in this chapter are the Consequence System and the Zero Tolerance System. Both of these require a Shout Spot, which I have indicated with the character @ in the following list.

CONSEQUENCE	ZERO TOLERANCE
FIRM INSTRUCTION	TELL
WARNING	ACT @
SPACE/TIME @	APOLOGISE
APOLOGISE	EXPLAIN
MOVE ON	MOVE ON

Every member of the family is allowed to use the Shout Spot. The principle is simple. If your child wants to shout and scream, he is only allowed to do so on the Shout Spot. This will teach him a very important life skill – removing yourself from a social situation when you begin to feel frustrated or angry. At first you will have to remind your child that when he starts to shout you will take him to the Shout Spot. You will need to do this several times before your child learns to control his shouting, but I have known children as young as two years of age take themselves to the Shout Spot once they know the system.

I recommend that the Shout Spot is in a safe place away from the family action. The kitchen is not a good idea. The bottom stair or a chair in the hallway would do. It needs to be a space where you can safely leave your child alone. Ideally there should only be one entrance, to help you contain your child there.

Many children of this age will arch their backs when you try to sit them down. They need to lie on the floor and thrash around while shouting. This is absolutely fine as long as they are close to the Shout Spot. Simply lie them on the floor when their back arches and give them firm direction, making sure not to get kicked, then walk away and give them the space they need.

Here's how it might work in a Consequence situation:

TELL

🦋 Firm instruction is given.

WARN

🦋 A warning follows (perhaps counting to three).

ACT

🦋 *"I have asked you not to do that. Now we need to go and [name something else that you want him to do instead]."*

🦋 Remove him from whatever he is doing. He is likely to shout and if this persists you need to take him to the Shout Spot.

SPACE

🦋 *"When you are ready to calm down and do as Mummy asked, we can continue our day. Sit here and when you are quiet Mummy will come and get you."*

🦋 Turn and walk away.

TIME

🦋 If your child gets up, keep returning him to the spot without talking. Don't answer any of his questions or demands.

🦋 After five minutes, or however long you feel is appropriate, remind him of the next stage in the day. *"When you are quiet we can do puzzles together."*

🦋 If he continues to shout, leave him again. Eventually your child will be sitting quietly on the Shout Spot. If he needs an hour to calm down, let him have an hour. Usually children will get bored long before this, and gradually he will calm down faster as he learns the system.

APOLOGY

🦋 Approach and say *"Well done, you stayed on the spot and were quiet. Let's have a 'sorry hug' and go and find those puzzles."* Don't push him to say sorry. A hug is the first step in showing you are sorry.

MOVE ON

🦋 Don't hold grudges. Be proud of yourself for seeing the system through.

When you first introduce the Shout Spot there will be a strong resistance but you must remain firm. This is what your child needs from you. Although you and your partner will decide on the behaviours you want to work on together, only one of you should discipline at a time. The other should make themselves scarce, but be available to provide moral support to you later.

Many parents have said to me "It doesn't work. My child keeps getting up from the bottom stair!"

The fact of the matter is that the system *does* work. What you need to remember is that you already understand the principle but your child is still learning. Everyone learns at different rates. He may need to be returned to the stair fifty times before he fully understands.

I have also come across some very determined children who want to push the boundaries to see if you will 'break' – but the moment you 'break' you have surrendered to your child. Remember that as you prepare yourself for Day One, with your list of behaviours to be changed at the ready.

You can address up to three behaviours at a time. Once your child understands the consequence system after your first three-day plan, you can extend it to further behaviours when necessary. There are examples showing how it can work with different kinds of behaviour on pages 159-170 of this chapter.

PLAN DAY ONE

After you have had breakfast and got dressed, now is the time to sit down with your child and create your 'praise and reward' aid. Introduce the jar that will be filled with marbles, or the naked doll that will be dressed, or maybe you would like to create a picture to which stickers can be added. Explain to your child what they will need to do to earn a reward, focusing on the positive and avoiding negative speak.

For example, let's say you have a picture of some cars without wheels and you have a sheet of wheel stickers.

Don't say:

"You know how you never do what I ask you to do? Well, unless you start being good you won't get any wheel stickers!"

Do say:

"Now this is going to be very exciting. I have made you a lovely picture, which we are going to colour together. Every time Mummy or Daddy asks you to do something and you do as you are asked, we will add some lovely wheel stickers to the picture so the cars are happy. Lovely good behaviour makes Mummy and Daddy and the cars happy!"

After this you need to ask your child to do something: *"Please can you take this piece of paper to the bin? It might help a car!"* Walk to the bin together if you have to. Once the first sticker is on the chart, the excitement will begin.

After this has been explained and you have played together for a while, sit down for a morning snack at the kitchen table and explain the Shout Spot to your child.

"It is fantastic that you are helping Mummy and doing things when I ask you to. Look at how the marbles are filling the jar. Well done! Now, there is something else Mummy and Daddy have decided and that is what to do if you do not listen or start to shout. We are going to call our bottom step the Shout Spot. If Mummy or Daddy ask you to do something and you don't do it and you start to shout we are going to take you to the Shout Spot and you need to stay there until you are quiet and calm. Then Mummy will come and get you and we will carry on with our day."

Your child may not respond but he will be slowly digesting what you said. You don't need to talk about it any more. The time will come when you will be acting out this system.

Your child is now aware of two elements of the day: the reward system and the Shout Spot. It is up to you to continue your day together and use both systems accordingly.

Discuss your plans for the day with your child. It will help him to feel secure. Only list the things that are definitely going to happen. Don't use the phrase "And if we have time we might ..." Children only need to know what is actually going to happen.

Up until now you may have been avoiding confrontations with your child by giving him what he wants and playing life on his terms rather than your own. You may even be slightly nervous of saying 'no' to him in case the situation escalates. My advice to you is the sooner it happens, the better. Once you have implemented the Shout Spot for the first time, it will become easier each time after that.

You are not being unkind to your child. You are teaching him a fundamental life skill – respect. Your child needs to learn that if you or any adult looking after him calmly and nicely asks him to do or not to do something, he must respond in an appropriate manner.

Throughout the day, make sure you notice and reward all your child's positive behaviour. Here are some things that might be rewarded.

- Sitting at the table for a meal when asked.
- Undressing for bath-time when asked.
- Remembering to visit the loo and wash his hands.
- Sharing when asked.
- Putting on his shoes and coat when asked.
- Helping you when asked.
- Asking nicely for something rather than just grabbing it.

❧ Saying please and thank you.

❧ Allowing you to turn off the television without a battle.

❧ Accepting that some things asked for are a 'not now but later'.

Some children will 'perform' for the reward, but make sure you are the one who decides when it is due and not them.

> Child: "Mummy, I just put your rubbish in the kitchen bin. Can I have a sticker now?"
>
> Mother (bending to child's eye level): "With this lovely system I am the one who notices when you are being fantastic and I decide when a reward is given. When you are a Mummy one day you can make the reward decisions."

Your child will accept this if you state it in a clear and confident voice. Look out for good behaviour and reward her as soon as possible to reinforce the fact that you are in control of the system.

Throughout the day I would like you to note down the reasons why rewards are given and why the Shout Spot has been used. Keep these lists separate.

EXAMPLE OF REWARD LOG

REWARD NUMBER	TIME	REASON
1	10.12	HELPED TIDY THE RUBBISH AFTER CREATING THE REWARD CHART.
2	10.50	PUT SHOES ON STRAIGHT AWAY WHEN I SAID IT WAS TIME TO GO TO THE SHOPS.
3	11.30	LEFT THE PARK NICELY AFTER FIVE MINUTES' NOTICE THAT WE WOULD BE LEAVING.
4	1.00	ATE LUNCH NICELY AND ASKED TO LEAVE THE TABLE.
5	1.15	HAD 45 MINUTES OF QUIET TIME IN HIS BEDROOM WHILE I MADE SOME PHONE CALLS.

EXAMPLE OF SHOUT SPOT LOG

TIME	TIME UNTIL QUIET ON SHOUT SPOT	APOLOGY HUG	REASON
12.15	35 MINUTES	√	REFUSED TO COME TO THE LUNCH TABLE, SAYING HE DISLIKED THE FOOD (A MEAL HE HAS HAD MANY TIMES BEFORE).
2.45	20 MINUTES	√	WANTED TO HAVE ICE CREAM AFTER HIS REST RATHER THAN THE BISCUIT I OFFERED HIM. KEPT OPENING THE FREEZER.
5.15	15 MINUTES	√	REFUSED TO COME TO THE MEAL TABLE AGAIN.
6.15	20 MINUTES	√	BIT HIS BROTHER WHILE IN THE BATH.

You don't want to spend your day going from one Shout Spot to the next. You must be realistic and realise that sometimes you can turn a blind eye to bad behaviour if it is not affecting anyone else. You need to have a clear definition in your head of what is acceptable and what is not and make sure you apply the rules consistently.

Pick your moments to distract and your moments to discipline.

At dinnertime, place the reward system in an area where it can be seen while eating. List to your child all of the positive things he did during the day that earned him rewards. This is an exercise that both of you will benefit from. The rewards are yours as well as your child's.

This positive reinforcement will stand you in good stead for Day Two. Tomorrow the systems will be clear to your child and things will run a little more smoothly. Just you wait and see!

PLAN DAY TWO

Your child will continue to test you today to see if yesterday's systems are going to continue. Show him they are by praising him for something as soon as you can and giving him a reward. Start the day as you mean to go on.

After breakfast and getting dressed, plan your day and relay this to your child so that you both have a clear direction. You're going to test the system today by doing an activity that would usually prove very challenging – maybe eating in a café, supermarket shopping or a car journey.

It's a good idea to keep a little bag full of entertaining items for your child to examine when you are out and you need him to sit still and be patient. This bag is only for times such as visiting a café, the dentist's waiting room, a train journey or car journey. It should contain the type of objects that you might get in a party bag, or grown-up items that he wouldn't normally be allowed:

- A notebook and pen
- A colouring book and crayons
- Your old mobile phone
- An old make-up compact
- A lip balm
- A bunch of redundant keys
- A little bendy doll
- A couple of necklaces
- Playdough
- A few matchbox cars
- A box of raisins (on occasion)

The idea is that you rotate the contents regularly so that there is always something new to discover. Hand the bag over as soon as you strap him into the car seat for a longer than usual journey, or when you sit down in the dentist's, or in the café after ordering the food, to give him something to focus on.

If he still starts to misbehave you need to find a quiet corner and implement the Shout Spot system. Here's how you could handle it if you were in a restaurant and your child began throwing the contents of his bag while waiting for the food to arrive.

- First things first – give your child advance notice of where you are going and what the consequence will be for misbehaving.

"Today I would like us to go out to a café for our lunch. We are going to take your 'bag of tricks' to keep us busy and I am going to give you lots of stickers for your good behaviour. But if you start being silly then we will find a Shout Spot in the café where you will stay until you calm down. Do you understand me?"

❧ The best place for a Shout Spot in a café is likely to be the loo. If you need to use the Shout Spot, lead your child in and sit him on the floor at one side of the room (assuming it is clean). Alternatively, close the lid of the toilet and sit your child down on it. If you have more than one child and there is no other adult you will need to take all of them along.

❧ Bend down to your child's eye level. *"Listen. I am not having that behaviour. You know we don't shout/throw. You need to sit here until you are ready to behave nicely. Then we can go and play with some playdough until the food arrives. I am going to wash my hands. You sit here and tell me when you are ready to go back into the café."*

❧ Wash your hands and ignore your child, even if he is shouting. This is the first time you have implemented this system away from home and your child is still learning. Give him the time he needs. Finish washing your hands. Deep breath! Bend down and make eye contact.

❧ *"Now let's wash your hands with the lovely smelly soap and go and see what we can make with our playdough, my lovely good boy."*

❧ Smile, have the hug of apology, wash his hands and take him back to the table. If the behaviour is repeated, you will need to go through the procedure again.

It may be embarrassing but it's vital that your child understands that consequences can be implemented out of the home.

Continue to log all reward reasons and Shout Spot reasons. Note the difference between Days One and Two. It may only be slight but there will be small changes to show you are heading in the right direction. Slowly your child is adapting and learning to control his own behaviour.

PLAN DAY THREE

Invite a friend over for a play date today so you can observe your child's ability to consider another person's feelings and share. It is important that the visiting child and his parent are aware of the systems you have recently put into place and the ways in which they are implemented. You may have to enforce them while they are there with a visit to the Shout Spot.

Let's imagine your child snatches a car from his friend's hand, causing the friend to shout and cry. Comfort the crying child and tell them that you need to talk to [your child's name] and you will get the car back.

FIRM INSTRUCTION

🦋 *"Now, we can see that you have lots of cars and you snatched that one from your friend. Let's go and give it back to him."*

🦋 Take your child's hand and guide him to his friend. Hold out your child's hand containing the car, if he won't do it himself.

🦋 If he still refuses to give it to his friend, proceed to a warning.

WARNING

🦋 *"You have a choice. Return the car or we are going to have to visit the Shout Spot. You choose: car or step."*

🦋 If he still refuses to return the car, lead him to the step and take the car from him.

SPACE

🦋 *"When you are ready to share nicely you can come and play. If you don't play nicely you can stay here. I will come back in a minute."*

🦋 Walk away and give him the space he needs.

TIME

🦋 Keep returning him to the step as long as he is shouting. When he is quiet go back for the apology hug.

APOLOGY

🦋 *"Let's go and continue playing. We need to give your friend a hug to say sorry."*

🦋 Help and guide your child to do this by creating a group hug between the three of you.

MOVE ON

🦋 *"Your friends only want to play with your toys. They will never take them home. Let's go and have a lovely afternoon."*

🦋 Create an activity for the children and then step back and let them play.

> A confident and happy parent leads to a happy and confident child!

If at the end of Day Three you can see fundamental changes in your child's behaviour, I recommend that you create a small certificate for your child for 'Amazing Behaviour'. Alternatively, you could buy a small present and place it under his pillow for morning.

Try to reward yourself in some way as well. You've done an amazing job. Your child is more understanding of the importance of respect than he was three days ago and you are both more confident and positive about your time together.

Once you have started using the Shout Spot you should use it consistently whenever your child displays behaviour you have decided you need to change.

Continue with the reward system for between five and seven consecutive days. You will notice after this that the rewards don't seem so important to him and that his behaviour has improved anyway.

Of course, there will always be new types of behaviour you need to address. A parent's work is never done. The golden rules are:

🦋 Keep the focus positive: praise rather than blame.

🦋 Accept that at times your child will misbehave and this is when the Shout Spot needs to be used.

In the remainder of this chapter I've addressed a number of possible scenarios that could cause problem behaviour and explained how to deal with them. The scenarios are:

- A new arrival
- Learning to say sorry
- Tidy-up time
- Hair washing
- Independence struggle
- Having a quiet time after lunch
- Tantrums
- Following simple instructions
- Always saying 'no'
- Running off in public places
- Spitting

See page 57 in Chapter 2 for advice on dealing with Zero Tolerance behaviours, such as:

- Biting
- Hitting
- Spitting
- Stealing
- Lying
- Spiteful words
- Deliberately damaging or breaking things

A NEW ARRIVAL

Many parents have a second child roughly two years after the first, and I always feel compassion for the first child who suddenly has to share his space with a baby. The build-up to the baby being born creates high expectations and then it arrives – and from a young child's point of view it does nothing interesting. All it does is cry and get lots of attention, and this can lead to the first child becoming frustrated and jealous and perhaps behaving in a challenging way.

I advise that you take note of the times your child finds particularly difficult so you can plan ahead. It's common for toddlers to object when their parent is sitting feeding the baby. My suggestion is that you create an art box (without paints!) that your child can use during baby's feeding times. Pull the box out just before a feed and set your child working on a creative project with crayons, stickers or playdough. Ask him to make something nice to show Mummy and baby (always use the baby's name). Sit at the table with him as you feed so he doesn't feel abandoned.

When feeding is finished, put the baby in her crib or chair and make a fuss of the art your child has created. You can create art at other times of day if you wish, but this special box is only for feeding times.

Babies are relatively strong little creatures and they can withstand an awful lot, so do let your child play with her. Perhaps he could lie with his sibling under the baby gym or sit cuddling her on the sofa. You will always need to supervise but try to relax and manage this bonding process without using the word 'no'. It is a positive exercise.

I often speak to the baby when I know that the older sibling is listening. *"Do you know how lucky you are [state name of baby]? I know you can't do a lot yet, because you are still learning. If you watch [say oldest child's name] you will learn how to be a big girl. Your big brother is cool."*

This gives your eldest child a confidence surge and makes him aware of his purpose as a brother – to teach the baby! Make your child feel that you need him to help you with this big adventure.

However, if the older child hits the baby, it needs to be a Zero Tolerance situation. See page 57 for instructions.

LEARNING TO SAY SORRY

The word 'sorry' doesn't always come easily to a child and when you demand that they say it, they may well refuse. I wouldn't turn it into a battle with a child under the age of three. When you have taken your child to his Shout Spot and he has protested and then eventually calmed himself, it is time for you to approach and ask him if he is ready to continue with his day. If he doesn't start to shout again then you know he is ready. Now's the time to introduce a form of apology by embracing.

> "Let's hug to say sorry. It is not nice to take toys from your brother. Let's go and give him a hug and find a toy to give him."

By doing this you are teaching your child to act out his apology. Build on this and in time you can encourage him to say the word 'sorry' during the embrace.

On the other end of the spectrum is the child who will behave badly and quickly follow it with a flippant 'Sorr-eee'. Don't be fooled. In this case, they should still be disciplined with a trip to the Shout Spot. Sorry is only a powerful word if it is said with true meaning.

> "I know that you have said sorry, but you are continuing to act the same way over and over again. You must not take your sister's toys. Now come with me to the Shout Spot. You need to sit there and think about what you have been doing."

If your child starts shouting in frustration, leave him to calm down and when you return, explain that when you say sorry it means you will not do that thing again. When you say sorry you must mean it. Time spent sitting alone will help your child to think it through for himself. Generally, it is only when the child feels the emotions of a consequence that they are truly sorry. When you hear your child starting to shout or cry, that is when you know that the consequence is working.

TIDY-UP TIME

At the end of the day when the floor is strewn with toys, it is important not to turn tidy-up time into a battle, especially since your child is likely to be getting tired. Do it together and make a game of it. I will often put music on when tidying up with children and dance as I go. This makes them laugh and they often choose to help.

Keep toys in large boxes so that throwing them in is an easy and noisy task. It's a good idea to keep tidying throughout the day when each game finishes so the mess doesn't get out of control. For example, if you have finished with the train track and your child is asking for puzzles, say *"Let's put the train track and engines to sleep in the big box while we build our puzzles."*

If he helps with the tidying up, you can reward him in some way. If he won't, don't make an issue of it. Leave it for a couple of weeks and address it at a later date. He may simply be testing you and if you ignore the behaviour for a while it may simply disappear.

HAIR WASHING

Lots of children hate having their hair washed. I recommend you start pouring water over your child's head from an early age so she gets used to the feeling. Be careful always to use shampoos that don't sting if they accidentally get into her eyes, because one bad experience could turn her against hair washing for good. She needs to get used to it because young children's hair should be washed an average of twice a week (or whenever it has sticky stuff or food in it!).

If your child is reluctant to have her hair washed, try blu-tacking a collage of pictures onto the ceiling above the bath. Ask her to look up at the pictures and tell you what she can see. Explain to her that with her head tilted this way the water will run down her back and nowhere near her face.

As you ask questions about the pictures, quickly pour a beaker of warm water onto her head. She will feel it run down her back.

Quickly ask a question to distract her. *"Can you see the cat/dog/ train/goldfish?"*

If she starts shouting, give her a choice: *"You can shout your way through this or you can look at the lovely pictures on the ceiling and let me gently pour water down your back."*

Pour the water and if the shouting continues just carry on. Take control and be firm. Some jobs simply need to be done.

It's a good idea to have a bath together and ask your child to shampoo your hair then pour beakers of water to rinse it. Let her start rubbing in her own shampoo. Show your confidence and belief in your child and she will absorb this confidence and begin to relax about hair washing.

It may be gradual but you will get there in the end by guiding confidently rather than forcing. When a child feels forced they will rebel.

INDEPENDENCE STRUGGLE

If your child believes she is capable of doing something alone, it is important not to crush that belief. It always puts a smile on my face if I walk down the street and see a child wearing their clothing back to front. They have dressed themselves and their parent has been relaxed about it.

The key to encouraging your child's independence is to give her limited choices that will suit you. Here are some examples:

Never crush your child's self-belief!

- Just before your child's bedtime, lay out two outfits that could be worn the following day. Place them in two piles, including knickers and hair bands, and let your child choose in the morning. Take a photo of her wearing the outfit of choice and keep it on your phone to boost her confidence.

- Prepare three vegetables at a mealtime and let your child choose the two she will eat. This will encourage her independence while you still have overall control.

- Lay six books on the carpet at bedtime and ask your child to choose the two she wants you to read. Step away and let her decide then meet her on the bed to read them.

❧ Choosing shoes can often be a challenge as children can want boots on a hot sunny day and sandals in midwinter. Ensure you only have appropriate shoes on display before letting your child choose.

❧ When you are out and about you can ask your child to make decisions about which side of the street to walk on, or whether to go to the dry cleaner's or the baker's first.

It is important that your child realises that she can't make all decisions and there are some you need to do. In this instance, say *"Thank you for letting me choose today. You can make the next decision about [state the next opportunity, such as how many library books we collect from the library this afternoon]."*

If your child starts to challenge your decision and the situation escalates, it is time for the Shout Spot followed by an apology, a hug and then continuing the day. You may have to be inventive in finding suitable places for the Shout Spot when you are away from home: a public toilet, a bench in a corner or even just a quiet aisle in the supermarket will do.

HAVING A QUIET TIME AFTER LUNCH

Between the ages of two and three, most children will give up their afternoon nap, but I still think it is important for them to have some quiet time for an hour and a half after lunch. They need to learn to be happy in their own company and to stimulate themselves for a period of time every day. Quiet time is a punctuation mark, dividing the day in two and allowing them to digest their food and build their energy for the afternoon. Here's how to get them to do it.

GUIDE

❧ *"Now that we have had our lunch we need to have our quiet time. You don't need to sleep but just have a relaxing time in your wonderful bedroom. This is a time just for you, when nobody asks you to share or answer their questions. It is your special time."* As you are speaking, lead them there by the hand.

STIMULATE

🦋 Visit the bathroom for a wee (if he is toilet trained) then enter his room. Set out some toys together and start him playing with a particular toy.

STEP BACK

🦋 Set an egg timer to ring when quiet time is over. Place it in a spot where you and your child can hear it – but not where your child could reach and tamper with it.

🦋 *"Now, I am going to send some emails and do the ironing. I want to get my jobs done before the timer. When the timer rings, our afternoon will start and we can go to the park. I love you. Enjoy your quiet time."*

Walk out of the room with confidence and belief that the system is going to work. It will take perseverance but after three consecutive days your child will grasp the concept. At first he is likely to keep coming out of his room. Simply return him and make him aware that the alarm has not yet rung. Keep calm but have the firm and direct tone in your voice.

Your child may attempt to spark a conversation to keep you in the room. Don't be fooled. This is your quiet time as well. Simply cut him short: *"We can have a big chat when the alarm rings. Not long now. Good boy."*

Stride out of the room believing in this system. If you believe, your child will sense this and accept the new system eventually.

FOLLOWING SIMPLE INSTRUCTIONS

I have met many parents who doubt their child's hearing because they just don't listen. They hear what they want to hear, of course, but ignore communication that doesn't interest them. This is extremely common. Children only want to do what they think is needed and to operate on their terms. Welcome to the world of toddlers – and beyond!

Selective hearing is exhausting and irritating but you need to deal with it calmly. If you have asked your child several times to put her shoes on or come to the table and she doesn't respond, you need to offer choices so she sees there will be a consequence.

Here's how I use the Consequence System to deal with being ignored.

ADVANCE NOTICE

🦋 *"When you have finished your toast, we need to go and get dressed."*

FIRM INSTRUCTION

🦋 *"Let's go and get dressed to start the day. Once we are dressed I am going to get the dolls' house out."*

WARNING

🦋 *"We need to go upstairs now. Ready... one ... two ... three!"*

🦋 Pick your child up and place her at the bottom of the stairs.

🦋 *"Ready, go!"* Clap your hands behind her and chase her to her room.

SPACE

🦋 If the warning has not been enough, now it is time to act. *"OK, young lady, you are clearly not getting dressed yet. You'll have to sit on your Shout Spot until you are ready to come and get dressed. Once you are dressed we are going to play."*

🦋 Walk away and leave her sitting alone to think. Do not let her leave the Spot for anything other than getting dressed.

TIME

🦋 Give her the time she needs but keep placing her back on the Shout Spot until she eventually calms herself.

APOLOGY

🦋 *"Now all is calm. Let's have a sorry hug and go and get dressed. Well done for calming down. Good girl."*

MOVE ON

❧ *"All dressed. Let's go and find the dolls' house."*

ALWAYS SAYING 'NO'

This is a phase most children go through and the best way of dealing with it is to stop asking questions and just give clear firm direction instead. Don't ask if your child wants to put their shoes on. Say *"Time to put shoes on so that we can head to the shops and choose something nice for lunch today."* Simply ignore the 'no' and put your shoes on and then your child's while talking about the next stage in the day.

If the protest becomes a shout and you can feel it escalating, take your child to the Shout Spot and continue with the Consequence System.

FIRM INSTRUCTION

❧ (Make sure this is not a question that requires an answer!) *"We're just going to the shops so put your shoes on now."*

WARNING

❧ *"Let's do it together on the count of three. One … two … three!"*

SPACE

❧ Take your child to the Shout Spot.

TIME

❧ Let him shout it out and return as and when you need to.

APOLOGY

❧ After a minute's calm, go to your child and have a sorry hug.

MOVE ON

❧ Make a positive statement about the next stage of the day.

Children will behave in a certain way if they get a reaction. If you stop reacting to the word 'no' and ignore it by placing your child on the Shout Spot, he will stop using it because it will feel pointless.

TANTRUMS

I believe tantrums are a natural part of a child's development. They are expressing an emotion and I don't think emotions should be suppressed. Adults have tantrums too, although most of us have learned not to throw ourselves to the ground and scream.

We shouldn't excuse a tantrum, but children need to learn that if they are going to scream and shout it is something they should go and do on their own.

> "OK, young man. If you need to 'shout it out' that's fine. Let's take you to your Shout Spot and when you have got it all out and have calmed down then we can carry on with our day."

If he is back-arching and rolling on the floor, simply leave him on the floor as close as possible to his Shout Spot and follow the system. If you are in a public place, you may have to lift him and carry him to an appropriate spot out of the way of passers-by. Put him down and go and sit or stand a little way off until he calms himself down. I often see parents hugging and trying to reason with children who are throwing a tantrum in public, but this will only encourage the behaviour.

Don't take the easy option and stop. Keep control and believe in the system.

RUNNING OFF IN PUBLIC PLACES

When in a public place I strongly advise that you hold your child's hand. It is a simple rule to instil and should be adhered to consistently whenever you are travelling from one place to another or out in any area where there are dangers such as traffic. If you are in a park or open space, he can run around but tell him clearly how far he can go and where he should stop: *"If you go into the woods, I will be very upset and you will have to spend some time sitting in the buggy."*

I sometimes put reins on children who have a strong tendency to bolt off without warning but I fully understand that some parents don't like the idea of reins because they feel they are treating their child like a dog with a lead. The art of wearing reins is that the rein is in your hand as well as the child's hand. It is held as a precaution for when your child slips his hand from yours and is certainly not an alternative to holding his hand.

ADVANCE WARNING

Decide what the rule will be before leaving the house and explain it to your child. Do you want him to:

- Hold hands all of the time?
- Wear reins at all times?
- Get into the buggy while you are walking along a busy road?
- Always hold onto the buggy handle?

There is no right or wrong rule. Just choose one and remain consistent. You could promise a reward when you get home if he manages to stick to the rules throughout a whole outing.

WARNING

- Mention to your child before leaving the house that if 'silly running' happens then he will have to stop and sit on the pavement, and may just end up in the buggy. Tell your child this in a firm and direct voice so that he believes what you are saying. Bend down to his level and make eye contact. *"Running off is NOT what we do. If this happens again it is straight into the buggy/the reins. I mean it."*

CONSEQUENCE

- If it happens, you will have to enforce the consequence even though it won't be easy. Safety comes first and I would catch him and put him in the buggy or his reins, even if he is resisting.

- Don't mention your disappointment. Remain silent no matter how much he is protesting. Believe in this tactic and it will work. This should only happen a couple of times before he realises that running off is not an attractive option. This is a challenge for you but it is a Zero Tolerance situation. Running away from a parent is dangerous and has to be stopped.

SPACE/TIME
🦋 If your child is in reins, you need to hold the strap and also hold his hand. He may refuse to walk, but be calm and wait patiently. Don't talk to him. Think of this as the Shout Spot. Let him sit or stand still and shout. The reins stay on until you reach your destination.

🦋 If you have put him in the buggy, follow the Shout Spot principle and don't start to push it until he is calm. He should stay in the buggy until you reach your destination.

APOLOGY
🦋 When your child has stopped shouting and has been calm for a minute, praise him. *"Well done, you have become calm. It worries Mummy when you run off. Let's hug to say sorry."*

MOVE ON
🦋 *"Now let's walk on and see how many cars zoom past us."*

This is not an easy consequence to implement ... but the bigger the challenge in life, the greater the reward!

SPITTING

Children often start spitting when they first go to nursery school and are trying to find their place in a class of other children. Parents hate it, though, and you may decide to implement a Zero Tolerance System before the behaviour becomes an ingrained habit. The moment you see your child spit at another child you need to act.

TELL
🦋 *"Spitting is something we never do. Mummy and Daddy don't spit at one another and you are definitely not to do this."*

ACT

🦋 Take your child to the Shout Spot. *"Sit here on your own until I am ready to come and talk to you. I am very upset at the moment."*

🦋 He may remove himself several times but just keep returning him. Perhaps he will try to explain his reason for spitting or start to shout and cry, but still return him to the Spot. If your child feels truly sorry for spitting, it will deter him from doing it in future.

🦋 *"When you are quiet and calm and staying in the Spot, I will come and talk to you."*

APOLOGISE

🦋 Once your child has remained on his Spot and is quiet for 30 seconds or more you can approach.

🦋 *"Well done for staying on the Spot and calming down. We need to say sorry then we can continue playing."*

🦋 Your child may find it hard to apologise, especially if the other party upset him. Guide him to give the other child a toy to play with or sit and build something together.

EXPLAIN

🦋 Now you can discuss what happened. *"No matter how much our friends upset us we never spit at them!"* The important thing is that the spitting was dealt with first.

FREQUENTLY ASKED QUESTIONS

My daughter will not remain on the Shout Spot. What should I do?
Everyone takes a different length of time when learning something new. Don't give up on your child and decide that she can't do this. Be consistent with your guidance and allow her to sense that you will not stop using the system. Tell yourself that it *will* work in the end, and persevere, leading her back to the Spot every single time she wanders off it until she can sit there quietly.

Where is the Shout Spot when we are out shopping?
You always need to be one step ahead of children. When you go into a shop or shopping centre, keep an eye out for a quiet spot, such as the public loo or a hallway or corridor. You can also march somewhere out of the direct sight of big crowds, such as a quieter aisle in the supermarket, and sit down there.

I have been known to leave items on a counter and announce to the sales assistant "Please can you hold onto my goods. I will be right back. We just need to address something." This often causes a little smirk from the assistant.

Most members of the public like to see parents managing their children's behaviour. It's ignoring it that causes people to pass judgement.

My child always refuses to hug to say sorry.
You need to guide him to do it by leaning towards him. Don't just stand in front of him saying "You must hug me." At first you give him the hug and build on it from there. You could give him the option of hugging or saying sorry, if he is able to speak by this stage.

If you lean in to hug him and he pushes you away, I suggest you tell him he needs to remain on the Shout Spot until he can apologise.

My child is quite happy to sit on the Shout Spot without shouting. I don't think it's working!
You're right – it isn't! You need to hear him shouting and complaining to know that the system is working. It sounds as though your child needs to feel there is more of a consequence to his actions, so I would take away a toy he really likes.

Here's an example: "When you keep pushing your brother like that, your little tractor doesn't want to watch. It upsets him. He is going to go and hide up high on the shelf. He will come back when he is ready."

If your child shouts in protest, he will find himself on the Shout Spot. The tractor stays up on the shelf for half a day or so and reappears later when he does something nice for his brother. "Your tractor likes it when you are nice to your brother!"

Make sure you choose a favourite toy. Some have more currency than others!

My child will be quiet on the Shout Spot until I approach, upon which he will start to shout again. Help!

This is quite common. You have simply approached before he is ready. He is still thinking and not quite calm. Just say "OK, you are not quite ready. You come and find me when you are ready for a sorry hug." He may want to approach you rather than you approaching him. Many children want to complete the Shout Spot process on their terms and this is fine so long as they have calmed down by the time he leaves the Spot.

What do I do on a play date if there is shouting in the playroom but I was not there to witness the initiating act?

As long as there is no serious injury, such as a bite, bruise or cut, I would embrace the situation in a positive way.

"Right then, let's not have all of this shouting. You are two lovely girls and you've got lots of toys. Let's have some fun."

If they each want to each tell their side of the story, this is fine but it can get a little out of hand. Simply listen and then conclude with: "Everyone is fine now, no harm done. Let's find something fun to do!"

Find an activity and set it up for them to continue playing. Step back and let them bond.

What do I do about 'telling tales'? My daughter is continually doing this.

There are times when it is an advantage for a child to come and report behaviour but in general it is not necessary. I suggest you remain calm and simply say "Unless someone is hurt or something is broken I don't really need to know. Go and have fun."

✿

Remaining consistent with discipline can be exhausting, especially if you have a child who continues to test his boundaries, but please remember that as time passes your child will grow in maturity and gain a greater understanding of the world. The challenges will change with each new stage in your parenting. It might be worth reading the next chapter now even if your child is not quite three, just so that you can stay one step ahead!

CHAPTER 5

Three-day plans for children aged three to six years

Your child's verbal skills will increase dramatically during these years, and one side effect of this is that they are able to discuss things with you – and argue back when they don't agree with you! They will have strong opinions and the ability to express them and it's important that you listen to them, while making sure they listen to you as well. I believe in being upfront and honest with children rather than trying to trick them into doing something. Explain what you want and don't talk down to them or underestimate their ability to understand you.

Most children start school at the age of five, and this requires a lot of preparation, especially if they haven't been to a nursery school first. Introducing them to a wide range of other children and helping them to form their first friendships is an important step along the way. They

> They need their sleep and their food at set times every day when they are coping with so many new things in their lives.

will be subject to peer pressure once they get to school and need to be ready emotionally, physically and developmentally. You'll notice them copying things they've seen other children doing – good and not so good things – and you'll find that a regular routine becomes even more important to them.

They will also need to learn to be away from you for a few hours at a time (if they are not already used to this), to put on their own clothes and shoes, and to sit obediently listening to the teacher. It's up to you, as a parent, to prepare them for all this, and in the Behaviour section of this chapter we'll look at some methods that can help.

However, you need to address the basics first. If your child has poor sleep patterns or eating habits, they may not have the energy to last through a school day, so it's important to set them on the right track.

I recommend that you address poor sleep habits before going on to any other plans.

THE SLEEP PLAN FOR CHILDREN AGED THREE TO SIX YEARS

Is your child always arguing over bedtime and trying to push it backwards, then refusing to settle and coming back downstairs again? It's disheartening as a parent if you sit down to your well-deserved relaxation time, only to hear the patter of little feet overhead. Or perhaps your child wakens at night and wants to come into your bed? Or is an early riser, often getting you up before the crack of dawn? All these problems need to be addressed, because if he is not getting the ten to twelve hours' sleep he needs at night, he is not going to be able to learn effectively at school or nursery during the day and by the time he gets home to you he will be tired and whining. That's why you have to take action – now.

Your child may try to resist changes to his sleep routine using all the powers at his disposal. If you have a Negotiator, he'll think of a dozen compelling reasons why he has to come back to the living room or kitchen again. A Fighter may start throwing toys around in his room. A Drama Queen might throw herself on the floor, acting as though you are the cruellest parent on the planet. (See page 35 for more on dealing with those types.) But you will have to stand firm.

If you follow the plan exactly for three days, your child will realise that change is here to stay. He may still kick up a fuss at bedtime, but will usually calm down faster than he did before because he will know he can't win. Three days should be enough for him to realise that. It might take longer if you have a particularly independent type, but the system should continue for as long as it takes. This is the way you want your child to sleep from now on, for the sake of his health, happiness and education.

PREPARING FOR THE SLEEP PLAN

It is very important that you choose your timing carefully. You need to be able to tick off the following statements.

- Everyone who lives in the house is healthy.
- Both parents can be fully focused.
- You will be sleeping at home for at least the next ten days.
- Your child won't have any other new activities during the next ten days.

I advise starting the process by talking about it on a Saturday morning and implementing it on a Saturday night. This means that you have two days away from school or work and both parents can be at home.

One parent will take the lead in the guidance process, but it's important that there's someone else to play a supporting role, whether that is your partner, another family member or a friend on the end of the phone. Ideally your supporter will be there at bath-time in the evening, and will help to make life as easy as possible for you. It's not going to be easy, especially if the poor sleeping habits have been ingrained for a long time now.

Although you will take the main role, your partner or 'support parent' needs to know how the system works as well, because they may need to settle your child themselves in future. I suggest they start by reading through the relevant sections in the book.

You will need:

- The child's bedroom should be as dark as possible with black-out curtains or tin foil on the window (see page 4)

- A small dim night-light should be placed low in the room away from the bed.

- A timer that is easy to read in dim light.

- Printed timings sheets.

- A guidance tool.

- A clock in your child's room, placed where he can see it easily.

In twenty years I've never yet met a child who couldn't be trained to sleep the night in his own bed, and yours is highly unlikely to be the first!

Now prepare yourself for a battle. It's not easy to listen to your child shouting from his bedroom after you've said goodnight, but you need to think with your head rather than your heart. It will get easier as your child begins to accept this is going to be a permanent change.

You have to believe it is going to work.

PLAN DAY ONE

Start by discussing the problem with your child and letting him know that you need his help and understanding to solve it. The key is getting him to make the right choice and understand that this is a good idea. Schoolchildren have to stay in their own beds.

I find that children are far more alert in the mornings so have a chat with your child after breakfast. Make sure the environment is calm and you have his full attention. There shouldn't be any other family members present and the television or computer should be turned off. Say something like this:

> "I want to talk to you about something I need your help with. Do you think you could help me? Mummy and Daddy have decided that it is time for you to stay in your own bed at night and to go to bed nicely and calmly. I have found a special book to help us do this. It's written by a lady who for years and years has been helping children to stay in their own beds."

Show your child the book and my photograph.

> "I think that together as a family we can do this, and this lady says that it won't take very long at all – maybe only a week."

In fact, the programme, when followed correctly and consistently, should only take three days but allow a bit extra so your child doesn't feel he has failed if he doesn't manage in three days.

Explain that his wakening in the night is disturbing everyone in the house and they are all tired at work the next day.

> "Daddy has to get up in the morning and go to work and so do I. You have school and so does your brother. We all need our brains and bodies to be super-fit in the day to do everything we need to do. Our bodies need two main things – good food and good sleep. You are a brilliant eater and now we are going to turn you into a brilliant sleeper as well."

Most children want to be big and strong. If he knows he only really grows when his body is resting this may prove a good incentive for him to remain in his bed.

Mention other things that he will be able to do when he is good at sleeping through the night:

Explain that the main time a child's body grows is when they are sleeping.

- Sleepovers with friends
- Staying at grandparents' houses
- Camping out in a tent
- Having a grown-up bed (or bunk beds)
- Summer camp or overnight school trip.

Some of these might sound scary to a little one, so choose the things that you think will appeal to your child. It is important that you remain positive and do not ask if he wants to try it. He doesn't know what it entails yet so the chances are he will say 'no'.

Next you need to introduce the guidance tool you are going to use. Examples are probably the best way to explain this.

❧ For a boy who likes trains, you could buy a train with a carriage and every time he is praised for his efforts a coloured gemstone is placed in the carriage as 'cargo'.

❧ A glass jar could be filled with colourful and interesting-looking gems or marbles.

❧ For a little girl, you could buy a ribbon and some pretty beads to thread onto it one by one.

❧ Magnets that click together to form a chain could be another guidance tool.

❧ Or you could buy a Lego kit and complete a stage after every step in the right direction.

❧ You could have a Barbie doll in her underwear who gets an item of clothing every time your child earns it. The aim is to dress the doll but you can continue beyond this so that Barbie gets several items of clothing to inter-change.

You know your child better than anyone so find a guidance tool that will be enticing for him. You will be using it for seven days so choose something that will appear full or complete at the end of that period.

If you are adding up to three gemstones a day, make sure you have 21 altogether. For Barbie, you will need several items of clothing – ensure you buy more rather than less. You will place the jar/carriage/ribbon/doll in your child's bedroom where it can be seen but not touched while the gems/magnets/beads/outfits are kept out of sight and controlled by you.

Show your child the guidance tool during your morning chat, and let him touch it, but explain that it will be the following morning before he is able to earn any of them.

Now you need to discuss the rewards he will get when he has earned three gems, magnets or beads. Suggestions could include:

- A bike ride in the park with Daddy
- A family picnic
- A visit to the shop to buy a magazine
- Baking cakes with Mummy
- A board game with Mummy and Daddy
- Building a den in the bedroom
- Thirty minutes of TV time
- Swimming with Daddy
- Visiting a café for afternoon tea as a family.

These are just a few ideas. You know your child best. Write a list of rewards and stick it on the kitchen wall.

Brilliant! So far, so good. You have:

- Introduced the concept
- Introduced the guidance tool
- Organised the reward system.

Continue with your day now but make sure that you have dinner with your child at a reasonable hour, preferably no later than 5.30pm. You should all sit down together and eat at least a small amount of the same food your child is eating.

If you have more than one child this is when you take the opportunity to explain what is going to happen later.

"After TV time tonight we are going to go to our rooms for stories and then you are going to settle to bed. We have a special system for [child's name] and when he manages to stay in his room he is going to get a marble in this jar, and a reward from the wall. Once he has filled that jar there is going to be a special treat for all of the family! I want everyone to be very supportive of [child's name] and be patient. He is about to do something he has never done before. Tonight when you are in bed Mummy and Daddy are going to decide on the Family Reward. It is going to be a special treat for all of us once the jar is full."

Plan for the Family Reward to take place the following weekend, but don't tell anyone yet in case your plans have to change at the last minute. Your child will be in a totally different place with his sleeping by this time next week. Believe this. You are going to take giant leaps as a family, remain consistent and not break and revert to the old ways.

After bath-time, when teeth are brushed and he has been to the loo and had stories read, it is time to tuck your child into his bed. Make sure that there is nothing he can ask for.

- There's a drink by the bedside (if this is usually requested)
- He has his preferred comforter
- The night-light is glowing
- It's nice and warm but not too hot!

Now you need to guide your child into bed, if he is not already there.

> Once you start this plan, there is no going back!

"You are such a good boy, I know that you can do this. We will put our first marbles into the jar in the morning and choose a reward. Well done. I am going to have some time downstairs with Daddy and then we are coming to bed. You are a good boy. We will all have breakfast together in the morning."

Don't talk for longer than 30 seconds. Leave the room and pull the door closed. You do not need to shut it totally if this is not what your child is used to.

If he is shouting, go to a place near the bedroom where you will be able to see straight away if he leaves the room. Now start the timer and the timing sheets, waiting for the Thinking Pause. Let him shout it out for ten minutes.

If your child has shouted continuously for ten minutes without a Thinking Pause then re-enter the room. Approach him and bend down to his level. Hug him if he will let you. *"Come on, calm down. That is enough now. You can do this. Into your bed and we will have a lovely day tomorrow."*

Keep your voice very direct and firm but stay calm. You are not cross. You knew the protest would occur. At this stage your child is confused. Reassure him, taking only 30 seconds, and leave the room. Do not be concerned if he refuses to get into his bed.

Start the timer again and listen for any seconds of quiet.

TIMER START	TIMER STOP	PROTEST TIME	THINKING TIME	CALM TIME
7.10PM	7.20PM	10 MINS	2 SECS	
7.20PM	7.30PM	10 MINS	5 SECS	
7.30PM	7.38PM	8 MINS	10 SECS	
7.38PM	7.45PM	7 MINS		15 SECS

You will only enter the room if there is a Crescendo Call (see page 47), and if you enter you will follow the same 30-second principle as before.

If he leaves his bedroom to come and find you, simply take him by the hand and lead him back again. *"Oh dear, come on, let's go back to your lovely bedroom with [the lovely blue bed, the teddies, your wonderful clock]."* Guide him into bed and say *"That's it, well done, see you at breakfast."*

If he refuses to walk back, carry him, but hold him low and facing away from you, almost as if he is walking in front of you. Don't lift him onto your hip. Put him back in bed as before.

You don't need to start filling out the chart until he has stayed in his room for five minutes.

Please remain consistent. This is going to be the most challenging night for both your child and you. You can do it. He is testing his boundaries and still remembers the old routine clearly. He is just making sure that you are not going back to the old ways. He may shout out questions to try and entice you in, or continually yell "I want my Mummy." Don't respond; just keep timing. Your child will eventually increase his thinking time and settle into sleep.

NIGHT WAKENING

If your child wakens in the night or gets up before 6am in the morning, you need to follow the same procedure as before.

- ❧ Return him to his room as quickly and calmly as possible, carrying him in front of you rather than on your hip.

- ❧ Place him in bed, saying *"Now, come on you can do this. Your room is a lovely grown-up boy's room. Head on your pillow and settle to sleep. Nice and calm and quiet. Good boy. I love you very much. See you at breakfast time."*

- ❧ If he decides to shout, start the timings chart and remain close to his bedroom but out of sight.

- ❧ Enter after ten minutes only if the shout is becoming a Crescendo. Calm your child for 30 seconds and then leave.

- ❧ Keep the timings chart until he settles himself to sleep.

You will get through the night and, if you remain consistent, your child will start to learn how the new routine is going to be. The first night is a big achievement for you and your child because you are learning something new together and you have refrained from returning to the 'old ways'.

PLAN DAY TWO

When your child wakens after 6am, enter his room and give him a hug. Praise him for staying in his own bed and returning each time he was guided and asked to do so. Explain that this is very different from how life was before but that this way is better for everyone. Make a point of telling him how proud you are of him (and quietly be proud of yourself – your child could not achieve this without your firm guidance).

No matter how disturbed a night you've had, aim to add at least one element to the guidance tool, and ideally two or three. This will encourage your child to continue to persevere and follow the programme the following evening.

🦋 He can have one marble/magnet/bead for 'going to bed nicely'. He may have shouted for a few minutes when you first left the room but if he remained in his bed and settled himself to sleep, that counts.

🦋 A second item might be awarded for returning to bed when asked or staying in bed all night!

🦋 A third might be for not getting up too early.

You may be feeling tired, as will your child, so take the morning slowly. Make sure that both of you have a good breakfast and discuss the reward for the day. Always give a reward of some kind. You can choose a small reward or a large one depending on the progress you feel was made, but don't point this out to your child. Encourage any other children to praise their sibling for his efforts.

Don't continue to discuss night-times during the day. Wait until later.

Once again have a family dinner at home at 5.30pm and bath-time about 6pm. During the bath, have a brief chat about going to sleep in your own bed and the marbles/magnets/beads plus the reward that will follow. Don't talk for more than a minute or two. It is not to be a big discussion. This is definitely not a time for negotiating.

If your child begins to rebel, simply remove him from the bath remaining calm and positive and say *We don't need to do anymore talking about this now. Let's go and watch some TV/find our stories.*

Follow the same routine after his bedtime stories.

🦋 Make sure teeth are brushed, he has been to the loo and everything is prepared and ready in the bedroom.

🦋 Now guide your child into his bed. As you are guiding him, talk about how good he is going to be: *"Last night you managed to keep coming back to your bed. Why not try and be fantastic and stay in your bed tonight. I know you can do this. You are such a grown-up boy. Soon we will be asking your friends to come and sleep over. Settle down now. I will see you for breakfast and reward choosing. I love you."*

❧ If your child is shouting, hold him close and talk positively into his ear. Place him in bed, tuck him in and leave the room.

❧ If your child will not let you near, just say calmly but loud enough for him to hear over his shout: *"I know you can do this. You are so clever. Into your lovely bed when you are ready. I will see you in the morning."*

The secret is to remain calm and firm. Your child needs to realise that you are serious about this process and that you believe in what you are doing and you believe that your child can achieve this.

❧ Leave the room and start the timings charts. Make sure your child cannot see you.

❧ Return to the room after ten minutes if he is still shouting to remind him to get into his bed. If he refuses just tell him that you love him and you know he can do this, you will see him at breakfast time.

❧ Start the timings sheet again. Remember to listen for the pause and re-start the timer.

❧ Do not enter into the room again unless there is a Crescendo Call.

If your child leaves his bedroom, remember:

❧ Return to bedroom

❧ Praise and reassure

❧ Timings

❧ Self-settled

If a child senses your doubt, they will resist believing in you, the programme and themselves.

PLAN DAY THREE

If you are remaining consistent, calm and firm, your child should now start to accept the change and should be showing signs of returning to his room with more ease, or settling sooner than he was on night one.

Look at the first night timings and note the differences.

When your child wakens (after 6am) enter his room (or, if he has come to you, return to his room with him). Praise and award him two or three elements for his guidance tool.

As you eat breakfast, talk about the day's reward and ask if your child is feeling pleased with himself. Tell him that he should be pleased because he is doing well at learning something new.

Carry on your day as usual. If your child has to go to school or nursery, I advise that you have a quick word with the teacher about what you are working on at home. She doesn't need to mention it to your child but she should be aware of the reason if your child is showing signs of tiredness.

Follow the same evening routine, with dinner served promptly at 5.30pm, bath at 6pm, and bed at 7pm. As you settle your child into his bed, praise him and talk about tomorrow's reward, but for no more than a minute. Say *"See you at breakfast time. You are such a good boy!"* Then leave the room and start the timings sheet if necessary. Don't return to the bedroom unless there is a Crescendo Call.

PLAN DAY FOUR – AND ONWARDS

You have now achieved three nights of the new routine and extensive changes will have been made. This does not mean that your child is now settling himself and sleeping through the night. He probably still has a few steps to take, especially if he is older, or a particularly independent character. It is important to continue with the routine of you returning him to his room, adding to the guidance tool in the morning and issuing rewards, although on school days the reward can be small – an ice cream after dinner or a treasure hunt for a little party bag treat. Don't forget to give the Family Reward you promised after a week of good sleeping. Make it something that everyone will enjoy.

After seven consecutive nights you will see an entirely new pattern forming and before long the nights when your child stayed up shouting will become a distant memory. He has a lot to thank you for. You guided him to make the change. You worked together, remaining calm yet firm. You have enhanced your family life. Well done to you.

Now comes a very important part of the programme – reward yourself.

❧ Have a game of golf.

❧ Visit a coffee shop and have a slice of delicious cake.

❧ Buy yourself a new item of clothing.

❧ Visit the hairdresser's.

❧ Have a lie-in one morning while your partner makes the breakfast.

Whatever it is, please find time for you. You and your child have been the stars of the show!

FREQUENTLY ASKED QUESTIONS

My child is scared of the dark and insists the light is left on.
No child is born scared of the dark. It's an idea that has been put into her head. Talk positively about the dark and agree to keep the night-light glowing and the light on the landing or in the bathroom on, which will shine through the crack in the door when you pull it to.

Don't let your child take control on this issue. It is a fact that we sleep better when it is dark. I often say to children "You must not trick your body. If the room is too light your body will think that it is the day and not fall asleep. Look after your body and teach him that it is night time."

I have two children sleeping in the same room. One is a good sleeper while the other is not. How do I manage this situation?
Treat the challenge as something that both of them need to work towards. They both get 'marbles' in the morning. Your second child will get them for being quiet when disturbed in the night and being encouraging towards her sibling. This means that up to six marbles can be rewarded each morning.

If your second child is still being disturbed a lot after two nights of the sleep plan, I might consider moving her into another bedroom

– even a mattress on the floor in yours – until the situation is resolved. You will need to explain that this is only for a little while, so she doesn't get used to the idea.

If your first child starts whining "It's not fair that my sister is sleeping in your room", you can respond with a promise: "You can have a sleepover in my room when you are able to be quiet all through the night. It won't be long now. You can do this, I know you can."

Should I separate my twins and sleep train them one at a time?
Twins normally share a bedroom, so it makes sense to train them both at the same time in the same room. Simply go for it! It's a challenge but it is possible to achieve. They will definitely challenge you on the first night but stay consistent and don't give in to any of their requests. As you enter the room, only address the one who is shouting but as you leave gently touch the other and say "well done".

If you trained them in different rooms and then put them back in together, you would most likely find yourself having to go through the same process all over again!

The bedtime battle starts as soon as my daughter gets out of the bath when she refuses to put on her pyjamas. Can you help?
Lay out two choices of sleep outfit. Let her help you choose the two outfits. It could even be summer shorts and a t-shirt, or a party dress. It really doesn't matter. You can turn up the heating if you are concerned she may be cold.

Discuss these outfits in the morning so that she can think about them during the day. While your child is in the bath, say "I am excited tonight because I don't know which of your outfits you are going to wear after bath-time." Don't mention the word 'bed'. "I am going to help you out of the bath and then stand in the hallway while you are in the bathroom deciding what to wear. When you come out it will be a big surprise for me and I will say 'Hooray! Let's put a marble in the jar!'"

This is giving your child the control she wants. Believe and trust her. Take her photo when she comes out of the bathroom and show it to her.

My son screams all the way through his bedtime stories because he knows it will be time for bed afterwards. What would you do in my place?

There is no point in reading to a screaming child. He needs to know this so mention it at bath-time.

"Tonight at story time I would like us to look at some books nicely together. If you are going to make lots of noise then we will forget the stories and jump straight into bed. Do you understand? [Mention his teacher's name] would not read to the children at school if they were all shouting at her, would she?" Give a little smile and then move on to washing him while he digests what you have just said.

You need to follow through and skip story time if he shouts, going straight on to the timing sheet and timer if need be. Keep doing the same thing every night and he will back down eventually.

My child plays with the light switch once I have left the room. Any advice?

Yes – remove the bulb!

As soon as I leave her in her room the shouting starts. She is too hot, too cold, too hungry, too thirsty – you name it and she'll try it.

I've heard all the excuses in my time and could fill the book with them. My favourite is "I fed my toy elephant today and I am scared he will grow in the night and squash me!"

Her kind of excuses need to be ignored, even the request for a drink of water (unless she normally has one at bedtime and you've forgotten). This may sound harsh but once you let the boundaries slip by giving in to one request, another will follow. Children are clever little beings and if they see you weaken, they will continue to push. Start as you mean to go on.

Ignore the requests and simply place her back into her bed saying "See you at breakfast time." Don't argue about it or even refer to what she is asking for, by saying something like "You don't need a drink. You can have one in the morning." If you enter into any discussion she will continue to pester.

Keep it simple. Don't steer off track!

My child calls out that he needs to go to the loo. Should I let him?
Take him to the loo, keeping the lights dim, and do not speak to him.
Walk him back to his room and place him in bed. Do not start a conversation. Now that he has been once, he does not need to go again.

The next night ensure he uses the loo before bed so that when he asks, you know it is attention seeking rather than a genuine need.

My son gets destructive when I put the lights out and close the door. He throws toys around and kicks hard against the door. I have to go back into the room just to make sure he's alright.
This would be a Zero Tolerance situation for me. You need to make eye contact and use your firm voice: "Do not kick the door like that. If you continue to do so it will break and then we will not be able to open it. You will not be able to get out of your room. I am serious. Do not kick this door. Do you understand me?"

Tell him that if he throws toys, you will take them away – and follow through.

As soon as something is thrown, remove it from the room and place it out of sight and reach in another part of the house. Toys can be returned as and when your child is behaving well, but leave them out of sight for at least 24 hours. Hard lessons are sometimes needed.

My child says she will fall asleep quietly if I stay in the room with her. Can I do this and leave when she is asleep?
No. As soon as she gets into a period of light sleep she will open her eyes, see you are not there and shout out for you. This will create a routine for your child. She will start to believe that she can only fall asleep if you are there watching her, and then you will be trapped doing the same thing every night without a break. You will have let her win!

It's tough implementing a sleep plan with children in this age group because they will try every trick in the book to stick to their old ways – but you simply must do it. Without enough sleep, they won't do so well at school and their health could suffer. Remember as you sit with a timer listening to your child's shouts of protest that this is all part and parcel of being a good parent. And you can do it!

THE EATING PLAN FOR CHILDREN AGED THREE TO SIX YEARS

Everyone likes to find their comfort zone – a place where they feel in control, safe and secure. Most of us get comfort from the security of a routine. We wake in the morning knowing we will have our cup of coffee, shower and brush our teeth and be out of the door at a certain time, and the day progresses from there. Children are no different. They like to know what will be happening in the day. They thrive on structure – and part of a day's structure involves three meals.

You may have a problem if your child is used to only eating certain foods and the thought of change sends her into a blind panic. However, if she is not eating enough different foods to get all the nutrients she needs, you must take steps to change her attitude to food before she gets too set in her ways.

This is where my three-day plan comes in. I'm not pretending it will be easy, because it probably won't. But within three days, your child should have tried some foods she has never tried before and have increased the number of foods she will eat by at least a bit.

Choose your timing carefully, as with all my three-day plans. If she eats lunch at school during the week, start the plan on a Saturday so that you have two days during which you are fully in control of the menu and can supervise mealtimes. Make sure everyone in the family is feeling healthy and ready for the challenge.

If she doesn't eat the meal on her plate, she will be allowed to have some fruit for dessert, but no substitutes.

Before you start, I want you to plan a menu for the next seven days. Breakfast is not usually a challenge, but you will serve a different lunch and dinner for each of the seven days, alternating meals your child has accepted before with meals she hasn't tried. The most important point to note is that no alternatives will be offered.

Get used to this idea, because it is crucial you don't give some bread and butter or anything else in place of the main meal.

Discuss the menu with your partner or any older children or other family members in the house. Get everyone to suggest dishes they like and organise them into a meal plan. Remember: this plan needs to include foods you know your child will eat, as well as introducing new foods. I find it's better to put the 'new' foods at lunchtime and the ones she knows at dinnertime, when she may be getting tired after her day, but your family routine may make this difficult. See if you can manage it during the three-day plan at least.

It can help if you try to make the new foods similar to ones she already eats:

- Sausages can have their skins removed and be rolled into meatballs or they can become the main ingredient in a dish such as toad in the hole.

- If your child likes food bread-crumbed, you can do this with chicken, pork and fish.

- If your child eats chips try serving potato wedges, which are better for her.

- If pesto or a pasta sauce is eaten, vegetables can be added, sliced very small to avoid detection.

- If your child eats spaghetti, they are likely to eat noodles.

- If your child likes tomato ketchup, they like the taste of tomatoes! This means you can have lasagne, bolognaise sauce, pizza and tomato-based casseroles.

Overleaf is a sample menu plan.

	LUNCH	DINNER
MONDAY	MINI PIZZAS MADE WITH MUFFIN BASES	TOAD IN THE HOLE WITH WEDGES, PEAS AND CARROTS
TUESDAY	TOASTED SANDWICHES	CHICKEN FAJITAS WITH PEPPERS
WEDNESDAY	SAVOURY PANCAKES WITH CHOPPED SPINACH AND CHEESE	SPAGHETTI BOLOGNAISE WITH GARLIC BREAD AND SALAD
THURSDAY	TOMATO SOUP AND CRUSTY BREAD	SWEET & SOUR CHICKEN WITH NOODLES OR RICE AND MIXED VEG
FRIDAY	A HOT DOG	BREADED FISH AND POTATO WEDGES WITH CORN ON THE COB
SATURDAY	PENNE PASTA WITH VEGETABLE SAUCE AND PORK MEATBALLS	MAKE YOUR OWN PIZZA NIGHT (CHOOSE YOUR OWN TOPPINGS)
SUNDAY	ROAST CHICKEN WITH CRANBERRY SAUCE, ROAST POTATOES AND GREEN BEANS AND CARROTS	BEANS ON TOAST

This is just an example, though. Make up your own plan, to suit your family, and shop for all the ingredients so that the fridge is fully stocked before you start.

Desserts should be small. Here are my suggestions:

- Berries and ice cream
- Banana and custard
- Apple crumble and custard
- Yoghurt
- Rice pudding
- Chopped fruit
- Dried fruit in yoghurt
- Fruit juice ice-lolly
- Jelly

Your child can also have two healthy snacks a day:

- Nuts & dried fruit mix
- Cheese straw

❦ Small sausage roll

❦ Piece of fruit

❦ Fruit juice ice-lolly

❦ Frozen yoghurt

❦ Flapjack

❦ Cheese cracker

❦ Hot chocolate drink

❦ Fruit smoothie

❦ Biscuit

Please remember that a snack is not a substitute for a meal. Only one snack is needed and if your child claims to be hungry, the next meal can be brought forward.

SCHOOL LUNCHES

If your child has school lunches, explain to a teacher or administrator about the plan you are following at home, and ask if it's possible to have a copy of the school menu plan so you can work around it? Most schools have a two- or three-week menu rotation. Discuss with your child what will be served at lunch that day and encourage her to put at least one thing on her plate that she knows she can eat, such as noodles, rice, bread or potato wedges, and one thing she is not so sure of. Tell her that she will get a reward if she does this. You may be able to arrange for a teacher or dinner lady to monitor discreetly what she eats and quietly encourage her to try new flavours.

If your child has to take a packed lunch to school I suggest following a similar principle: place something in the box you know she will eat and introduce a new flavour. Encourage her to try the new flavour first followed by the known food.

Avoid crisps and chocolates, as they will inevitably be eaten first and have minimal nutritional value. Many schools now ban sweets from lunchboxes. Try giving her a cereal bar with dried fruit instead.

THE DAY BEFORE PLAN DAY ONE

After breakfast, have a chat with your child on her own and explain clearly what is going to happen. I've suggested a possible 'script' but choose your own words.

> "I need to talk to you about something. Now you are [state age], I know that you will be able to understand. I want to tell you about our 'stop button'. Everybody in the country has a 'stop button'. You can't see it because it is inside your brain. It sleeps when we are playing and busy at school and it wakes up at mealtimes. We start to eat our food and when our body has had enough to eat it sends a message to our brain and our brain presses the 'stop button'.

> "The thing with your 'stop button' is that sometimes it comes on too quickly. Your brain presses the button before your body has had any food. Foods like [list three foods your child will not eat]. Your body needs food inside it to help it grow and become stronger and stronger. Food helps with your muscles [demonstrate with your arm], your bones [demonstrate by tapping your leg], your teeth [smile] and it gives you energy to be able to work hard at school and run around the playground.

> "Do you understand? Have you any questions you want to ask me?"

Answer any questions but keep the answers short and simple to avoid confusion. This is a lot for your child to take in.

> "The reason I am telling you this is because you are grown-up enough to understand and I have a way of helping you with your 'stop button'. Together we can fix it so that it only comes on at the right times."

Once you have explained to your child about the 'stop button' you will have started a thought process. Now start to write a list together of the foods that your child does eat. Make it as long as possible, listing foods she may have eaten in the past or has at least tried before.

Once this is done let your child have some free time to play on her own. Let her escape into the garden or potter in her room. She needs to think about what you have told her.

Remember: only one new meal to be tried each day. Never two.

While she is playing I suggest you devise the meal plan for the coming week. You already know the family favourites and you now have the list of foods your child will eat in front of you.

Go shopping for the ingredients for the week's meals and store them all in the cupboards, fridge and freezer. Nothing further needs to be done now until tomorrow.

PLAN DAY ONE

After breakfast I suggest that you announce to the whole family that you have created a meal plan for the week. This is the time to explain to any other children in the family about the 'stop button'. Keep the talk concise so as not to make your child alarmed.

The next thing you need to do is make the eating plan a fun activity, which your child sees as a rewarding process. I suggest getting a small box or jar and decorating it together. Use paints, glue, glitter and stickers. While you are decorating this jar or box, explain to your child that every time she tries a new food on her plate – and swallows it – something special will be placed in the jar. Don't tell her what this is going to be. Anything that engages your child will do.

- Micro machine cars
- Marbles
- Magnets
- Beads
- Little Lego men

🦋 Gems or jewels

🦋 Seashells

🦋 Miniature animals

Objects need to be small enough to be inserted into the box or jar one at a time, and you can hide them and have a treasure hunt, if you wish.

You should also make a wall chart where you note each time your child tries a new food. You can either:

🦋 Get your child to draw a picture of it on the chart

🦋 Write the food type in letter stickers

🦋 Draw several plates and each time a new food is tasted, draw the food onto the plate

🦋 Make the food type out of fimo or clay.

The importance of doing this is so that your child (and you) can see what is being achieved. You'll do this after every new taste and the chart will be kept on display.

As you explain the principle behind the chart, it is important to remain very positive in both your tone of voice and your body language. You need to truly believe in what you are saying. If you show any doubt this will make your child doubt the entire process.

Now have an area in the kitchen where everything is on display.

🦋 The new foods chart

🦋 The menu plan for the week

🦋 The box/jar that will be filled.

MID-MORNING

At around 10.15am, when you have finished all your preparations, if your child can read, ask her to take a look at the menu to see what you are going to eat later. Get the ingredients out to make the main meal and start cooking it together.

Ideally, your child will help you each morning of the three-day plan to prepare the meals for the rest of the day. Give her tasks she can do, such as mixing ingredients in a bowl, cutting mushrooms or pears with a very blunt knife, washing fruit and vegetables, or stirring jelly until the cube dissolves.

Have music playing in the background and keep praising your child for her efforts. This is a totally new experience for her.

As you are cooking, if there is an opportunity to taste something I strongly advise it. This is preparing her for the flavours that will greet her at the meal later. If a new food is chewed and swallowed, this deserves a piece of treasure. It doesn't only have to be at mealtimes that food is tasted.

Once you have made the meal and a dessert, repeat the explanation about the 'stop button'.

"When we sit down at the table at lunchtime we want to try very hard to beat this stop button. So don't start talking or hesitate, simply pop a mouthful in. We need to see how many mouthfuls you can eat before the stop button comes on. Let's try for two mouthfuls today. We can do it. I know we can!"

LUNCH

Today is the first day of this plan and your child may feel overwhelmed by it. Don't expect any new foods to be eaten today. The main achievement will be to cook the meal. But if she manages even a tiny taste, reward it with a piece of treasure. I advise that you eat lunch around 12 to 12.30pm.

- Let everyone serve themselves, if possible. Encourage your child to put a very small amount on her plate, even if she is reluctant to eat it. If it's a dish she can't serve herself, give her a maximum of three tablespoons. Huge portions on the plate are off-putting. Mention the stop button once more: *"Let's try and beat that button."*

- As you sit at the table, eat your own meal and make conversation with your other children. If only the two of you are at the table,

I suggest you tell your child a story about something you have done in your life. Don't comment on what your child is eating (or not eating) to avoid giving her performance anxiety!

🦋 Stop talking after a couple of minutes and place a small amount of food on your child's fork or spoon. *"That's it, let's nibble on this little bit to work towards treasure. Well done."* Leave the fork resting on the plate and continue with your story.

🦋 Once your story or conversation with a family member is over, continue to eat your own meal.

🦋 Look over at your child as you are chewing, direct your eyes towards her fork and give her a smile. *"Give it a try when you are ready."*

🦋 Now mention what the afternoon is going to involve and finish your meal.

🦋 Ask one last time: *"Would you try one little nibble?"* If there is still resistance, leave the plate in the centre of the table and bring out the dessert. Serve at the table.

🦋 Praise your child for remaining at the table and tell her she is doing very well. She is making fundamental changes. Thank her for her part in cooking the meal. *"That stop button won today but I am sure you will beat it when we have this meal next week. Let's try dessert."* You have made your child aware that this meal is going to be served again next week and that eventually she will eat it.

🦋 Follow the same principle with dessert as you did with the main meal. Encourage only three times: at the beginning, middle and towards the end.

🦋 If your child has earned a piece of treasure, give it to her and let her add it to the box or jar, and if any new foods have been tried, add them to the wall chart.

Remain confident and calm, even if she hasn't eaten a bite. This is only the first meal of Day One.

In the afternoon around 3pm I suggest you offer a healthy snack. Remember it is only small to tide her over until dinnertime. It is not a meal substitute. Try to get outside for some fresh air and exercise during the afternoon to help build her appetite.

DINNER

If lunch was an unfamiliar meal, dinner should be something you know your child likes. Serve it two hours before your child's bedtime. If she goes to bed at 8pm, dinner should be around 6pm. If there is still reluctance to eat, follow the same principles as before.

- Remind her as she is serving her own meal: *"You can do it, sit yourself down first and go and beat that stop button."*

- Only encourage three times at the meal table.

- Praise for any little achievement and aim for a piece of treasure to be awarded before the end of the day (you could have a treasure hunt if you like). Add any new foods to the wall chart.

This will have been a draining day for both you and your child. Give her a warm bath and make sure she gets to bed in good time (at least twelve hours before she needs to get up in the morning).

If you are concerned that she may be hungry you can offer a drink of milk. Remember that breakfast and one meal should have been eaten today, as well as a morning and afternoon snack, so she will be absolutely fine. She will simply wake in the morning eager for breakfast.

> Food is a fuel. It is not needed in order to sleep.

PLAN DAY TWO

After having breakfast and getting dressed, take a look at the day's menu with your child and decide what needs to be cooked. Give her jobs she can do and offer little tastes as you go along. Once this is done, let her play outside, if possible, to build up an appetite.

Serve lunch at the table. Exude confidence and positive attitude and your child will pick up on it.

- Remind her as she helps herself to the food: *"You can do it. Sit yourself down and go and beat that stop button."*

- Start eating and then after a couple of minutes encourage your child.

- Tell a story or chat to another family member.

- Encourage again (if needed).

- Eat and talk about the afternoon plans.

- Encourage one final time towards the end of your meal.

- Praise your child and tell her that you are sure more will be eaten next week when you have this meal again.

- Dessert.

- Reward and new foods (if any) added to the wall chart.

It's good to get out of the house in the afternoon, to distract your child from the new routine. Spend some time at the local park, feed the ducks or visit the shops. Have an afternoon snack, if needed, around 3pm. Make it small and remember not to eat too close to dinnertime.

Eat dinner around 5 to 5.30pm, before your child gets too tired. This is now the fourth meal you have had under the new system and the routine is slowly becoming familiar. Treasure should have been hunted for on both days and new foods should be noted on the wall chart. Have a look at the treasure jar or box and the chart together and feel proud. You are making changes together. Say: "You are doing brilliantly. Just look at that list! You have now tasted [state the foods]. I am so proud of you."

> Little steps have been taken towards a healthier diet and a happier relationship with food.

PLAN DAY THREE

Follow the routine as on Day One and Day Two, but today you will invite friends over to play in the afternoon and stay for dinner. Invite a friend who is a good eater and check with her mother that she will eat the meal you are going to serve. If you like, you could serve the two children in a different place – maybe in the garden or in a playhouse. A different environment will encourage independence, and peer pressure could mean your child is more likely to eat well. Serve a dessert they both like, such as ice cream, and then organise a treasure hunt with hidden treasure for both your child and her friend.

You have now completed three days using the new system. You have stepped away from your old ways and are working towards your child having a more balanced diet.

Take a look together at the list of foods your child has tried. Praise your child and let her know this is a system that is going to continue and that you are going to follow the same meal plan for two weeks. Tell her that her body must feel happy knowing that it is going to get lots of lovely food to make it big and strong. Say that her brain will feel happy knowing that it is going to be fed lots of brain food so that it can concentrate in the classroom and produce great pieces of work that you will see on Parents' Evening at school.

"Together we can do this. You can do this. Let's beat that stop button!"

Give your child a big 'High Five' and a hug and say....

DAY FOUR ONWARDS

Use the meal plan you have created for the next fourteen days (in other words, repeat it once) and then it will be time to reassess. After that, you may want to change some of the meals or elaborate on them. When you introduce new meals please try to prepare and cook them with your child and produce them for at least two consecutive weeks. The key is that your child becomes familiar with them. It may take five or six consecutive weeks before she is comfortable with a meal and starts to eat it, as opposed to just tasting it. Persevere, and you will see a change eventually.

Always keep the meal plan on display. It is important that your child can see what each day holds. This makes her feel more secure and prevents the fear of the unknown. If she can't read, look at the plan together in the morning and tell her what is in store.

After a week or so, you may find that your child is less interested in the reward system so it is time to change it.

For the second week of the meal plan, I recommend that you sit down as a family and devise a list of activities you find fun.

- A trip to the zoo
- Swimming
- A family bike ride
- A picnic in the park
- A trip to the cinema
- A sleepover with friends
- A family board-game afternoon

Write every idea on a piece of card and place them in an envelope then say:

> "We are all working really hard with the new system and I think we need a reward at the end of every week. Everyone works hard at school and work and [child's name] is getting better and better at beating her stop button. This is why we are having these rewards, because of all the effort [child's name] is making. On a Friday night after dinner Mummy and Daddy are going to chat about what reward you will all have at the weekend. On Saturday morning at breakfast time the reward card will be waiting on the breakfast table. That reward will happen over the weekend!"

Even if your child hasn't tried many new foods, focus on any positive steps and offer weekly rewards. It's crucial that you make sure they happen during the weekend they have been promised. Children don't understand rain checks! Without these weekly rewards your child could lose her incentive to make changes, so do keep it up.

FREQUENTLY ASKED QUESTIONS

My child says he tries lots of new flavours at school. How can I be sure?
I would contact the school, explain the situation and ask if you can talk to a dinner lady or member of staff who is normally present in the dining hall. Tell your child that the person in question is aware of the situation so that he knows he can't lie about his eating.

If he mentions a new meal he has tried at school, cook it at home. He may then say "it's not like the one at school" but continue to present this meal weekly until he eventually realises that it is there to stay. I have even gone to a child's school in the past and got the recipe for a food he claimed to have eaten then copied it exactly. This sounds like a lot of effort but it's worth it if it increases the variety in your child's diet.

I've tried to start your eating plan but my child sits silently at the table and refuses point blank to eat.
Many children will start the process with a 'stand off'. Continue to eat your own meal and remain calm. Pay no attention to this behaviour on Day One. On Day Two make your child aware that you expect her at least to eat the part of the meal she knows she likes. "Don't rob your body of the food it needs."

Keep calm and give her time. She still thinks that you are going to return to your old ways and she will try everything she possibly can before she starts eating. The plan will work eventually if you give it enough time.

I have a child who won't even come to the table. It's my own fault because in the past I took his food to him in his play corner. How can I change this habit?
Make it clear to him that you are following a new eating plan now. The old days are gone and they aren't coming back. Say: "You need to choose. Sit on the stair in the cold hallway or come and sit at the

table. I know what I would choose. The plate does have [name what he likes] on it. Come when you are ready."

Give him the space he needs. If he still hasn't come to the table by the time the meal is over, he will get a shock when you announce that it is bath-time without bringing any food to him. This may sound severe but the chances are your child will only miss a meal this once. Tomorrow he will come to the table.

After bath-time, if he complains he is hungry I would return downstairs and re-heat his meal. If he still won't sit at the table to eat it, he is not genuinely hungry. If he does eat it, tell him firmly that mealtimes in your house are not after bath-time and that this will not be happening again.

My daughter will carefully pick around what she doesn't like and eat only what she knows. Any suggestions?

It's amazing the delicacy with which children can pick around a plate, avoiding getting so much as a morsel of the dreaded food onto their forks. Some will even refuse favourite foods if they have touched something they don't like on the plate, as if they are somehow contaminated! Obviously you can't let this behaviour continue.

Start by putting only a small amount of what she likes on her plate and letting her know that she can have seconds if she tries a little bit of something else. "Just one pea or a teeny bit of carrot would be a wonderful start."

Stick to your word. Don't give any more of the food she likes until something else has been tried. It will work in the end.

My other children are teasing my 'non-eater' and I fear this is escalating the situation.

The other children need to be disciplined according to their age and then spoken to in private at a calmer time. The last thing you need is increased tension around the dinner table.

If the teasing doesn't stop, I would ask the culprit to leave the table and go and sit on the stair. Tell him he can return to the table once he is ready to say sorry and eat nicely. If he refuses to apologise, wait until the 'non-eater' has finished his meal then sit him at the table in silence on his own to eat the rest of his meal.

During the evening, talk to your other children at a time when there are no background distractions. Tell them that if there is any more teasing at the dinner table they will not be included in the weekend reward and will have to stay at home. Remember that you will have to follow through with this consequence if the teasing continues.

My son will announce a food is 'disgusting' before even trying it.
He is trying to get a reaction, so don't give him what he wants. Ignore the statement and continue with the meal.

How much dessert should I give if my child has not eaten any of his meal?
I would offer a very small pot of yoghurt and some fruit. Make your child aware that no dinner means a very, very small dessert. Bigger dinner, bigger dessert!

At what age should I start teaching my child table manners?
If your child is a picky eater, I would focus on getting her to eat a wider range of foods first before focusing on the correct use of cutlery and so forth. But there's advice about table manners on page 226, in the Behaviour section of this chapter. Don't leave it too long!

❧

There may be some foods that your child will never eat, even as an adult, such as liver, spinach or curry. Some children don't like the idea of eating animals and go through a vegetarian phase. The main thing is that you take away their fear of food at an early age and get them used to trying new things, until there is a broad range of fruits and vegetables, grains and protein sources that they will accept, covering all the bases of vitamins and minerals they need. That's when you've done your job as a parent.

THE BEHAVIOUR PLAN FOR CHILDREN AGED THREE TO SIX YEARS

A client with a four-year-old son once said to me "Life revolves around him because it is easier that way. We have been living like this for so long we are nervous of what his reaction would be if we started telling him what to do."

If you read that statement and heard your own voice then please read on. By following some simple guidelines and approaching things differently you will start to see your family life in a whole new light.

Unlike the 'terrible twos' stage, your child is now able to communicate and has a broad vocabulary to get across what he wants to say. Tantrums may still occur but with the added complexity of the use of words. He will often want to have the last word or feel that he has made his own decision and he does not want to be told what to do. At this age you have to hand the decision-making over to your child and guide him to make the right decisions.

> Everyone wants an independent and confident child – and you can have one. It all starts with trust.

We all like to feel that we are making our own decisions in life. Nobody wants to feel ruled by another person. Most importantly, if we allowed others to make our decisions we would lose the ability to make them for ourselves.

By saying this, I mean that you need to take a step back and allow your child to make his own decisions. Even a three-year-old is capable of doing this.

All children behave inappropriately at times. It's part of being a child! They are still learning and at times they will learn through their mistakes. As a parent it is important to allow your child to learn in the way they want to.

My system involves giving children of this age two choices and then letting them make the decision about how they want to proceed.

Let's imagine a situation in which a four-year-old boy keeps taking his younger sister's toys. This is causing the younger child to scream and shout out. You say:

"OK [child's name]. You have a choice to make here. One: you and I find something else for you to do and you let your sister have her toys or…Two: I ask you to leave the room and sit on the stair for a while until you are ready to play happily. You need to make this decision. One: play and share. Two: go and think about it on the stair."

In doing this you have shifted the focus onto your child. He has to make the decision for himself. You have not threatened him or enforced your authority. Instead you have passed on the responsibility.

If the child chooses option one and stops taking his sister's toys, you praise him and do as you promised, either sitting down to help him build a Duplo tower or simply placing the playdough or some puzzles on the kitchen table for him. *I am so pleased with you. You made a brilliant decision there. Now everyone is happy.*

If the child chooses option two and continues to bait his sister, you take hold of his hand and walk together to the stair. Remind him that he made this choice.

"You made the decision to come out here to the stair and think about what you were doing. When you have thought of something nice to play, come back to the room and we can do it together."

It is at this stage that your child may start to scream and shout, whinge and moan or possibly try to negotiate. Keep your head clear and stick with the system. Return your child to the stair as many times as necessary until he is quiet and calm. *"When all is calm we can talk about this. Calm first and then we talk."* Keep it simple and consistent. Eventually your child will quieten down.

It is once your child is calm that you can reason with them. Now is the moment to ask your child if he can hug and say sorry. Hug him and explain: *"When Mummy gives you two choices you need to think about which is the right one to do. Let's try harder next time. What should you have chosen to do?"*

If he cannot answer you must help him.

"Next time, let's let your sister play with her toys and we don't take them away from her. OK?"

You need some recognition that he understands. A nod of the head will suffice.

- Give your child his two choices
- Allow him to make his choice
- Act on his decision
- Offer praise or consequence.

> There is one key element to discipline and that is to know in your heart that you mean what you are saying.

If you have a sense of determination and confidence your child will hear it in your voice. The one thing you don't want to do is hesitate or waver.

When your child has started to behave in a way you don't like, don't always feel you need to act immediately. Unless there is violence or danger involved, you can step back for 30 seconds and think about the situation and what it is that you are going to say. Once you have the script clear in your head you'll be able to continue with confidence.

BOUNDARIES

Children thrive on routine and boundaries. They feel comforted by knowing what is 'right' and 'wrong' behaviour and what the consequences will be if they don't behave well. This is as true at home as it is at school. That's why it's important to agree on a set of house rules that all the family know about. It may be worth writing the most important ones down so that everyone is singing from the same hymn sheet and any childminders or other people who care for your child can follow them as well.

Some examples might include:

- No shouting in the house
- Remain seated at the table during mealtimes
- Do something when you are asked
- Ask permission to leave the meal table and thank the cook
- No hitting or spitting at other people
- Help to clear the meal table when asked.

❦ Share your toys and books

❦ If you are feeling cross, go to your Thought Space

❦ Apologise when necessary

❦ Be happy rather than whiney

❦ Talk about your feelings

❦ Ask for snacks. Don't just take them from the fridge

❦ No splashing water out of the bath.

I feel very strongly that you should encourage children to stop and think about how the other person in a situation is feeling. I was raised hearing the phrase: "Put yourself in their shoes for a moment." When children are born they think they are the centre of the universe and it is only through your guidance that they will grow to understand that consideration of other people is a vital life skill.

Here are some discussion points you can raise to encourage empathy.

❦ *"Do you know that you make me very sad when you scream and shout?"*

❦ *"How do you feel inside when you shout like that?"*

❦ *"Let's hug and make the happiness come back."*

❦ *"Which feels better – a smile or a frown?"* Act this out with your child.

❦ Notice other people around you and read their facial expressions together.

When you decide to follow my three-day plan in order to establish some new boundaries for your child, make sure you have plenty of time to focus on him. Ideally you want to start this plan when both you and your partner can be involved, so that might mean starting on a Friday afternoon, after nursery or school. Time off work is not essential as long as you both understand the rules and one parent can continue during the coming weeks.

I advise choosing a time when the diary is relatively free, but you don't need to remain housebound. The first two days involve family time at home and also out in the park. On the third day an afternoon play date needs to be organised.

I also advise that you have a fridge full of food and all meals organised for both the children and adults in the house so you don't have to think about shopping and cooking. Your focus is behaviour.

THE PRAISE AND REWARD SYSTEM

This system is not just for the child; it's also for you, so that you can see progress being made and aren't tempted to give in under pressure.

With children aged three to six, I have been known to use:

- Magnets that click together
- Gems or marbles in a jar
- A Lego kit that is constructed in stages from the instruction manual
- A family portrait jigsaw

The principle is straightforward. Thank your child for behaving in a certain way and then place a magnet on the tower, or a gem in the jar, or construct the next stage in the Lego kit, or put the next few pieces in the jigsaw. This gives you both a sense of achievement. You are working on a project together.

Arrange to have 30 to 40 rewards to get you through the three-day programme, and the same again if you want to continue for six days. I have found that after this period of time the reward system is not needed in the same way as the change in behaviour is starting to become the norm.

The weekend after the project is finished, you will reward yourselves as a family. This is usually done in the form of a day trip or outing. Rewards could be:

- A trip to a safari park or petting zoo

🦋 A cinema outing with popcorn!

🦋 Camping in the garden

🦋 A meal out together

🦋 A bike ride with a picnic

🦋 A day at a theme park

🦋 Going swimming

Every time good behaviour is noticed, it should be written down and at the end of the day you can look over the list together.

DATE	BRILLIANT BEHAVIOUR
09/09	JAMES PUT HIS SHOES ON THE FIRST TIME HE WAS ASKED.
09/09	JAMES SAT AT THE TABLE UNTIL THE END OF THE MEAL.
09/09	JAMES HELPED CLEAR THE TABLE.
10/09	JAMES STOPPED TEASING HIS SISTER WHEN HE WAS ASKED.

Make sure you don't use the reward system as a bribe, though.

🦋 Don't say: *"If you put your shoes on you can have a magnet."*

🦋 Do say:*"Can you put your shoes on so that we can head out to the park?"* Pause and see if the act is completed, then say: *"Remember, we are building a magnet tower!"*

If your child says "I'll do it if I can have a piece for the puzzle," you need to explain that praise is something you wait to be given. It is not something you ask for.

THE CONSEQUENCE SYSTEM

The system we are implementing basically involves giving your child two options and then letting her decide. The positive choice leads to a reward but the incorrect choice will lead to a consequence.

In certain situations, one of the options you offer your child will be to take time away from the family and go to her Thought Space. This is the same idea as the Shout Spot you used for younger children, but I've renamed it because this age group need to be encouraged to think about the decisions they make and this is a place where they can have peace to do just that. Once your child reaches the age of five or six, you may choose to ask her to spend time alone in her bedroom instead of in a Thought Space.

For many children, the frustration they feel at spending time alone is a great enough consequence. However, for older children you may find that one of their privileges has to be removed as well in order for them to truly understand the importance of behaving nicely. The most effective privilege to remove is whatever they are looking forward to next in the day.

"You can stop splashing water out of the bath now and play nicely with that fantastic boat or you will have to get straight out of the bath and go to bed without any TV time this evening. You choose!"

If the splashing continues, you must follow through the consequence: she has to go straight to bed without any TV. When a consequence is implemented you need to see that the child is genuinely upset.

If you are going to remove something from her life, it needs to be something she will truly miss.

If she doesn't seem upset, then it is not an effective consequence.

- With younger children, a favourite toy can be confiscated for a day.

- For older ones, the day's screen time (on computers, TV or games consoles) can be banned.

- A play date or sleepover at a friend's house can be cancelled.

After you have implemented a consequence three times for a particular behaviour, you will see a change. Your child will begin to stop and think before making her choice. She will consider the previous consequence and this should stop her in her tracks.

I tend to only implement consequences as a last resort. When you do, the immediate behaviour can be a challenge but the long-term result is very rewarding.

If you show your child clearly the way you want her to behave, and make sure she does it, you will earn her respect. If a child does not respect you and the house rules, and feels she can do as she pleases, she is not going to thrive in the outside world, which is full of rules and regulations. You

> When you sign up to parenting, you sign up to the challenges as well as the fun stuff!

want your child to have the best possible start in life, and this is an important part of it.

Are you ready to begin? Tick off the checklist:

- A weekend has been set aside starting with a clear Friday afternoon after school.
- You have full support from your partner and any other adults in the house.
- You have agreed upon the house rules and written them down.
- The consequences have also been written out but these are not displayed.
- The fridge is full and meals are organised.
- You have agreed on a Thought Space.
- The reward system is organised.
- You have a book or chart in which to write down all of the good behaviour.
- A play date is organised for the afternoon of Day Three.
- A 'prize' is organised for the following weekend.

PLAN DAY ONE

Explain the reward system to your child first but don't let him hold the reward tools at this stage.

- *"We have decided to give our family a challenge. We want to build a magnetic tower but the bricks are only going to be placed on top of one another after good behaviour. So when I say 'Please can everyone come to the table because dinner is about to be served?' if you come straight away and sit down then you are given a brick to add to the tower. Sounds easy, doesn't it? Once we have built our tower we are going to get a prize! A family prize. What do you think would be a good prize for us all?"*

🦋 Give a few examples and then see what your child(ren) suggest.

🦋 *"Mummy and Daddy are going to think about the prize and we will announce it once we have built our tower."*

🦋 Aim for the outing to take place the following weekend but don't let the children know that's when it will be. Once you feel that your child(ren) understand about the rewards and the prize, you need to explain the house rules.

🦋 *"Mummy and Daddy have written some 'house rules' to help us get our magnets. If we can all follow these rules we will have built a tower in no time at all!"*

🦋 Read out the rules and give a short explanation if you need to.

🦋 Finally you need to mention the Thought Space and make your child(ren) aware of where it is. Take them to it. *"If at any time you make the choice not to behave then you will need to come to the stair and sit here until you are calm and ready to have fun again."*

This is all you need to say. You have explained it and now you are going to have to act when necessary. Your child(ren) will not gain a full understanding of the system until it is actually used.

Let the child(ren) play for a while until the first time you need to give them a choice, and then follow through with a magnet for good behaviour and the Thought Space otherwise.

If this is a Friday afternoon after school you will be proceeding with dinner, bath, screen time, stories and bed.

Next morning, when everyone is dressed and teeth are brushed, I suggest you sit down and plan the day ahead. I will often write out the structure of the day as I say it so that everyone knows the routine. If you are an organised person you might find that your child thrives on the idea of ticking off the list as each stage passes.

- A small morning outing, such as going out to get a newspaper, post a letter, or buy some milk
- Home for a play before lunch
- Quiet time after lunch for an hour
- An afternoon trip to the park or walking the dog
- Home for dinner
- Bath-time
- Screen time
- Stories
- Bed.

Remember to notice any positive behaviour. This is not just when you ask your child to do something and he does it; you may choose to comment on how he is playing: *"You are playing so nicely together as brothers I think we need to put a magnet on our tower!"*

When you notice good behaviour, write it down on the list, ready to read out at bedtime. The children do not have to be made aware of this at the time.

When a 'situation' arises, take a deep breath and assess it. Decide the two choices you are going to offer: good behaviour or Thought Space. If necessary, take your child to the Thought Space.

- Lead him there by the hand, sit him down, then crouch and look into his eyes. He is likely to be shouting with anger or crying at this stage.
- Hold his arms. *"You were asked to choose and you chose to carry on [state behaviour] so now you have chosen to sit here. When you calm down we will carry on with our day."*
- Turn around and walk away.

The moment your child steps away from the space, return him and sit him down.

 "When you are calm and sitting nicely we can carry on with the day."

 After explaining twice, simply return him to the space in silence each time he removes himself.

 This could last for as long as half an hour or an hour the first time. Do not give up. Your child is testing the system. He is testing you. Stay strong and believe in yourself and the system.

 The moment your child is quiet, or whimpering quietly, bend down and say *"Well done, you have become calm. Good boy."*

 Hug and encourage your child to say sorry. At this stage it may be said in the form of a hug.

 "Now, let's carry on with our day." Suggest an activity and start to play together.

 Don't mention this incident again. Your child is still absorbing the process you have implemented.

 Note the incident in your book when you get a chance. This is for your reference only. You will notice that the number of times you need to use the Thought Space will decrease as the days continue.

At dinner, put the reward system in the centre of the table, but tell your child not to touch it while you are eating. Talk about all the positive elements of the day.

"This morning we did not have a tower but now we have eight magnets!"

"I have enjoyed my day watching all the good behaviour."

"There were only two trips to the Thought Space."

"I wonder how many magnets we will get from now to bedtime?"

"Everyone is sitting nicely at the table. I think I will add a magnet now."

"Hooray for us – soon we will get a prize!"

Aim for seven or eight rewards to be given daily so that the project is complete after five or six days. You can then have a family prize at the weekend.

When you put your child to bed, read through all the positive elements of the day. Tell him how proud you are of him and how much you are looking forward to tomorrow.

Your positive energy will be absorbed by your child and very soon he will see absolutely no point in behaving negatively. He will strive to earn your praise. Just remember to keep giving it.

PLAN DAY TWO

Today both you and your child will wake up knowing that new systems are in place to change behaviour. Your child is still likely to test you and push the boundaries to see if you are continuing with the new way or returning to the old ways. Please stay strong.

Try to begin the day by rewarding your child as soon as possible. This will remind you both that you need to stay positive and focus on the good stuff!

Get a piece of paper and write down what is going to happen in the day, listing events in order so that they can be 'ticked' by your child as the day progresses.

Today I advise you to set yourself a challenge and do something with your child that you may have shied away from in the past. Many parents say that eating out or a trip to the shops is a challenge, or even that simply having a conversation on the phone can prove tricky.

I am going to guide you through these three challenges and I would like to think that by the end of the day you will have achieved at least one of them.

EATING OUT

It is unrealistic to expect a child to sit at table for any length of time with nothing to stimulate him. It is also a challenge for him to be given food that he does not recognise or has not tasted before. That's why you should:

❧ Take your child to a 'child-friendly' restaurant

❧ Take activities to entertain your child

❧ Order the meal as soon as you arrive.

Remember to take some rewards with you. I understand you can't transport the entire magnet tower, Lego construction or jigsaw puzzle but you could bring some pieces to award when they are earned.

The first thing to do is prepare your child without making too much fuss. Explain that you are going out to eat and that you need to pack a bag of things to keep him busy at the table while waiting for the meal. I advise that you place something in the bag he has not seen before, such as a small tub of playdough or a sticker book. A key thing to remember when taking a child to a restaurant is that you want them to be hungry. Don't fill him up with snacks beforehand or allow him to have a big drink while waiting for the food.

On arriving at the restaurant order the food and then visit the loo together. Ask your child to use the loo and when you are washing hands say *"Now, if at any stage you think you need your Thought Space we are going to come in here. If there is any shouting or silly behaviour we will come here to calm down. Do you understand?"*

Wait for a response. If there is no answer continue with a very positive tone: *"We have washed our hands nicely and your behaviour is great. Let's go and get a reward!"*

Hold hands and walk tall to the table. You can do this! Take control and be a strong leader and he will follow!

While waiting for the food, play a game such as 'I spy'. Talk about your surroundings and count how many people you can see. I will often play the question game:

"I can see a man in a blue jumper. What colour are his trousers?"

"How many waiters can you count?"

"I can see a vase of flowers. What colours are they?"

The key is to keep your child engaged. Please remember that this is a challenge for him as well.

Once your game comes to a natural end, ask him if he would like to look in the bag for things to do, but explain that when the food arrives the bag will have to be put away because the waiter does not like toys at his table.

Let your child explore the bag on his own. Only talk to him if he asks you something. If your partner or another adult is present, you can have a conversation at this stage.

When the food arrives, calmly ask your child to put his belongings back into his bag. Start to praise him: "*Well done, darling, you are packing up. I think that will definitely earn you a reward!*"

> Remain positive. Believe that your child is capable of conforming and he will.

Try to avoid a confrontation but if you see behaviour escalating, take his hand and say "*Let's just go and have a chat. Excuse us, we won't be long.*"

Get yourselves to the loo before the meltdown happens. When you get there, use the loo if you need to but don't talk until you are both at the basins. This is your child's thinking time, and it is also giving you a chance to think about what you will say next.

If he has quietened down, you can say "*OK, now are we ready to return to the table and finish our last few mouthfuls. Then we can open up your bag again while we wait for our ice cream.*"

Note that you are guiding your child and making them aware of the positive elements (bag and ice cream). Take your child's hand and say "*Come on, let's go.*" Walk tall and exude confidence.

If your child hesitates, ask what would make this situation better for him. Listen to what he has to say and answer his questions with short clear answers. This is not the time to start a huge debate. Negotiation is not an option. Use a 'chop chop' approach and return to the table.

At the end of the meal you will decide whether your child is happy with his bag of activities or ready to leave the restaurant. To a degree children will dictate this. Coffee might have to be a takeaway to drink at home.

I always find that after sitting in a restaurant children want to run and play so take the 'long walk' back to the car or visit a park or pond to feed the ducks on the way home.

When you arrive home praise your child strongly. Be proud of yourselves as a family.

VISITING SHOPS

When parents say to me "He is a nightmare shopping" my natural response is "Why do it to yourself?" Most children don't want to go to the shops and now that your child is at nursery or school there should be time in the day for you to shop alone in peace. However, if you work when he is at school, this might not be an option, and there are always times when it could be necessary to shop with a child, so here's my plan to make it as stress-free as possible.

The key is to know the shops you are going to and what it is that you need to purchase. The moment you start to browse your child will get restless because you are doing something without purpose as far as they are concerned.

Before leaving home, let your child know the three shops you need to go in and what it is you need to buy. Write your list on a piece of paper in front of him while he is having a snack at the table. Tell him that after those three shops you will be going to the park or playground and doing something just for him: *"Because you are going to be so kind and help Mummy with her shopping, I want to say thank you so I am going to take you to the park."* Your child now has a reason to behave.

In the shops give your child responsibility:

🦋 Ask him to hold the door for other shoppers.

🦋 Ask him to make choices where appropriate. *"Shall we get the blue or the red one?"*

Three shops maximum is my rule. Stick to it if you possibly can.

🦋 Ask if he can find a particular item in the supermarket aisle. *"Can you see your favourite cereal?"*

🦋 Let him hand over the money or bank card.

Tell your child how well-behaved he is being and that he is earning rewards as you are shopping.

If your child knows that the maximum is three shops and the park is to follow, he should manage to behave. Keep to the rule and don't attempt a fourth shop if the deal was three!

If his behaviour becomes unbearable you may have to terminate the trip.

- Return home in silence. Don't talk to your child at all. He has behaved badly and deserves to be ignored.

- When you get home, take him to the loo first if you think he needs to go then lead him in silence to the Thought Space.

- Sit him down and say *"I'm really disappointed. You have made me sad."*

- Remove a privilege. *"There will be no television for you today. Sit here until you are ready to show me you are sorry."*

- Leave him there. If he gets up from the step, keep returning him to it in silence. Don't look at him. Walk away each time. Take deep breaths and stay calm.

- When he is quiet, approach him. *"Are you ready to say sorry?"*

- Wait for a response and if it is yes, instigate a hug. *"You cannot behave like that, [child's name]. Next time we go shopping that is not going to happen. Do you understand me? I love you very much but I will not have that behaviour. Now, let's carry on with our day."*

- Move on. Set up an activity and give your child space to play alone. Then calm yourself. Well done.

MAKING A TELEPHONE CALL

I advise setting an egg timer before making a phone call.

- Engage your child in an absorbing activity.

🦋 Tell her you are going to make a phone call. *"I need to make an important call but it is only going to take five minutes. I have set the timer and when it 'pings' I will come straight off of the phone and reward you with a gem/magnet but I need you to help me by being very quiet. Let's try it."*

🦋 Set the timer and place it out of reach.

🦋 As you make the call, walk in and out of the room your child is in.

🦋 When the timer pings you must stick to the deal and terminate your call.

> Five phone calls spread out over the course of the day is probably the maximum your child can manage at this stage.

Practise the system by calling friends and family rather than making business calls, so you can cut them short abruptly if you need to. Start with five minutes and build up to ten.

If your child shouts and plays up during the call, you will have to terminate it and take him to his Thought Space, as before. Remove a privilege, wait until he has calmed down, explain why the privilege has been removed, then get on with your day.

AT BEDTIME

By the end of Day Two I would like to think that at least seven rewards have been given and the reasons for the rewards have been written down. At bedtime tell your child that every time he misbehaves from now on, he will have to spend time on the Thought Space. Move on to list the positive points of the day, reading them out from your book, and praise him for any achievements.

Take time in the evening to glance at your book and count how many Thought Space moments you have had versus the rewards given. I am sure you will find that your child is behaving better than he did on Day One, but remember that you are both still learning and you have only been doing this for two days. Be proud of the changes you have made!

PLAN DAY THREE

Consistency is the key. You need to see the changes you have made as changes for life.

🦋 Give your child two choices

🦋 If the behaviour continues take him to the Thought Space

🦋 Wait for calm

🦋 Apologise

🦋 Move on.

> Time to think is fundamentally important. The sooner you teach your child that, the better.

Invite a friend with her child for an afternoon play and dinner. When they arrive, explain your system to them so that your child sees that it will continue whoever is in the house. (He already knows from yesterday that it continues outside the house.) Guide the children to a fun activity and sit down for a chat with your friend.

During the afternoon, use the Thought Space if you need to. Your child should be beginning to understand the important of removing himself from a situation when tensions start to build. In time your child will naturally go to the Thought Space and later on (from the age of five or six) this may be replaced by spending time alone in his bedroom.

At teatime, place the reward system on the kitchen table and talk about how pleased you are with the amazing behaviour in your house. If you think your child will be embarrassed if you do this in front of his friend, let him overhear you telling your friend how well he is doing.

There are only a few days to go before the Family Reward. Plan an event that excites you all. Remember, you are being the parent your child needs you to be, and one day, in years to come when he stands taller than you, he will thank you for everything you have done for him.

In the next part of the chapter we are going to look at how the systems can be used for different types of behaviour – some that your child needs to learn and others that he needs to 'unlearn'.

🦋 Following instructions

🦋 Taking responsibility for her own belongings

🦋 Table manners

🦋 Continual negotiation

🦋 Whingeing and whining

🦋 Sibling squabbles

🦋 Anger management

🦋 Swearing

FOLLOWING INSTRUCTIONS

By the time a child is three years old she wants to feel she is making her own decisions, so you need to persuade her that's what she is doing. It's time to get clever! Rather than simply issuing an instruction, stop and take note of what she is doing. The chances are that she is engrossed in something.

🦋 *"I can see you are busy so I am going to set the timer. When you hear the 'ping' can you please put your schoolbag in your room? Did you hear what I said?"*

🦋 Wait for a response of "Yes, schoolbag."

🦋 Set the timer.

🦋 When it 'pings' give her a moment.

🦋 Approach with the bag and hold it out.

🦋 *"Thank you, [child's name]. You can come straight back to that."*

🦋 Praise her on her return.

Failing to do as she is asked after the timer has rung leads to the Thought Space. You will only need to do this three or four times before your child realises life is easier if you simply do as you've been asked.

Young children, boys in particular, find it hard to follow more than one instruction at a time, so don't overload them. If you instruct a child to go upstairs to collect a jumper, brush his

Only issue one instruction at a time. Don't overload.

teeth and put on his shoes, chances are only the last of those tasks will be completed.

TAKING RESPONSIBILITY FOR HER OWN BELONGINGS

This is something that has to be taught – children rarely do it naturally – but it is important once they start school or nursery. My system can be used for children as young as four or five.

The night before school I advise that your child lays out her clothes for the following day. It is also important that she checks the correct shoes are waiting by the front door and her bag is packed. I often create a tick list with a child that we photocopy and place on the bedroom wall so we can run through it and tick off the items before bedtime.

You may already have completed some of the tasks, while your child will do others. It all helps her to build an understanding of the importance of forward planning and organising for the day ahead.

TASK	MON	TUE	WED	THUR	FRI	SAT	SUN
LAY OUT CLOTHES	√						
SHOES BY FRONT DOOR	√						
SCHOOLBAG PACKED	√						
HOMEWORK	√						
READING	√						
HOMEWORK BOOK SIGNED	√						
MUSIC PRACTICE	√						

Don't expect her to remember everything all the time, but reward her for anything she does achieve. By starting this process early it will encourage independence and give her strong management skills for the future.

TABLE MANNERS

All parents have their own opinions on table manners. Agree with your partner the rules you want your children to follow, arrange them in a list according to priority and address one type of behaviour at a time. You can use the trusty jam jar with marbles to reinforce it. Wait until the behaviour you want has become more or less second nature before moving on to address another.

> "Today we are working on sitting up straight at the table. Food to our mouth not mouth to our food! I would like everyone to try very hard and every time I notice nice straight backs I will place a marble in the jar."

Barking at the children if they are not obeying won't help. Keep it positive. If you notice bent backs, say *"I hope everyone has a straight back! I have a whole pile of marbles here!"*

Ensure that you praise everyone at the table (your partner included) at least twice.

It's wonderful to see the response. It reminds me of a sea of children in assembly suddenly sitting up straight when the headmaster arrives!

CONTINUAL NEGOTIATING

This is an exhausting trait, if you let it happen. There are times when a child can have his say and others when he just needs to do as he is asked. If you are managing a Negotiator, give him as little information as possible. The more you tell him, the more he can question and challenge. Read the following example.

> Parent: "I need you to put your shoes away so that the floor is clear for when the cleaner comes in the morning."
>
> Child: "If the cleaner is not coming until the morning I will put them away then. I don't need to put them away now."
>
> Parent: "Please pop your shoes away and then come to the table ready for dinner."

Child: "What is for dinner?"

Parent: "Shoes, [child's name], and I will meet you at the table."

When you ask your child to do something (or not, as the case may be), stop and think "Am I happy to negotiate on this?" If the answer is no, then stand strong.

Firstly, if tasks need to be done use the timer as a warning of what is going to have to occur. Don't entertain any negotiation.

> "This is not open for discussion. You heard the timer just as I did. Now you choose. Are you going to do the task straight away or do you need to go and sit on the Thought Space to think about it first?"

Step away and allow your child to make his choice. If he continues to argue simply take his hand and sit him down on the Thought Space.

> "When you are ready, please can you [state task]."

When the task is complete don't make too much of a fuss. Just say "Thank you for doing that." Don't make any negative comments that might deter your child from obeying next time.

It may be very boring but with consistency you will get results. The negotiator will often dig his heels in and opt for the Thought Space but in time the task will be completed.

WHINGEING AND WHINING

I have great sympathy with parents who find themselves listening to whingeing and whining. The key is to nip it in the bud before it even starts.

> ❧ "I am very sorry but my ears just don't listen to that funny noise. I need to hear your lovely voice and then I can help you with what you want or need."

❦ If the whining continues, ask her to make her choice. *"Do you want to use your lovely voice or talk in that funny way sitting on the Thought Space? You choose. Lovely voice or Thought Space?"*

❦ The moment the whine occurs again, take your child's hand and guide her to the spot.

❦ *"When you have got all of that silly voice out we can then carry on with our day."*

❦ Return your child to the spot every time she removes herself and continues to whine.

❦ When she is staying on the spot and the noise has stopped, approach her. *"Have you found your lovely voice? Now shall we go and do something nice together [state activity]?"*

❦ While you are engaged in the activity together you can take this opportunity to ask your child to look at you and when she is focused say: *"I need you to know that when your silly voice comes you need to sit on the Thought Space and get it all out. I only want to hear your lovely voice."* Nothing further needs to be said unless she has any questions.

SIBLING SQUABBLES

In order for siblings to play well together, they need to learn how to disagree and resolve their own disagreements. They should be able to be physical with one another in a kind and fun way, and to respect each other's space. It is important that you manage their behaviour while also giving them room to learn these vital skills.

When siblings get physical with one another, our instinct may be to stop them tumbling and rolling around the floor in case they get hurt, but this is not always the best course of action. Instead, say something like "Think about your strength, please." If you watch and wait, the tumble will either come to a natural conclusion or one child will start to inflict pain on the other.

- ✿ Once shouts of pain are heard, stop the mini-battle. *"That's enough of that. You have had your moment of tumbling around. Let's find something else to do."*

- ✿ You may need to pull them apart and place them at opposite ends of the room. *"Now, we need to find something else to do now."*

- ✿ Consider whether they need to head outside and burn off their energy. Guide them to another activity.

- ✿ If there's been an injury, the children need to hug and ideally say sorry to one another.

- ✿ Once you have them engaged in another activity take a moment to talk to them both about strength. Ask who is the stronger child and why. Ask what could happen if they kept fighting and Mummy didn't stop it. Ask them questions to get them to think for themselves. *"When we get angry let's think of what we could do rather than hit another person and get into trouble? Do you know what happens in our country if two men are fighting in the street and one gets hurt?"* Talk to them about police and prison. Children of this age are very capable of understanding that the country has laws.

If your children are stealing toys and/or baiting each other, don't jump in straight away. Leave it for a while to see if they can resolve it themselves. Only intervene if you truly believe you are needed. In this case, give your child his two choices.

> "Either you return the toy and we find some nice things for you to play with or I will remove the toy and you have to go and sit on the Thought Space and think about sharing. You choose. Return the toy or Thought Space?" Give him to the count of three.

Follow through with either praise or the Thought Space. While one child is on the Thought Space, focus on the other. Your child needs to identify failing to share with a feeling of isolation. Once he is sitting calmly, you can initiate a discussion about sharing.

If you have a child who is a Negotiator encourage him to work out a deal, whereby they swap one toy for another. You could be creating a future leader of industry!

ANGER MANAGEMENT

If your child is showing symptoms of anger for whatever reason, he needs to be taught how to manage it. In particular, anger leading to violence needs to be isolated. You may find that you can understand the violence – it could be that the other child was in the wrong – but this does not excuse it.

There's a world of difference between rough and tumble with a sibling, and losing your temper and trying to inflict pain on someone else, and children are well aware of the difference. If your child gets cross and lashes out, you need to act immediately.

- Say *"We don't hit people in anger in this house. Not ever."*

- Take your child's hand and march him to the Thought Space.

- *"You are staying there until I have calmed down and you have calmed down. I get very upset when I see you hurting others like that. Very upset."*

There's a strong possibility that your child will still need to vent his anger. Keep returning him to the Thought Space and let him shout it all out. Rather than suppressing this emotion, your child needs to express it.

Once the anger is released and the child is calm, you need to talk to both children. Make them aware that violence can get you into serious trouble. Ask them to apologise to one another and then continue with the day.

SWEARING

The first piece of advice I would give is to ignore your child the first and second time you hear him use a swear word. Let it pass. Children will often swear to get a reaction, and the greater the reaction the more frequently the word will be used. The third time you hear the word I suggest you play ignorant.

"What does that word mean? I've never heard it before? Can I say it as well? Can we say it to Daddy?"

Wait for a reaction. Children tend to go quiet at this.

"What does that word mean?"

If they can't give you an explanation – which is most likely – say "*If you don't know what a word means then it is silly to use it. You have lots of brilliant words in your head. Why don't you use some of these instead?*"

If the bad language continues, now is time for a pep talk. Sit down at a quiet moment, just the two of you. Make sure there are no distractions and make eye contact with your child.

"As you get older you learn more and more words. These words you are using are not nice and we cannot use them any more. Your brain is only four-year-old size [or whatever age they are] and it will not be able to understand the meanings of these words. When your brain is able to understand I will talk to you about them. For now I need you to use words you understand. Those words could get you into trouble. We don't want that to happen, do we?"

Pause for a moment, retaining eye contact, then say "*Do you want to tell me anything or ask me anything?*"

Speak with authority but not with anger. Your child was experimenting and the language should cease with this calm explanation. If it continues, I would simply send the child to his room and tell him to close the door behind him and continue that language where no one can hear him. He can come down when all of that rubbish is out of his mouth!

FREQUENTLY ASKED QUESTIONS

Can the Thought Space be my child's bedroom?
The Thought Space is a consequence for bad behaviour and making the incorrect decision. If your child is happy to go to her room and play then this is not a consequence. If she doesn't like going to her room on her own and being isolated from the family, then it can be used.

My child is verbally rude when I ask him to do something. The standard response is "No. Shut up, Mum!" How should I deal with this in public?
Take him to the nearest quiet spot and bend down to his level. "I have told you how ugly it makes you look to talk like that. We don't speak that way. I am going to give you one last chance but the moment you speak to me like that again today you are going to be going to bed early without any television. I mean it! Do you understand me?"

Wait for your child to respond with a yes. Don't move until he has replied.

Choose a consequence that is really going to upset him. Most children of this age dislike the thought of going to bed straight after their bath. You will know what you need to remove. Just make sure it is something you can carry through.

My child is nearly seven years old. Can I still use the Thought Space?
Yes. Most children dislike being excluded and forced to sit in an area with nothing to do. Sitting on a stair or chair in the hallway is 'boring' and will aggravate and frustrate them. However, if you feel the Thought Space is no longer effective, remove a privilege instead.

My daughter keeps wandering off when we are in shops. How can I stop this?
The simple way is to give her a warning and then let her know that if she walks away again, the rest of the trip will be spent holding hands and every time you need to stop and look at something she will have to sit on the floor at your feet.

She will not like the sound of this but if she continues to walk away, you will need to follow this consequence through. (See also 'Visiting shops' on page 220.)

My child never lets me check my emails. He will bat my phone away when he sees me looking at it.

I suggest allocating a time of day when you check emails. It is not the fact that you do this but the irregularity that frustrates. Remember: children like routine. Find a time that suits your routine and call this your 'email time'.

It is different if you are waiting for an important email. If this is the case, make your child aware of it and have an activity on standby for when that mail comes through. (This could be bubbles in your pocket at the park, or playdough and a snack at the kitchen table.)

Try to put yourself in your child's shoes and understand his frustration at not knowing when and how long you are going to spend on the screen.

My boys (aged five and six) would fight all day long if I let them. It starts as a game but will often end in tears.

I suggest you separate them and distract them at the first sign of fighting, and if it starts again I would tell them to take it upstairs to their room. Say: "I don't want to have to watch this any more. Upstairs right now. Go!" Clap your hands and chase them up the stairs and return downstairs alone.

By the time they are upstairs, children tend not to fight any more, and if they do it is short-lived. Siblings usually fight when they have an audience and know that a referee is present. When they are on their own, they can see little point.

Believe in your children. Feel confident that the fighting will cease. But the first time you try this, listen carefully to make sure that World War Three is not breaking out above!

How do I get my child out of a sulk? It can last for ages!

If your child is sitting in a sulk on the Thought Space, I would leave her there for as long as 20 or 30 minutes then make her aware of an activity going on elsewhere. This could be art work at the kitchen table, baking or rearranging the dolls' house furniture: something she will find engaging.

If she is sulking around the house, ask her to go to her bedroom and lie on her bed with her face in the pillow. Go to her room and show her how to do this.

Say: "Come downstairs when you are ready to leave the ugly look in the pillow and put on the pretty happy face." Physically show her how to do this. She may laugh but you should still ask her to carry it out.

"I will leave you to change your face then I will see you in the kitchen for baking [or whatever activity is next in the day]."

Kiss her on the head and go downstairs.

When she arrives in the kitchen, don't ask if it worked. Just look in her eyes and say "That's better, now let's bake!" No further discussion is needed.

❋

It is not easy to change the patterns of a child's behaviour when they are aged three to six. It is a far more difficult challenge than when you have a toddler – but still easier than waiting until she is a teenager! If you put in the hard work now, you'll find the results extremely rewarding. Once your child sleeps well at night, eats a healthy diet and behaves reasonably, you are well on the way to creating a rounded and balanced little individual. You'll feel confident that you can trust her to make the right decisions for herself and other people once she is out of the house and out of your care, whether at school or in the home of a friend.

Children love praise, and generally they love to please.

Children thrive when they know right from wrong and are clear about the boundaries you have put in place. Once they believe that you will follow through with consequences should they behave badly, they will try their best to avoid it. Your child now knows her place in the family structure. She knows what you expect of her and how to keep you happy.

Continue being consistent and clearly stating the boundaries in each new situation your child finds herself in, and you will all continue to grow as a balanced, content and confident family.

CHAPTER 6

Potty training

It's easy to get anxious about potty training, but the simple fact is that unless there is an underlying health condition nobody walks down the aisle on their wedding day wearing a nappy, and sooner or later your child will crack it. One of the keys to making it a success is not to focus on it so heavily that it becomes a concern. Your child knows you better than you think: when you are feeling anxious he will often sense this without you realising. So remaining relaxed, calm and consistent when teaching your child something new is extremely important – and potty training is no different.

> Make sure you exude positive energy.

Another key is that you need to feel 100 per cent confident that your child is ready and have total belief that he can do it. If you show doubt or uncertainty this will, in turn, cause your child to question his own ability.

WHEN SHOULD YOU START?

This is the only section of the book that is not written according to age, because in this instance my three-day plan refers to the process of training at whatever age the child is ready. Potty training must be viewed in relation to the individual child's emotional and physical ability. So while my basic principles are the same here as elsewhere in the book, my visual praise aids vary depending on your child's age.

Potty training can be a smooth process, but it is essential that you allow your child to take the lead. As a very rough guide, I would say it's likely to take place between two and a half and three and a half years old, although it may be earlier or later.

In order to avoid any sort of 'power struggle', be aware that all children tend to go through a stage when they discover the word 'no' and desperately want to use it; if this is where your child's at, it's not the right time for potty training.

Your child is the decision maker for this milestone – not you!

LOOKING FOR SIGNS

It is a good idea to start noting how often your child is urinating at around two and a half years old. If you change his nappy every one and a half to two hours and find that at times it is dry, that means he is starting to gain control of his bladder – the first step towards being ready to do without a nappy.

It is important that you observe him for at least three consecutive days, maybe even noting in your diary how often he urinates. And if you find over this period that there are several dry occasions you might want to take the next step.

Consider the following statements to find out if he is ready:

- My child's nappy is often dry when I change him on a one-and-a-half- to two-hourly basis.

- He informs me when he has done a wee or a poo in his nappy.

- He is showing signs of discomfort when wearing his nappy.

- He wants his nappy changed as soon as he has soiled it.

- He will remove his own nappy at any given opportunity.

- He is happy to talk about potty training and read books about it.

- He has a clear understanding of what potty training involves.

- He happily watches both parents using the loo.

- He announces doing a wee or poo in advance.

- He is not at the stage of continually saying 'no'.

If you agree with seven or more of the statements above, and you are going to be based at home for the next two weeks with no weekends away or holidays arranged, you are ready to go ahead with the purchase of a potty or loo seat and begin the three-day plan!

PREPARING FOR THE PLAN

Once you feel the time is right, you can start the process by talking about the potty. You don't need to buy one at this stage, but with the help of storybooks and images printed from the computer you can start to help your child understand how the transition from wearing a nappy to using the loo is made.

He will have seen you using the loo many times, but now you can build on his familiarity by talking through what you are doing each time you go:

- *"Pants down, sit down and relax. I am going to think about my afternoon at the park."* Silent pause as you sit on the loo.
- *"Now my body is ready to have a wee!"* Listen together for the 'tinkle', then announce: *"Finished."*
- Next, say, *"Wipe"*, and follow this with the action.
- Then, *"Flush"*, and, again, carry out this action.
- Finally, move over to the basin, say, *"Wash and dry"* and show your child how you wash your hands.

At this stage your child is simply an observer. You do not want it to become a game where you visit the bathroom together and your child just wants to flush and then spend time washing his hands. I suggest that the only time you visit the bathroom is when you actually need to use the loo and your child wants to come with you. Don't fall into the trap of you sitting on the loo while he engages in water play at the basin! Ensure he engages in what you are doing before the taps are turned on after the loo is flushed.

If, on the other hand, your child does not want to accompany you to the bathroom, don't push it.

The next stage is to talk to your child gently and explain that you're going to be removing his nappy while he's playing at home and/or in the garden, and that he will sit on the potty you're going to buy together when either a wee or poo is coming.

"Now, I think that we are ready to do something really fun. Today we can play around the house and in the garden without you wearing your nappy. You can wear your fantastic big top [describe the top] and we'll have some fun together. When you feel a wee or poo is coming you can sit on your potty. Your potty would love to catch your wees and poos. Wees and poos will lead to [stickers/magnets/marbles]."

Once again, if your child clearly says 'no' and puts up resistance, you should leave things as they are and not broach the subject again for at least three to four weeks.

If he seems positive, this is a good time to look at relevant books and stories together. You can even start to look on the Internet at images of potties you might buy.

Your child needs to learn that we always wash our hands after we have used the potty/loo. I advise that you keep a step close to the basin and soap within easy reach so that your child can show independence in this area. After all, he will eventually be carrying out the entire process alone.

To start the three-day plan, you will need:

Remember: you need to feel 100 per cent sure that your child is ready to take this step.

- Several pairs of shorts/trousers with elasticated waists and a long t-shirt/top
- A clear diary for at least three days
- Fun cups and sports bottles to encourage liquid intake
- Visual-aid materials (see page 242 for ideas)
- A calm and relaxed approach.

Choose a time when he is 100 per cent healthy, and when you will be with him all day long to show him the new routines. Make sure you have the time and energy to give it your focus, and then get started.

THE THREE-DAY POTTY-TRAINING PLAN

Here are the dos and don'ts of the plan in a nutshell:

DO

- Keep calm and smile a lot.
- Allow your child to visit the bathroom with you when you need to use the loo.
- Make sure your child knows where the potties have been placed.
- Give your child plenty of fluids using sports bottles, drinking straws and fun cups.
- Let your child go naked from the waist down when you are at home together.
- Put your child in shorts or trousers with elasticated waists (both girls and boys) when you go out.
- Give physical praise (kiss, hug, spin around/swing).
- Use visual praise aids (see page 242).
- Keep all nappies out of sight.
- Aim to guide your child towards the potty/loo every one and a half to two hours. If he says 'no' he probably means it. Leave it be.
- Take note of regular bowel movements (often a short time after a meal has been eaten).
- Both of you use the loo/potty before leaving the house and when returning home; make this a consistent routine.
- Take a potty and spare clothes (two sets) on all outings.
- Truly believe your child can do this.

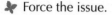 Remember that accidents are not intentional.

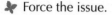 Stop the process if your child is clearly not ready.

DON'T

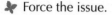 Show frustration because you want to start potty training, but your child is not ready.

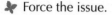 Force the issue.

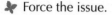 Inform your child that 'everyone else we know wears pants'; your child is an individual.

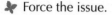 Keep reminding him that he is 'a big boy and should be wearing pants'.

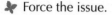 Continually ask him, *"Do you need a wee? Do you need a wee?"*

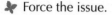 Show disappointment when an accident occurs; this is part of the learning process.

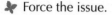 Grimace when emptying the potty or use words such as 'disgusting'.

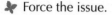 Overpraise; this can unsettle and embarrass a child.

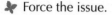 Think he is not capable of potty training.

 Continue with the process if your child is showing signs of not being emotionally ready.

When the inevitable accidents happen, whether in your child's pants, on the floor or on your furniture, keep calm and simply clean up as quickly and quietly as possible. There is no benefit in showing disappointment. Simply make eye contact with him and say, *"Accidents happen. Let's try a little harder next time to get to the potty. When you feel the wee-wee feeling, don't wait – go straight to the potty. Your toys will still be waiting for you when you come back."*

PLAN DAY ONE

On the morning of the day you decide together that you are going to say goodbye to nappies, sit with your child when he wakes up and read one of the potty-training-related books you've previously looked at.

I then suggest that over breakfast you discuss visiting the shops this morning and going to buy a potty and some pants. Talk about where you think the potties will need to be positioned around the house. I would guide your child with this if he is unsure: *"Well, we'll need one in the kitchen/playroom"* (depending on where the toys are in your home); *"we'll need one in the bathroom upstairs and I think we should buy a special seat just for you to put on the loo. This can go in the downstairs cloakroom."*

This will be a lot of information for your child to absorb, so I suggest that you change the subject after this (unless he shows that he wants to go on with the conversation), continue with your breakfast together and then get dressed and head out to the shops. At this stage your child is still going to be wearing a nappy.

The shopping trip is important and I suggest you do it as early in the day as possible. Large supermarkets are open as early as 8am and most other stores are open by 9am. It is important that you and your child go together, as by doing this, you are helping to focus his mind on the action he's undertaking. This is a significant part of the process. (If you already have potties in the home, whether from an older child or donations from friends, that's great; however, I'd still like you to visit the shops to buy underwear, then when you return home you can introduce the items you already have.)

I'd recommend buying a potty for each level of your home, plus one you can take with you in a large bag when you are on outings. If your child is nearer the age of three and is looking too big to sit comfortably on the potty, cushioned loo seats might be better. This is something you can discuss with your child. If uncertain, try both!

As for underwear, ten pairs should be ample. Make this a positive purchase. Don't think in terms of needing dozens to allow for accidents – these are inevitable, but rinsing out tiny underpants is a minor task.

On arriving home, remove the nappy as soon as possible and allow your child to run around in a long t-shirt. This should be seen as fun. It is now important to ensure that nappies are not visually available to your child; seeing them can cause mixed messages. However, don't throw them away altogether at this stage either.

Position the potties strategically around your home, as already discussed with your child, and place a book or toy next to each one. These should be left in place as distractions for when your child is using the potty.

IDEAS FOR VISUAL AIDS

The next task I would like you to do with your child is to create some visual aids, so that as he 'performs' your child can log his successes and thus see his progress. It is a great incentive and creates an association between using the potty and a sense of purpose. Here are some ideas (you'll need to choose from these as appropriate to your child's age):

- Decorate a glass jar together using glass paint and stickers. Then, each time your child has a successful wee or poo a gem/rock may be placed in the jar. The jar and gem sizes should be such that the jar is filled within a week.

- Tie a ribbon to a door handle, then every time your child performs he can thread a bead on to the ribbon. The idea is that eventually you will create a necklace. You could even buy beads with letters on them in order to spell out your child's full name.

- Placing stickers on the potty each time it is used is a simple but effective visual aid. If your child wees or poos on the potty while you're on an outing, simply place the sticker on his shirt and he can decide where to stick it when you return home. Ideally, it should go on the main potty at home, but the decision is his.

- Some children respond extremely well to sticker charts. You could draw or paint a big picture of a potty and attach it to the wall close to the potty you think will be used the most. Then, every time the potty is used place a sticker on the chart.

- Building also works: each time the potty is used give your child a brick and he has to place it on the previous brick to create a tower. You can purchase little clay bricks and 'cement' to add interest, or use Duplo, Lego or wooden bricks that can be painted as the tower progresses.

Visual aids do have an expiry date, in that your child will eventually lose interest in them. But usually, by this stage, he will be happy to use the potty or the loo without an incentive other than emptying his bladder or bowel!

So just to recap, we have now reached a stage where:

❧ There is a little bottom out in the open

❧ A visual aid has been talked about and created

❧ The potties are distributed around the house.

It is now mid-morning, approaching lunchtime.

MORNING PLAY

It is important to give your child some space and let him play in the way he usually would. As he begins playing simply remind him of where the nearest potty is. This can be a time when you catch up on your household chores or sit down with a cup of tea. While he is playing, I recommend that he always has a drink available to him. This can be in a sports bottle or a cup with a straw, according to his age and ability. I am sure you will know the kind of drinking aid that will entice your child to drink! It needs to be something appealing to him, perhaps with a favourite character on it (Postman Pat, Thomas the Tank Engine, Peppa Pig or Dora the Explorer). You could even add a little juice to the water to give it a more interesting flavour. And try to vary the cups or bottles to maintain interest.

It is tempting to keep asking your child, "Do you need a wee?" but try not to.

Just give your child his drink and let him play. He needs to get used to the new system in the house and also to relax.

After your child has been playing for fifteen minutes, I would ask him to stop for a moment while you remind him where his potty is (it needs to be where he can see it). Look in his eyes when you are talking to him so that you know he is fully engaged in what you are saying. Then ask him for a response: "*So when you have the 'wee feeling' where are you going to go?*" When he responds, praise him: "*Well done!*

That potty must be very excited about you sitting on him and filling him up! And we can put a sticker on our potty" (or refer to whatever visual aid you have chosen to use).

It is helpful to monitor the time for your own reference to see how long it is before your child needs a wee. You will also find that the opening of his bowels occurs at a similar time each day. You will start to see a pattern after three or four days and it then becomes easier to manage.

MONDAY	WEE	POO
10.05AM	√	
12.30PM		√
1.10PM	√	
3.20PM	√	

ACCIDENTS HAPPEN!

When your child first learned to walk he probably fell to the ground many times before getting successfully from A to B. This is no different. You may very well find that first attempts do not reach the potty. This is not unusual. Please remember your child is learning a new skill and this event still requires praise:

"Look at you! Well done. This is our first wee not in a nappy! I think we need a sticker for that." Then place a sticker on your child's shirt and let him know how pleased you are by giving him a big hug.

With boys, it can help to address their penis directly: *"Now, listen to me, Mr Willy. You did a great job of having a wee without the nappy. Could you now ask [child's name] to take you over to the potty next time? It's that big, shiny red thing over there. Could you try that please?"* This may sound daft, but I've tried it many times and it does seem to work. I then pretend that I've had a response: *"OK then,"* I say, in a funny voice, and I reply, *"Thank you very much, Mr Willy."* This will often make the child laugh, but also,

When a boy is sitting on the potty/loo, don't forget to explain the importance of aiming his willy downwards!

more importantly, makes them realise that this is a part of their body they need to 'take ownership of' and control.

You can do the same thing with girls, using whatever name you use for her 'front bottom'. I use the word 'vagina' but choose whatever you like and use it consistently.

Make sure that you clean up as quickly and quietly as possible. This is not something your child is to be involved in. If he asks questions, simply say, "*This won't take a minute. What are you going to play with before lunch? It is nearly time for some sandwiches/soup/pasta.*"

LUNCHTIME

Before lunch it is a good idea to go to the bathroom together: "*I always have a wee before my lunch and dinner. Let's go together and then wash our hands for lunchtime.*"

Encourage your child to sit on the potty and spend a period of time sitting on the loo yourself. This is not to be a 'social event', so try not to engage in conversation; encourage your child to look at his book/toy instead. Be aware that if your child has urinated within the last hour he may not need to go again. You are instilling a routine, rather than expecting a result. Spend no longer than three to four minutes with your child sitting on the potty. Then wash hands and go for lunch.

Most importantly, remain positive: your child *can* and *will* do this. All he needs is your clear and positive guidance.

Over lunch, I suggest you talk about what you are going to do that afternoon. It would be nice to go for a little outing for a couple of hours (say 2–4pm). Everyone should get some fresh air daily, so a trip to the park or the shops, feeding the ducks or visiting a friend are perfect.

Talk about how you are going to manage the need for a wee or poo while you are out. "*Now, we are going to have to choose a pair of pants for you to go out in and a pair of shorts/jogging bottoms/leggings you can easily pull down. I am going to take the potty out with us and we will find a place to put it in the park/friend's house.*"

This needs to be said in a very positive and direct manner, using your 'firm' voice, so that your child has clear direction. Ensure you smile and express positive body language at the same time.

Don't be hesitant about leaving the house. The worst-case scenario is that you'll need to change your child's clothing. Most parents have to do this at some stage in their child's potty-training stage.

AFTER LUNCH

It's very common for a child to open their bowels after lunch if they have not already done so at some stage during the morning. You may already be aware of a regular time at which your child fills his nappy.

Let your child down from the table to go and play while you clear the kitchen. Before doing so, bend down so that you have eye contact with him and say in a positive tone with a smile on your face: "*Now, when you go and play, you might need a wee or a poo. When you feel this happening, try your best to go and sit on the potty. We can then look at your wee/poo* [children love doing this] *and get a sticker/a brick for our tower/ thread a bead on our ribbon. I am going to clean up the kitchen while you have some play time. Please remember that your potty wants a wee or poo in it. Good boy.*" (While there is a school of thought that the phrase 'good boy/girl' should not be used, I feel that when a child hears that they've been labelled as 'good', this is something that they believe and will act upon.)

While your child is playing after lunch, keep an eye on him and note if you can see him concentrating on opening his bowels. When you see this, say: "*I think you might need a poo. Let's sit on the potty and have a story.*" Then let him sit himself down while you spend a few moments looking for a story (you are stalling the process here in order to keep him on the potty). Remain quiet while you choose a story and do not look at your child. Delay finding the story for as long as possible and only start reading when he says he wants to leave the potty.

"*OK, I am going to read [state the title] while you sit on your wonderful potty.*" Start reading the book in a calm manner, then, after a minute, give your child the book and tell him you just need to empty the washing machine/find your phone/go to the loo yourself. Say, "*I will be right back. You carry on looking at the pictures in the story book.*"

Now leave the room. You'll have to wait patiently for as long as your child needs. Most children want privacy when they are opening their bowels. They are happy to show the result, but the act is something they generally want to do alone. If your child gets off the potty or calls you to continue the story, he is simply not ready. In that case, finish the story and then ask him what he wants to do next. Let him guide you. If he wants to continue to play, this is fine. If he requests more stories, ask him if he needs a poo/wee. If he says yes, read him one more story and then leave him alone again for a moment.

Next, say, "*You have had two stories now. I think if you want to poo, I am going to just fold the laundry while you do that and then I will be back to play. See you in a minute.*" Say this in a positive tone and leave the room.

If after this he requests more stories, ask him to remove himself from the potty and have stories with you on the sofa or rug, keeping the potty in sight. What you don't want is for your child to think that the potty is synonymous with story time.

Throughout the process, remain relaxed. If you are anxious and nervous your child will pick up on this.

Success!

Everyone has their own 'celebration' style. I personally put on some music and do a ridiculous little dance, which usually sends the child into fits of laughter. If we're out of the house, I still do the dance but have to sing as well! However you choose to celebrate, it's important not to go over the top or embarrass or confuse your child. You know him better than anyone, so find a way that will please him and then proceed with the visual aid.

LUNCHTIME NAP

If your child is still having a sleep after lunch, ensure that he plays for 20 to 30 minutes first. If during this time he urinates or opens his bowels, you might want to make a considered decision about whether or not you want him to go to bed in a 'sleep nappy' (it's important to call it this) or to let him sleep in his pants. If he has not performed a great deal during the morning or after lunch, it might be a good idea to put the sleep nappy on. It is important to be absolutely clear that this nappy is only for when he sleeps. I also recommend placing disposable mattress covers or pads under the fitted sheet on your child's mattress.

Let your child have a nap of no more than an hour and fifteen minutes and when you wake him gently, make him aware that the sleep nappy is being removed.

Remember to make a note of the times your child urinates. If the nappy is wet after the afternoon nap, you can try asking him when the wee came. It's useful to find out if he urinated in his sleep or as he was waking up. It's a hard question, though, so don't be surprised if he doesn't answer. If he tells you he just did a wee, and the nappy is still warm, it means he knows when he is urinating. This is a positive step towards understanding bladder control. Note it in your diary. If he doesn't answer, just note in the diary that he urinated while he was sleeping.

If you put your child to sleep without a nappy and he urinated in his bed, don't worry about it. You may want to ask yourself whether it is worth using a sleep nappy at this stage. It is best to approach bladder control during the day before working on 'dry nights'.

If you wake your child and his nappy/bed is dry, praise him and give a reward of a sticker or brick. If you have three consecutive dry daytime sleeps, you can start to assume that your child understands that sleep is not the time to urinate. This is progress indeed.

You are likely to find that he will need a wee before he starts his afternoon play. When he is fully awake, visit the bathroom together and you sit on the loo as your child sits on the potty. Do this quietly. It is not a moment for conversation.

- Finish your motion and flush and wash your hands.

- Ask *"Do you want to sit a little longer while I go and make your bed?"*

- Act according to the decision he makes.

This is introducing the routine that every time he wakes from a sleep he visits the bathroom. Your child may have woken with a wet nappy but this will not always be the case and you need to implement this routine from Day One.

AFTERNOON OUTING

If your child woke from his nap with a dry nappy and didn't perform when you went to the loo together, I suggest playing at home for 20 or 30 minutes before heading out for the afternoon. Give him a snack of some watery fruit, such as halved grapes or chunks of melon, and a drink.

Before you leave the house, you should both visit the loo/potty. This is good practice and helps to instil a routine.

When you are out, remain calm and positive. Once at your destination, explain to your child where you will take the potty if he needs a wee or poo.

🌿 If you are in the park, for example, find a secluded spot (behind a tree) and say firmly and directly, *"That will be our Loo Tree! If you need to do a wee or a poo we will go to that tree."* Take him to the tree and show him how you will place the potty on the ground. *"This is where we will come. Do you understand?"* You need acknowledgement before allowing him to go and play. I would allow an hour and a half playing in the park before returning home for a play with 'a bottom in the air' before dinner time.

🌿 If you are visiting a friend I suggest placing the potty in an area of the house he knows and feels comfortable with. I would only suggest visiting a friend who understands the situation and will be forgiving if there's an accident on her carpet or furniture. When you arrive at her house take your child's hand and visit the bathroom together, taking the potty with you. Use the bathroom together if he is willing. Return to the play area and place the potty in a secluded spot with your child. This needs to be done before any toys are played with. *"Now I am going to talk to [friend's name] in the kitchen. You can see where the potty is and we can visit the bathroom together if you want. Have fun playing … wees and poos in the potty remember."* Now leave the room and relax. Let him enjoy his playing time.

🌿 If you are going shopping, I suggest visiting one or two shops and then going to a café. In the café, visit the loo while your drinks are being prepared. Take the potty with you and see if he is ready to do anything. If not, drink your drinks and sit for five or ten minutes. If your child has not urinated for more than two hours, visit the loo in the café one more time before returning home. Some children prefer to urinate at home rather than in public places and can show amazing bladder control to achieve this.

If your child has an accident when you are out, he will tell you. If he doesn't, don't leave him for more than fifteen minutes without changing his clothing. Note in your diary that he was not concerned when he urinated in his clothing. If this continues you may need to consider stopping training and returning to it at a later date.

> Remain positive at all times, both for yourself and your child. Negative energy takes you nowhere.

Remember that this is the first day and children will often have an accident when they are outside and preoccupied. This is NOT a concern.

While you are changing him, ask, *"Did you feel your wee when it came into your pants?"* Wait for his reply, then say, *"Think about it next time, please. Now let's go and play again. I love you."*

The moment you arrive home, remove your child's trousers or shorts and advise him to go and sit on the potty. If he has managed not to urinate the entire time you were out of the house he is now very likely to need to go.

Ask him to sit on the potty while you unload the buggy and start to prepare the dinner. You will need to take him and guide him to lower himself on the potty. This is still early days. He is not yet ready to take himself to the potty when you ask him to. Lower him onto the potty and then continue with your chores, all the while telling him what you are going to do.

Leave him sitting for as long as he needs to; don't force it if he leaves the potty and wants to play. Just ensure that now you are home he is naked from the waist down.

EVENING ROUTINE

Before dinner follow the same principles as for lunch (see page 245). Then after dinner, let your child play for twenty minutes while you tidy the kitchen and remind him of the potty. This may be the time when your child usually opens his bowels; be aware of this if so, and follow the same principle as at lunchtime (see page 246).

- Just before you are ready to start the bath-time routine, praise your child for the day's efforts and tell him that he has been really good. Ask him if he has had a nice day. This will give him the opportunity to say if he wants his nappies back (although it is very unlikely he will). Whatever you do, don't put the thought into your child's head by asking him outright, *"Do you want to wear your nappies again?"*

- Continue with your usual bath-time and have a potty with you in the bathroom. Ask your child to sit on it before getting into the bath (again, creating a routine) while you run the water.

- After the bath carry on with a little television or some books and give your child milk if you are still offering it to him.

- This is a winding-down time and a wee will often come now. Keep the potty close at hand and if your child is sitting on the sofa or your lap I suggest placing a towel discreetly between you. Mention to your child that the potty is there if it is needed. If your child urinates on the towel, make him aware of this and the following day start story/TV time on the towel and then proceed to sitting on the potty while watching TV or having a story.

- At the end of the day, after teeth brushing, tell your child that everyone in the world sits on the potty/loo before bed to try and say goodbye to the last wee of the day. This again instils a routine.

- Before bed, add a bead/sticker/brick to your visual aid to show your child that you are pleased and to show that there has been progress. At this stage there should be at least two items on it: one for the first time your child urinated without a nappy, irrespective of where it was, and one for today's efforts overall.

🦋 The last thing you do before saying goodnight is to put your child in his 'sleep nappy'. Most children learn to train themselves during the day before taking the leap to remaining dry through the night, so take things one step at a time.

If your child is older, getting towards the age of four, and he objects to wearing a sleep nappy, you could put him in bed without one so long as you have a plastic cover on the mattress. It might be worth waking him gently when you are going to bed yourself and taking him to the loo or sitting him on the potty. I would only do this if your child has shown very good bladder control during the day, with two and a half or three hours between urinating and no more than one or two accidents. To train your child both day and night in one step is a huge leap but with an older child it is possible. This is a decision you need to make.

> You have done it! You've got through the first day of potty training…

If your child is younger than three and a half, explain that you will use a sleep nappy but that if it is dry in the morning with no wee in it, then you can talk about going without a sleep nappy.

Once your child is in bed, take a look at your records and see if a pattern is emerging. If so, take it into consideration when making plans for Day Two. Then sit back, relax and be proud of yourself. You achieved a lot today – as did your child.

However, if your child has been very disturbed today and there have been a lot of tears and upset you need to make a considered decision about whether you think it is beneficial to continue or if it would be better to leave toilet training for another month. You will know in your heart of hearts the best choice to make for your child.

PLAN DAY TWO

As soon as your child wakes in the morning remove the 'sleep nappy' and wait five minutes before asking him to sit on the potty, as he may still be a little sleepy. Give him a book if you think he needs distraction while sitting on the potty and leave the room for a few minutes (no more than four or five). Tell him: *"I am just going to turn off my alarm clock/find my phone/visit the loo myself. I will be right back. You see if you can have a wee while I am busy."* Again, you are implementing a routine here – after all, most of us start our day with a wee!

Next, prepare for another day at home with your child naked from the waist down. As on Day One, note when your child urinates or opens his bowels.

MORNING ROUTINE

If there is more than an hour between your child first waking up and breakfast being served, I'd recommend sitting him on the potty again and then washing hands ready for breakfast. You will discover in time whether he does his first wee of the day immediately on waking or just before breakfast – and until you do, I'd encourage that he try on both occasions.

Sitting at the breakfast table together is a nice time to talk. Remind your child of his visual aid and that he's going to tell his willy he wants lots of wees in the potty. After this you do not need to discuss the potty any more. Your child will now have a better understanding of what he needs to do and he should be left to think about it on his own. Continue with your breakfast and talk about the day ahead. You can plan a morning activity at home and then an outing in the afternoon.

Give him time and space – he might just surprise you!

After breakfast is often the time when bowels open. While you are tidying the kitchen, give your child his space: *"I am going to tidy up while you have some fun with your toys. How about you make a hospital for your cuddly toys and I come to help when all is tidy in here? Please remember the potty."* It is at this point that you need to truly believe that your child *can* do this. He knows what to do.

Once you enter the room, continue to do as you had promised (i.e. help build the train track).

🦋 If you notice signs that he needs the potty, guide him accordingly and give him a book or small toy. A stress ball can be a fun thing to play with, so maybe you'd like to keep one close to the potty. While your child is trying to perform don't pay him any attention. Busy yourself with something else and reduce communication to a minimum. Don't forget your celebration technique if the potty is filled!

🦋 If an accident has occurred when you enter the room, simply clean it up with the least fuss. "Can you try and get to the potty next time young man?" Continue as you had originally promised to do, for example helping with the toys' hospital.

I recommend there is just one outing a day during the three-day plan, while he is still learning how it works. Look at the diary you created on Day One and decide whether it would be easier to go out in the morning or afternoon. Ask yourself:

🦋 When did he last urinate?

🦋 How long did he hold on between urinations yesterday?

🦋 When does he tend to open his bowels?

Judge whether it will be easier to be away from home before lunch or later in the day.

AFTERNOON ROUTINE

As we've seen, sitting on the potty and then washing hands is an important part of the routine. It's enforced in nursery schools and schools throughout the country, so it's helpful if you've introduced it in the comfort of your own home. It can also be frustrating further down the line if your child gets into the habit of needing the loo half-way through family mealtimes then refusing to finish his food as it's cold and everyone else has finished. You can avoid this by encouraging him to visit the loo before every meal.

After lunch, this is the time when you clear the kitchen and prepare for the next part of the day while your child has some time alone playing. Follow the usual routine:

❦ Explain what you are doing: *"I'm cleaning up the kitchen."*

❦ Point him in the direction of a toy: *"Why not have a tea party with your tea set?"*

❦ Remind him of the potty: *"Don't forget to use the potty if you need to."*

❦ Give him space for ten to fifteen minutes.

If your child needs an afternoon nap, take him to his room and put on his sleep nappy. If this is the time of the day when your child usually opens his bowels, leave at least 20 to 30 minutes after lunch before putting him to bed. You don't want him to get into the habit of soiling his nappy every day during his nap (see page 246).

Your child should sleep no longer than one and a half hours, and once he's awake you should remove his nappy immediately. The rule is that nappies are only on when your child is on his mattress. The minute he is no longer horizontal the nappy is removed.

Remember to note if the nappy is wet. Praise your child if he has been dry through his sleep by adding to the reward system.

If you stayed at home in the morning you can go out now, remembering to pack the potty, two sets of clothes and a drink. Visit the loo together before leaving the house and remind your child that the potty is coming with you. If you are going to the park, make for the Loo Tree, or find a spot at your new destination where you can discreetly use the potty.

Some boys like the idea of standing and take to it immediately, while others prefer the security of sitting on the potty and standing comes later.

Standing by the Loo Tree in the park could be a good time to talk to your son about weeing standing up: the principle of weeing 'up the tree' or 'helping the grass to grow'. You can mention that this is what Daddy would do if he needed a wee in the park or in the woods where there was no loo. Then let your child go and play. He will digest the new information and make you aware of how he wants to wee now he knows the options.

Your afternoon outing should be no longer than a couple of hours. Once home, if your child has not urinated in the last hour, guide him to his potty as soon as you get in and ask him to spend a moment there while you prepare for dinner.

Now you are home, your child can return to being naked from the waist down. You might find that it becomes part of his routine not to urinate while you are out, but that he'll need to do so the moment you get home.

I find that children inevitably want to visit the bathroom as soon as they arrive home from nursery. I think the majority of us are creatures of habit and prefer using the loo in the privacy of our own home. Children are simply mini versions of us!

If you have been out in the morning and are spending the afternoon at home have your child bare from the waist down and continue as you did yesterday morning (see page 243).

Make sure that you spend time playing together but also give your child periods when he is playing alone as you carry on with your afternoon tasks. Don't keep asking if he needs the potty. He should be able to go one and a half to two hours between urinating, and even longer if he doesn't drink during this time. Give him space.

EVENING ROUTINE

As usual, visit the potty/loo and wash hands before sitting down to dinner together. Talk about your day and ask your child what he liked best about it. Remember that potty training is only one aspect of the day and life should not revolve around it.

After dinner give your child some time alone as he may need to sit quietly on the potty for a bowel movement (about 20 to 30 minutes before heading to the bath). If you have worked out when your child's bowel movement occurs, you can make him aware of it so it becomes a conscious part of his routine: "*I think that your body likes to do a poo after dinnertime/lunchtime/breakfast time each day. Let's make sure we sit on the potty at that time.*" And remind him about the visual aid that will follow.

Once more, establish the habit of going to the loo before getting into the bath. Then follow your usual post-bath routine, be it stories or TV time, perhaps with your child sitting on a towel, drinking his milk.

Once the milk is drunk you may want to transfer him to his potty for the rest of story/TV time. The reason for the towel is simply to protect your sofa. Often when children are sitting watching TV they will concentrate on nothing else but the moving images, especially if it is at the end of the day and they are tired.

Make one last trip to the potty if your child has not urinated in the last hour, then brush his teeth and put him to bed. Praise his efforts through the day and reward him using a visual aid. At least two rewards should have been given, so there should now be a minimum of four. The last thing to do, before giving him a hug and a kiss, is to put on his sleep nappy.

> Remain positive and keep calm – this method will achieve the results you want.

Now look at your record of your child's potty training thus far. After two days you should be seeing a pattern of how his body works. Hopefully, you'll be feeling positive about the last two days and your child will be showing enthusiasm rather than resistance. You'll need to reflect on this and decide whether to continue or whether your child needs another month in his nappies.

PLAN DAY THREE

Now that Day Three has arrived, if a routine had formed and you are seeing steps in the right direction, your day should look something like this:

(BM = bowel movement/poo)

6–7am	Awake and slowly start the day. Remove your child's nappy while he is still lying in bed/cot or immediately after he gets up. Put him on the potty within five minutes.
7.30–8am	Sit on potty again if he did not urinate when first getting up. Wash hands and have breakfast, followed by quiet playtime. (Check your records, as this could be his BM time.)

8–8.30am	Get dressed (naked from the waist down or pants/trousers – your choice today depending on the last two days) and brush teeth ready to start the day.
8.30–12pm	Morning activity at home or outing, remembering to offer plenty of liquids. When your child has managed a period of one and a half to two hours without using the potty you could mention that it might need to be used. Make eye contact and ask, *"Would you like to sit on your potty now and see if you can make a wee come?"* If he refuses, drop the subject.
12–12.30pm	Sit on the potty before lunch and wash hands. Over lunch talk about your plans for the afternoon. After lunch your child can have another quiet play as you tidy the kitchen. (Check your records again to see if this is his BM time.)
1–2.15pm	If your child has a nap, put him down 30 minutes after lunch. Suggest using the potty if it has not been used for a while. Read a story if this is part of your routine and once your child is horizontal in bed put his sleep nappy on. Let him sleep for one hour and fifteen minutes.
2.15–2.45pm	Wake your child if he has not woken naturally and remove his nappy. Put him on the potty, with a book if necessary, and leave him to it for three to four minutes.
3–5pm	Afternoon outing or time at home (reverse of morning). If you're going out, both of you visit the bathroom before leaving the house: *"Potty before out to play."* Remember to take a potty and spare clothing. Once home, immediately remove your child's clothing from the waist down. Direct him to the potty while you get organised for dinner.
5–5.30pm	Wash hands and have dinner. Talk to your child about how successful the day has been and how proud you are of him. Look at the visual aid

together and praise him highly. Let him play quietly after dinner while you tidy the kitchen. (Again, this could be BM time.)

6pm	Bath-time. Guide your child to sit on the potty while you fill the bath.
6.30–7pm	Stories or TV time with your child sitting on a towel, then transferred to the potty.
7pm	Brush teeth. Final potty visit. Put on sleep nappy last thing before saying goodnight.

Continue to keep a record throughout the day whenever your child urinates or has a bowel movement.

With Day Three complete and the visual aid standing proud as a sign of the achievement you've made together, you may now continue on this journey. Your child still needs your guidance, and it will be some time before he is visiting the loo alone and washing his hands without you even realising. But that day will arrive … in time.

> One step at a time and before you know it your child will have progressed from the potty to independence.

ROUTINE POTTY/LOO VISITS

We've talked about the importance of establishing a routine when it comes to using the potty. Here's a summary of the routine 'visits' to aim for:

Good morning	Five minutes after sleep nappy removed
Before breakfast	Only if he did not perform when first placed on the potty earlier
Mid-morning	An hour and a half to two hours after last wee
Before lunch	Visit potty and wash hands for lunch
Before afternoon nap	Put sleep nappy on for nap time
On waking from nap	Five minutes after sleep nappy is removed
Before going out	Visit the bathroom together

Returning home	This is a common time for the potty to be needed
Before dinner	Visit potty and wash hands for dinner
Before bath	Guide to potty while the bath water is running
Before bed	Just before the sleep nappy is put on

At routine times, don't ask your child if he wants to go to the potty – just take him. Let him take the toy he is playing with.

At other times, only ask him if he looks as though he wants to go or if he hasn't been for an hour and a half or two hours. If he has drunk a lot, that's another time to be on guard. And keep an eye out around the time he normally has a bowel movement. This may happen more than once a day.

The table below is taken from a three-day programme I carried out with a girl aged two years and eight months. These were the findings on Day Three:

MONDAY	WEE	POO
7.30AM	√	
8.45AM		√
11.30AM	√	
1.20PM		√
3PM	√	
4.45PM	√	
6.30PM	√	

ONE TOO MANY ACCIDENTS?

If at any point during the three-day plan you feel that your child has no interest in using the potty and you have spent more time cleaning the floor than emptying the contents of a potty down the loo, I suggest you reassess. It may simply not be the right time for your child. Try to relax about this. Your child now fully understands the concept of using the potty, so your efforts will not have been wasted. He might just need a little extra time. Give it a month to six weeks and start again.

Everyone has a different body cycle, taking into consideration factors such as exercise, food intake and water consumption. Your child is no different and he will soon establish his own routine and become familiar with it.

As a rough guide, by Day Three at least 50 per cent of his efforts should reach the potty/loo.

There will be accidents because he is still learning, but you should see progress as each day passes. By Day Seven, 90 per cent of his efforts should reach the loo and you may find that the visual aid is no longer needed; only use it for as long as your child is engaged by the concept.

If your child starts having accidents again after a period of managing to use the potty, take him to the doctor to check that he doesn't have a urinary tract infection. If there are no medical causes, it may be worth introducing a new visual aid to get him back on track.

FREQUENTLY ASKED QUESTIONS

The first day has been non-stop accidents with no successes and my daughter doesn't seem interested. What do you suggest?
I advise that you stop the plan and put your daughter back in nappies. Try again in four to six weeks' time.

Every time I ask "Do you need a wee?" he answers "No". What do you suggest?
You need to establish set times of day when your child sits on the potty, whether he thinks he needs to or not. Guide him to the potty, lower him onto it and give him some space. If he performs when you do this, there is no need to keep asking whether he needs a wee.

Can we eat out over the first week of potty training?
I wouldn't advise it, especially not at a time of day when your child's bowels tend to open. Start by taking small trips to friends' houses or cafés close to home for a snack before venturing out for a full meal. Wait until your child is comfortable with potty training first.

My child only has a poo every three or four days. I am worried she is constipated.

It is not uncommon for children to resist opening their bowels for as long as possible. Just ensure that your child is drinking plenty of water, and add a little fruit juice for flavour if necessary. Offer watery fruits such as melon and grapes (halved) and avoid white bread, which can be binding in the digestive system.

Do not draw attention to it when she has a poo. Eventually she will relax and start to poo more often.

My child is refusing to drink water. How can I persuade him?

Add a little fruit juice to his water to give it more flavour. Ice lollies made from juice can be given as a treat. Ensure plenty of fruits and vegetables are being eaten, as these all contain water. Not all children are big drinkers so don't be overly concerned, but try to tempt him to stay hydrated on very hot days.

My child only poos in his sleep nappy when I put it on for his lunchtime nap. What should I do?

Some children don't like the thought of something leaving their body, especially from behind. They prefer a nappy or pants to catch it. To break this inhibition they need to poo without any clothes on, so I suggest that you place your child in his bed with a bare bottom.

Ensure that he has his lunch reasonably early (midday) and has at least 30 minutes of play before you put him down for his nap. If he is already having this long, increase the play time by ten minutes. If he has not opened his bowels by then, try putting him to bed without a nappy. He will probably call out to you when he feels the poo coming, or wait until he wakes up. Many children can suppress a bowel movement for some time.

By placing him in bed with no nappy, you run the risk of him soiling the sheets but you may actually break the cycle of him using a sleep nappy.

Alternatively you could skip his afternoon nap for a day and see if he performs elsewhere.

My son will happily continue playing in the park after soiling his pants. How do I deal with this?

Avoidance is the best remedy. Don't take your son out of the house immediately after a meal. Make sure he sits on the potty before leaving for the park. When you arrive in the park, show him where the potty is going to be placed. And don't stay there for any more than two hours.

If he often seems to have a bowel movement in the park, I suggest visiting it at a different time in the day and being at home at the time he normally performs.

If this has only happened a few times and it is due to him being excited and distracted, I would simply clean him up and continue with the day. Accidents happen!

My child wants to keep her pants on, rather than playing in the house with a bare bottom. Is this OK at the start of the plan?

Ideally you want her to be able to see her first wee when it happens, which is usually on the floor. I would place her in a knee-length dress and explain that no one would be able to see her pants anyway.

If she still insists, let her put some pants on but tell her that if they get wet they will have to go in the washing machine. Leave out one spare pair but no more than that. Once they are both wet, she will have to have a bare bottom under her dress, and you can explain that the pants will be washed and dried by tomorrow.

To keep your child warm enough in winter, she could wear a woollen dress with a cardigan, socks and slippers. A boy could wear a long top with a vest underneath, along with socks and slippers. As long as the top half is warm enough, your child will be fine.

If my child has not urinated all morning can I still take her out in the afternoon?

During the three-day plan, I don't think you should leave the house until urine has been passed. Get her to drink plenty of liquids and suck a fruit juice ice-lolly, if necessary.

How long should we use the potty before introducing the loo seat?
Some children become attached to their potties and want to continue to use them. I would let that happen but once accidents are few and far between leave the potty behind when you go out and encourage the use of public loos in restaurants and shopping centres.

Let your child guide you. Most children reach a stage when they are too big and choose not to sit low down on a potty any more.

🦋

The important message with potty training is to remain as relaxed as possible. What's the worst that can happen? An accident on the floor is easy enough to clear up and urine is sterile. A few accidents are likely at the start of the learning curve. Sooner or later your child will learn good bladder control and won't need to visit the loo every couple of hours.

Your attitude to the process will be picked up by your child. The last thing you want is for them to sense that you are stressed and become tense themselves. Tense is not something that works well with potty training!

There will be times when you forget and an accident might occur. Simply learn from it and accept that you need to make this your focus for three solid days. You and your child are learning together.

The key is to remember the moments in the day when you take your child to the potty as part of a routine.

Remember what I said at the beginning of the chapter: nobody walks down the aisle wearing a nappy under their wedding dress or morning suit. Hardly any children start school wearing a nappy under their school uniform. So relax! Your child will get there when he is ready. All he needs is your positive energy, guidance, belief and enthusiasm.

Conclusion

I would like to think that by the time you are reading this, you have implemented a three-day plan in your household and found just how effective it is. And if you've done it once, you'll feel more confident if you ever need to repeat the experience because of another challenge.

As your child grows and routines change, there are bound to be some difficult moments. Life is full of them. The key is to communicate. Listen to your child, tell him what is happening and never underestimate his ability to understand. Explain any alterations in their routine, and why they are necessary. Give him time to adjust.

Holidays can be difficult for children because there's suddenly a new routine and they don't know the rules. Remember that when you get into a car or onto a plane you generally know where you are going and what is about to happen. Your child has no idea. Reassure him every step of the way by giving him a running commentary and you will help him to understand and accept that change is very often a good thing.

If your child finds it difficult to slip back into the old routine after a holiday or to adapt to a new routine if there have been changes in the household (such as a new baby, or a divorce) then read the relevant plan in the book and consider implementing it when the time is right.

I have helped many families in the last twenty years and it was wonderful to watch them benefit from my plans. Some parents even appeared to walk taller after the three-day programme because their confidence in their abilities as parents had grown!

The fact is that three days is all it takes to get back control of your family life. You now have clear direction and a book you can refer back to if there is a problem. The most important thing I want is for parents out there to enjoy their children.

About the author

Kathryn Mewes was born in 1973 in London and lived there for the first seven years of her life. She then moved to Wiltshire and in 1984 a final family move took her to Hampshire, where she completed her education.

In 1992 Kathryn attended Norland College in Hungerford and in 1994 she graduated with a Distinction and The Gifford Hall Award for Excellence. She then began her career as a Norland nanny, staying with families for a period of time and learning and growing alongside the parents. It didn't take long before her fascination with the dynamics of family life became an on-going study.

After nine years as a nanny, Kathryn went to Australia, where she lived for three years and spent time with many families helping to resolve concerns they had about their children's behaviour. It wasn't long before she realised that she only needed to be in a home for three days in order to bring about long-lasting change.

Kathryn returned to London in 2007 and launched her business in the UK. She is now based in Southwest London but travels the country every week working with different families on their own particular 'family challenges'. She goes by the name of Bespoke Nanny, and will arrive with her little suitcase, live in for 72 hours and then continue to guide that family for the next month by telephone.

Although she visits one and sometimes two families a week, by writing *The 3 Day Nanny*, she hopes to share with parents the techniques she uses when visiting homes for a personal consultation.

Kathryn continues to help families with challenges, and can be seen cycling the streets of London on her vintage bicycle complete with basket and shiny bell.

"With a new baby and a terrible two-year-old, life was reasonably stressful. Our nights were being broken by baby feeding and by a toddler who had never really established a night-time routine and demanded frequent comforting. Most nights felt as though the two were tag teaming and we were a long way away from a full night's sleep.

When Kathryn arrived at our home she immediately fitted in. Within a very short space of time she had befriended our toddler and worked out the ways of our household. It was a welcome break to have Kathryn take both girls off to the local playground during the afternoon when I got some time to myself, and also during the evenings when my husband and I got to have a meal out together and some adult time.

By the time Kathryn left she had established a structured day- and night-time routine for both of our girls. They were taking their daytime naps at the same time and for a lengthy period and sleeping through the night.

I can genuinely say that now our girls are 7 till 7 sleepers. The best money we ever spent!"

Emelye, Greenwich

"What a difference three days and one woman can make! We contacted Kathryn to help us with our twins, George and Stella, who were five months old at the time. We had got ourselves into a really difficult place where the twins would only fall asleep if they were breastfed or walked. In addition, they were 'snackers', who would drink little amounts up to 15 times a day, each. I was near breaking point – walking round and round and round parks by day, and imprisoned on the couch at night. Also we were up most nights, through the night. Kathryn stayed with us 72 hours (three days and three nights). During that time she turned our lives around! She gave us and our babes a routine. She taught them to self settle, so we now put them into their cots for their day naps and night sleep and they get themselves to sleep. This was previously impossible – a dream. In addition she regulated their feeds and sleeps, so they no longer snack and rarely become overtired. One of the best things for me was that Kathryn didn't leave George and Stella to cry it out. There is, of course, some crying, but it wasn't distressing as she obviously has a very good understanding of children. A month on, and everything is different. We have our lives back and our babies are smiling more than ever! I am spending more quality time with the babies during the day and even have a night life! We put the babies down at 7pm and they don't wake until 6–7am."

Lauren, Clapham

"Kathryn made ground-breaking progress with my son, aged 7 years, in terms of getting him eating, getting involved with cooking and communicating how he feels. She taught both him and me so much. I realised we were in a rut when I contacted Kathryn but only now do I realise quite how far we had sunk. An immense weight has been lifted off my shoulders and instead of dreading the weekly food shop, I now look forward to it due to Kathryn's ideas and guidance.

Kathryn walked into our lives seamlessly. She is sensitive, support-ive, encouraging, kind, professional and great fun. My only wish is that I had found her sooner!"

Emily, Fulham

"We all loved having Kathryn in our home. She sat with Lucien and they created a weekend menu together and cooked all of the weekend food. She believes in children making their own choices rather than feeling food is forced upon them.

After eating the crunchy chicken Kathryn asked 'What did your taste buds tell you, Lucien?'

'That was quite nice,' he replied!

Our three days with Kathryn helped iron out Lucien's issues with mealtimes."

Rosie Millard, Daily Telegraph journalist

"One day with Kathryn completely transformed my relationship with my son – I feel so much more confident and relaxed as a mother now, which has helped my little boy learn his boundaries and also react in a calmer manner. I had read numerous books on babies and toddlers but always came up with excuses why none of their findings would work for my 15-month-old son. But having Kathryn come into our home and tailor her advice to the specific quirks of our family and the set-up of our house was incredible. She knows children so well that she instantly found easy fixes for most of our problems and broke down the big issues into manageable steps so that nothing felt too difficult or overwhelming. She also helped me realise how much my little boy already understands and gave me a new respect for his abilities. We had a wonderful day with her and are truly benefiting from all of her advice. I would highly recommend her services to every family!"

Jennifer, Clapham

"This woman is incredible! We tried everything to get our toddler to sleep in her own bed but to no avail. Kathryn Mewes came into our home and worked her magic. As working parents we became exhausted by our toddler waking in the night. This led to us all bed hopping and eventually all ending up in our bed. Needless to say this made us feel like total failures as parents. Kathryn cleverly offered us practical and easy-to-follow instructions and our daughter's behaviour changed rapidly. We now have our bed back to ourselves and we tuck her in to her own bed every night! Never did I believe that anyone could fix our daughter's sleep problem, as many sleep experts had tried before. But somehow Kathryn's approach has transformed our daughter and enriched our confidence in being parents again. We cannot thank her enough for introducing her easy-to-follow programme specifically tailored to our family.

I challenge anyone to follow Kathryn's advice and not get results!"

Sammy, Clapham

"Inviting you into our home was the best decision we could have made. We now have a contented, relaxed and happy little boy. You made the process stress-free and verging on enjoyable! We adored having you in our home and it was incredible to watch you work with our son and obtain the required results with minimal disruption. You were so kind and generous, for which we are all extremely grateful."

Georgina, Parsons Green

Index